THE VOLCANO,

MONTSERRAT,

AND ME

LALLY BROWN

DEDICATION

*This book is dedicated to all those who died on 25th June 1997
including my friend Beryl, who was known to everyone as
'The Fruit Lady'*

MAP OF MONTSERRAT

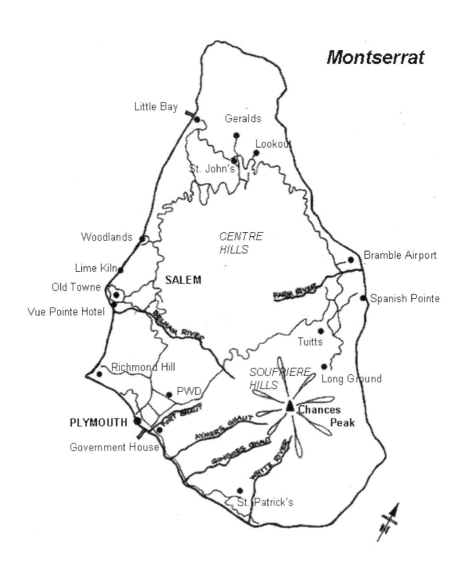

CONTENTS

INTRODUCTION

The pretty little island of Montserrat is just one of the dazzling Caribbean jewels in the necklace of the beautiful Leeward Islands.

Only fifteen minutes flying time from Antigua it is known as *"The Emerald Isle of the Caribbean"*. A romantic reference to both the verdant landscape and the island's association with Irish settlers who left St. Kitts and moved here in 1632.

The pear-shaped island is small, approximately 16 km by 11 km. The bulb of the south, now dominated by the grey mass of the smouldering Soufrière Hills Volcano, used to be the lush and fertile area of Montserrat with the harbour and capital Plymouth. The narrow neck of the north, currently developing into the vibrant commercial and residential centre of the island, is more arid with sparsely clad and rocky hillsides.

I first arrived on Montserrat in early July 1995. My husband had been appointed Deputy Director of the Public Works Department on a two year contract for the British Government.

We fell in love with the island and her people instantly. The 10,000 or so residents of Montserrat were a warm and exotic fusion of indigenous charmers and wealthy expatriates.

In early 1995 there was a feeling of optimism in the air. Rebuilding after the devastation caused by Hurricane Hugo in 1989 was complete and life was looking good for this diminutive British Overseas Territory in the Caribbean.

There was the anticipated opening of the brand new Glendon Hospital, and the completion of an impressive new Government HQ in the capital Plymouth, and talk of extending the runway at W.H. Bramble Airport to accommodate larger aircraft to bring in more tourists, the life-blood of this popular vacation destination in the Caribbean.

Then on the morning of Tuesday 18th July 1995 life on this beautiful piece of paradise called Montserrat changed, abruptly and without warning.

Nothing would ever be the same again.

But let me tell you the dramatic story as it unfolded, through the pages of the Journal I wrote at the time.

1 - JULY 1995

IN THE BEGINNING

My husband arrived on Montserrat in early May 1995, two months before me. I was left behind in Sussex, England to support, supervise and soothe our teenage son who was taking his GCE Advanced Level examinations. Our daughter was at University, temporarily resident somewhere in Russia while studying for her Degree but due to join us all in Montserrat on 8th July.

Stressful exams safely negotiated, I arrived on the island with our son at the end of June as *"the accompanying spouse"* to the Deputy Director of the Public Works Department and began the happy task of settling in to life on a beautiful, friendly Caribbean island.

It was in my capacity as the wife of an expatriate Government official that I found myself invited to coffee at Government House on the morning of Tuesday 18th July. I was without transport and still adjusting to my new life so I was very grateful when one of the other guests kindly volunteered to be my escort and chauffeur.

The morning was hot and humid as we drove along the waterfront of the small capital town of Plymouth towards Government House. We crossed the narrow bridge over the dry bed of Fort Ghaut before turning sharp left up a steep hill. Halfway up the hill on the right a sentry box guarded the entrance to Government House. A policeman, immaculate in his uniform of regulation white jacket and dark trousers, grinned cheerfully as we approached and waved us through into the drive.

Lawns bordered with rose beds and dotted with trees, and several historic and impressive large black cannon graced a pleasant garden that overlooked the sea. I thought the house itself, built at the beginning of the 20thC, was modestly pretty and unpretentious. A late Victorian two-storey construction mainly of timber it had three small saw-tooth peaked roofs, the gable boards of which had been painted an emerald green. A huge bronze bell was mounted beside the front door. A wide veranda circled the house with an upper balcony supported from below by short columns, and from a pole on the first floor, the British red, white and blue Union flag was hanging limply in the tropical heat.

As we parked the car a blur of tan fur skittered down the steps to greet us and I was introduced to Winston, resident dog of uncertain parentage, a foundling discovered in the gardens of Government House and subsequently adopted by the Governor's wife.

Winston expertly herded us up the entrance steps to meet the mistress of the house who was waiting, crisp and cool in white slacks and silk blouse, to gather us in. Gracious, charming, and chirpy, she bestowed warm embraces and brushed cheeks with known and new acquaintances alike.

Her Britannic Majesty's representative in Montserrat is His Excellency the Governor, currently Frank Savage, and an invitation from his wife to attend for coffee is generally conceded to be something of an honour. As a very new recruit in the circle of expat wives on the island I was suitably flattered.

The coffee morning had been arranged to introduce the wife of the newly arrived Police Commissioner to a few female friends. It seemed to me we were just a group of colonial ladies gathered together for a good old gossip. It was a bit like musical chairs. We sat in the lounge, a dozen of us, sedately sipping coffee and juggling pieces of cake while we moved from seat to seat to meet and greet as the fancy dictated. The overall impression was of amiable, middle-class, middle-income, English ladies who were either entering or leaving middle age. An hour or so of convivial chatter and then the group rose in unison to depart.

It was while we were saying our farewells on the steps of Government House that I became aware of a strong, acrid smell in the air reminiscent of rotten eggs. I sniffed cautiously and glanced around at the assembled ladies. No-one commented and unaccustomed as I was to Montserrat I simply assumed it was the fetid fumes of drains steaming in the tropical heat, and taking my cue from the other guests I politely refrained from mentioning it.

It was 9.00 p.m. that same evening when the phone rang. Abruptly and without warning life in Montserrat had changed dramatically and forever.

A colleague from work was calling my husband. He urged us to switch on the radio. There was an emergency announcement by His Excellency the Governor Frank Savage. We scrambled to obey.

The Governor was speaking in slow and sombre tones. He was saying that after 350 years of sleepy dormancy the volcano in the Soufrière Hills above the capital of Plymouth had become active. There was, he reported, rumbling and roaring coming from deep within the bowels of the hills and thick clouds of steam and fine ash were being vented high into the air.

So it hadn't been the smell of drains I had noticed at Government House earlier that day, it was hydrogen sulphide given off by the awakening volcano with its distinctive and offensive odour of 'bad eggs'.

The Governor continued his broadcast by advising everyone in the very vulnerable Kinsale area of the island to the south of Plymouth to pack an overnight bag and be prepared to leave the vicinity.

The Chief Minister of Montserrat, Rueben Meade, followed the Governor on the radio to give more detailed news about the situation up in the Soufrière Hills.

"Do not be alarmed" he said reassuringly, and his final words *"enjoy a pleasant evening"* were, we decided, a polite civility not intended to be flippant.

After the broadcast we gazed at each other in bewilderment and disbelief and in common with every other resident of Montserrat we spent a long night absorbing the news and discussing the implications of what we had heard.

This time of the year, from June to October, is the hurricane season, and we would normally have been focussed on the daily forecast coming from the Weather Channel, but the unexpected events at the volcano monopolised our attention. So it was a double surprise on the morning after the startling revelation that the volcano was active to discover that a tropical wave was passing over our area of the Caribbean which had just been upgraded to a tropical depression.

Were we to expect an erupting volcano coupled with a hurricane? Fortunately not, but the storm brought strong and gusting winds with heavy rain to the island and the normally placid blue sea looked grey and ominous with whipped white-caps rippling across the surface. This only served to fuel our feelings of vulnerability.

In spite of the brooding weather HMS *Southampton* the Royal Navy vessel on duty in the Caribbean as the West Indies Guard Ship (WIGS), changed her course and came racing towards Montserrat. On arrival, the Commander echoed the words of the Chief Minister. *"No need to be alarmed"* he beamed reassuringly, stressing that the arrival of the ship was *"A purely contingency thing!"*

We were told the Lynx helicopter on board would help with observations of the volcano since no-one really knew what was happening. A Nimrod aircraft also appeared and flew over the old crater in an attempt to take photographs, but the thick smoke billowing out of the hillside made visibility poor. The Nimrod's sensitive equipment had registered sulphur gas emissions from the awakening volcano at a distance of over two hundred miles away.

The volcano was producing something the scientists called 'acoustic energy explosions' at approximately half-hourly intervals. These sent ash and vapour three to four hundred metres into the air.

Dr. Ambeh from the Seismic Research Unit of the University of the West Indies flew into Montserrat in an attempt to determine more accurately what was happening inside the Soufrière Hills. He came on the radio saying he had collected a sample of fresh vented ash and 'chewed' on it to determine whether it contained beads of glass from the 'heart' of the volcano. This would mean it was new material rising to the surface, a very bad sign apparently.

I drove into the capital Plymouth with my daughter and we could see quite clearly that an area up in the Soufrière Hills was belching dark grey clouds in intermittent puffs up into the sky. These spread as they rose hovering over the hillside dissipating a little with the wind but hanging as a thick misty smog pressing in on Plymouth.

We parked on the waterfront and covered our mouths with scarves as we dashed across to the Post Office. All the cars wore shrouds of ashy grey dust and the smell of sulphur was incredibly strong. It made our throats sore and our eyes sting. Most of the shops were closed and shuttered or simply empty. People were scurrying, like us, with handkerchiefs over their faces. A lorry driver had found a surgical mask from somewhere and sped through town in a cloud of dust, his mouth and nose covered.

We ran up the street into the bank which gave us air-conditioned comfort for a few minutes. The bank was packed with people withdrawing 'hard cash'. On the radio the Chief Minister had been appealing to people not to take their money out of the bank but no-one seemed to be listening.

An American pushed into the bank after us and keen to air his knowledge about volcanoes he loudly volunteered the information *"The gas rolls down first, before the rock blows"* and followed it with the advice *"if you survive that, run for your life!"*

We decided to cut short the visit to town and hastily returned to the relative safety of our home at Old Towne, four miles from the volcano as the crow flies.

Old Towne 1995

We had been instructed to pack an overnight bag in case we needed to evacuate in a hurry and to include all important papers and some drinking water. Working on the premise 'if it could be replaced leave it, if it couldn't pack it' our daughter's priority was to save her precious degree thesis notes. She was, however, also persuaded to include money, passport, torch, a box of matches and water.

There was a scramble to leave the island. Over a period of ten days immediately after the emergency broadcast on the 18th July the Immigration Department reported the departure of 1200 people. With a passenger capacity of less than forty the three daily LIAT flights out of Montserrat to Antigua were fully booked for several days. LIAT abandoned the usual booking procedure and resorted to suggesting that people just 'turn up' at the airport.

The small charter company Montserrat Air were bombarded with requests to charter on an hourly basis. A shuttle that put an impossible strain on the pilots. Instead they tried to spread the charters to one every 90 minutes.

The two most common questions in Montserrat these days are *"Where will we go if we have to leave?"* and *"Will it really blow or will it just quietly pop and bubble for several years?"*

The UK press reported that Montserrat was being evacuated, and during a live broadcast of the Test Match between the West Indies and England the commentator told listeners around the globe the alarming news that Montserrat was erupting and two British warships were evacuating people. The Governor quickly gave an interview to the BBC trying to replace this misinformation with detailed fact. The volcano had not yet erupted and there was no mass evacuation. The situation was being closely monitored.

Behind the scenes a great deal of preparation was taking place for the worst-case scenario. The Montserrat Defence Force (MDF) was mobilised and busily erected tents and dug open latrines (*"shitters"* they call them) in the northern hills of Montserrat as far away as possible from the Soufrière Hills.

They had hoped to accommodate 8,000 people but they don't have the area recommended in the World Health Organisation instruction book.

We are currently on High Orange alert. The signal for evacuation to the north will be when we are put on Red Alert. When it comes the church bells will ring the radio will broadcast a message from the Governor or Chief Minister, and the police will patrol the areas to be evacuated with screaming sirens. At that time we have been instructed to gather up our things and meet at our respective pick-up points. Or if we have our own transport we must wait for instructions. We will not be allowed back to our homes.

No-one has mentioned the animals. In Montserrat it is a familiar sight to see a cow or bull chained up beside the road or tethered goats, particularly in the southern hills where the initial evacuation is expected to take place.

Again and again we are being advised to have a bag packed. We are only allowed one small bag in which we are expected to pack passport, bank books, land titles, savings books, marriage certificate, medicines, clothes, and enough food for *"a couple of days"*. But I have seen cars heading north loaded with tin baths, plastic pipes and an amazing assortment of household bits and pieces.

During this unsettled period of anxiety, Rose Willock, the warm-voiced and motherly Station Manager of ZJB Radio Montserrat, keeps telling us to *"Slow down, and calm down, and take a deep breath!"*. She plays gospel music and hymns, and songs she thinks will soothe our tension, like Phil Collins and *"Just Another Day in Paradise"*.

The preachers are exhorting us to pray. Some say that this is God's way of punishing us for our sins. The Pentecostal Church has started daily prayers at 5.00 a.m. each morning and the Glad Tidings Pentecostal Church recently held a Thanksgiving Service for 'being spared so far'.

Our teenage son is totally unaffected by the rising hysteria around him. He listened to the morning bulletin while making his breakfast of scrambled eggs recently with the blasé comment *"Sod the cholesterol if I'm going to die today!"*

He is spending his time building a canoe designed by his friend Angus. They launched it in Angus's swimming pool and baptised it *"Sea Agouti"* before it rolled over and sank. Our son jokes that if the order comes to evacuate Montserrat he and Angus will paddle off into the sunset in their strange craft.

People are beginning to talk openly of the initially unthinkable, appalling to contemplate, awful possibility of a complete off-island evacuation.

Although we are repeatedly assured that the northern one-third of Montserrat will be safe in the event of a major eruption, the scientists are comparing our volcano with that of Mt. Pelée, Martinique, which erupted in 1902 destroying the town of St. Pierre. Over 29,000 people were killed in a matter of minutes. The pyroclastic flow of hot gases and ash shot from the volcano at a searing 400°C and raced through the crowded capital of St. Pierre at a speed of well over 100 mph. The residents did not stand a chance.

At the end of July we decided to take a drive up into the Soufrière Hills towards the site of the venting volcano to try and see for ourselves what was happening. As we climbed upwards we met trucks and cars crammed with people and possessions, slowly, carefully, winding and bumping down the hillside towards us.

Passing abandoned homes we entered the low, grey, cloud of ash, but still we had not managed to reach the site of the actual venting although we could see columns of white vapour rolling powerfully out of the folds of the virgin green hillside, just like a train under a full head of steam.

We had gone some distance when we decided it would be wise to be prudent and turning the car around we headed back down, this time passing a truck grumbling towards us with MDF soldiers hanging on to the sides.

As we move into August and the height of the hurricane season the future is uncertain.

2 - AUGUST 1995

PLYMOUTH EVACUATED

As we moved into August preparations for evacuation to the north of the island accelerated.

An emergency evacuation jetty was proposed at Little Bay and British marines arrived to survey the seabed. *"A really cushy job!"* one of them was heard to say with happy satisfaction.

An RAF C130 Hercules like a giant bloated grey cigar, lumbered into the airport and from its belly off-loaded containers packed with tents and provisions.

Five containers with rations for two days were moved up to the north of the island and parked at Gerald's Bottom where several very old green canvas army tents, sufficient for four to six sharing, had been erected. Before the invasion of the tents and containers Gerald's Bottom served as a recreation and cricket ground and also as a place for tethering donkeys and goats.

From our house we watched as the navy Lynx helicopter thumped overhead and flew busily in and out of the cloud that surrounded the Soufrière Hills.

The Soufrière Hills consists of five 'domes' in close proximity to each other. Chances Peak at 3002 ft. is the most prominent of these hills and the highest point in Montserrat. A large, old volcanic horseshoe called English's Crater lies behind Chances Peak and within the confines of the crater, surrounded by a rocky moat, sits the dome of Castle Peak. The open side of the horseshoe faces east and rolls gently down Tar River, Hot River, and in less than a mile reaches the sea to the south of W.H. Bramble Airport.

It was on this flank that vents had opened up and were producing the gas, ash and steam emissions which sounded like a jet-engine taking off.

It became apparent to us that the volcanic activity was increasing when the Governor and Chief Minister reported swarms of earthquakes on the evening of the 6th August. They also warned us of an additional hazard associated with recent rains from passing tropical depressions. Mudflows are running down the mountain ghauts with Fort Ghaut in Plymouth particularly badly affected. A thick silty bed is building up and we have been warned not to use the ghauts as pedestrian short cuts.

The annual Emancipation Day celebrations were supposed to take place on Holiday Monday 7th August. Belham Bridge had been decorated with large crimson blossoms from the flamboyant tree and a sign beside them read *"Firs' o' August come agen, Hurrah for Nincom Riley"*. This being a reference to the slave who was chosen to read the Emancipation Proclamation to his fellow Montserratians back in 1834.

But before dawn on Holiday Monday the scientists monitoring the volcano contacted the Governor and Chief Minister to tell them that seismic activity was increasing further, and advised evacuation from vulnerable areas in the southeast of the island. Measurements taken on Holiday Monday showed the volcano had discharged 1200 tonnes of sulphur dioxide into the atmosphere. A sure sign, said the scientists, of increased activity.

The Governor and Chief Minister came on radio at 5.15 a.m. to inform anyone who happened to be up and listening at such an outlandish hour that people living in the area from Trant's to Spanish Pointe (close to W.H. Bramble Airport) must evacuate immediately.

That included the villages of Bramble, Bethel and Long Ground, the area we had been exploring the previous week.

The Chief Minister tried to reassure us saying *"It's not yet time to panic!"* maintaining that it was *"Only an increase of a notch in the state of alert"*. But while the broadcast was being made we were woken from our bed by a phone call from the Governor's Office informing us that the families of British Government personnel were being advised (they stressed it wasn't an order) to evacuate the island immediately. After a short family deliberation we decided to ignore the advice, preferring to stay together in Montserrat for as long as possible. But although we personally chose to remain, some families of government employees hastily packed to leave and by mid-morning six adults and eight children had flown off to the safety of Antigua.

Those of us who had elected to remain in Montserrat started packing suitcases in earnest. We also checked our provisions, replaced the cooking gas cylinder with a full one and generally tried to organize ourselves.

However, after an anxious twenty-four hours we were told the activity had 'gone quiet' and stabilised although the Governor did confess privately that we were still technically on Red Alert.

Normal daily chores continued and a reminder that it was the hurricane season came as a tropical wave headed towards us from the east Atlantic and we experienced the calm before the storm, with a mill-pond sea and humidity which brought out biting insects and a plague of tiny black flies.

Montserratians call the invisible biting sand flies *"no-see-ums"*. They are a real nuisance and come in their thousands when the weather is hot, still and sticky and a storm is brewing. They have a sweet, sickly, smell and swarms of them appear from nowhere, wriggling in black heaps on the floor before dying. The swimming pool attracts them and within minutes an undulating blanket of black corpses turns the pool dark grey.

Although activity at the volcano seemed to have slowed, evacuation of people from the vulnerable areas continued and on Thursday 10th August I received a desperate phone call appealing for help to *"put the old folks to bed"* at Brades School in the north. The school had been taken over as a temporary shelter to accommodate the 'infirmed' and 'shut-ins' and included the elderly who are not ill enough to be in hospital but are unable to look after themselves. Three Montserratian volunteer Red Cross workers were at Brades School struggling to cope with over seventy elderly people who had just arrived.

My daughter volunteered to help too and night was drawing in as we set off northwards to find the school. The road was unfamiliar to us and no signposts guide the way, so it was a question of memorizing a long and complicated verbal direction. But when we arrived at Brades we spotted a small group of single-storey buildings tucked away on a rough patch of land. Driving into the schoolyard we were confronted by a chaotic scene.

The three exhausted Red Cross staff, Adelle, Ann and Sonia, were using the Headmistress' small room as their HQ. Ignored in the corner a radio was playing the now familiar reggae tune *"A weh ya garn a go wen de volcano blow?"*

Two doors led off the tiny office. The one on the left opened into a classroom that had been hastily prepared as a women's room, and a door to the right led to a toilet. Two old gentlemen vague and confused were waiting outside the toilet door, and as we entered the office an old lady carrying a very full bedpan walked slowly across in front of us from the women's room to join the queue. There was the unmistakable stench of stale urine.

Adelle introduced herself as the Special Needs teacher at the small Red Cross School in Plymouth. In her mid-twenties elegant and tall she was very, very, tired. She said she couldn't remember when she had last slept. An ex-army 'cot', a sort of canvas camp bed, had been squeezed in beside the office desk a few feet away from the toilet door and Adelle was trying to snatch some rest as and when she could.

Sonia had her toddler with her. Small and serious little Sonny wandered around in the confusion while Sonia attempted to give care and comfort to the perplexed elderly evacuees.

They told us to expect around seventy people for the night but as we worked more kept arriving, and ultimately there were 107 people to care for, deposited by relatives and friends and members of the Emergency Services.

We had diabetics, the incontinent, the handicapped, and the confused. On canvas cots or mattresses hastily placed on the bare floor they were squashed together. One young girl, mentally and physically disabled, sat in a corner in her wheelchair and on a nearby mattress lay an old lady with both feet amputated, watched over by her equally elderly husband. Every inch of the school floor was occupied and in the narrow gaps between the mattresses brown paper bags bulged with precious personal belongings gathered in haste. The old folk were very grateful for anything that we did for them, but in their confusion they were completely unable to articulate their needs or desires.

We helped with the old ladies for a while and then my daughter and I were nominated for kitchen duty. We found Sylvia, Frances and two ex-girl guides trying to prepare supper in the small school kitchen.

Frances is the school cook and as elderly as some of those we were attending to and also partially deaf. Born and raised in the tiny settlement of Brades she has a natural regal presence. Her tightly balled black hair is in ringlets compressed beneath a red scarf bound across her forehead. Her speech was slow and distinct but with such a strong local accent that at times I found it difficult to understand.

After introducing ourselves we were put to work. On the kitchen table we found a paper bag which on investigation appeared to be full of extra-long bridge rolls, but was the locally made 'dollar' or grease bread. Extra fat in the recipe makes this popular bread unbelievably heavy giving it the advantage of resting like a rock in an empty stomach.

Plastic plates were lined up and we rationed out a small piece of the bread onto each. A large tin of processed cheese was opened, thinly pared, and miraculously divided on to seventy plates. Thoughts of Jesus and the loaves and fishes came unbidden to my mind. Then five cans of corned beef were scraped, mashed and tipped into a pot and heated through and a generous tablespoon dropped onto those plates empty of cheese.

The supper menu was therefore either a paring of cheese or a dollop of corned beef hash, while on the stove a large vat of boiling water was prepared in readiness for 'bush tee'. Frances told us that she was making 'cow's tongue' tea, so called because the leaf of the tree is shaped like a cow's tongue.

Sylvia explained to me that 'bush tee' (depending on which bush infusion is used) can be relaxing, invigorating, and healthful but always very good for you. It is best served, they all assured me, as an early morning pick-me-up. Cans of evaporated milk were tipped into another pot and Ovaltine and chocolate added. The bright new plastic mugs just delivered were colour coded, red for sugar and yellow for diabetics.

It was a long and exhausting night as we moved between the old folk, distributing the meagre rations, helping them to eat, and settling everyone down to sleep.

There were moments of crisis. One of the blind men became irritated with his ninety-two year old female helper and they began to bicker. His equally aged blind friend tried to intervene, by sitting on him. A frenzied tussle between the two blind men ensued quickly brought under control by a gently efficient Adelle. A geriatric lady, bedded down in the female classroom, cackled with delight when she discovered that her soaking incontinence pad made a marvellous missile, and she had to be restrained from targeting fellow evacuees. Tired but amused, Adelle put the trouble down to the effects of the full moon and too much bush tea.

When my daughter and I eventually returned home, we were greeted with the disquieting news that Hurricane Felix was 750 miles away moving steadily towards Montserrat and packing winds of over 80 mph. We fell into bed exhausted wondering whether we would be battening down for a hurricane when we woke.

Mercifully for Montserrat Hurricane Felix abruptly changed course during the night and veered north towards Bermuda and we experienced nothing more than strong winds and heavy rain.

During the evening of the 12ᵗʰ August the seismicity increased alarmingly and over 100 earthquakes were recorded overnight. Dr. Ambeh was being interviewed on ZJB Radio Montserrat when one of them shook the island. Simultaneously we heard the rumble from the radio and from outside and the villa began to shake around us with a loud cracking sound as the structure stretched and moved. Dr. Ambeh paused, and as the vibrations died away he said *"I think we should bring this interview to a close!"* and disappeared rapidly.

Our most alarming experience was early the following morning on 13ᵗʰ August at 2.22 a.m. when we were shocked awake by the loud noise and strong vibrations of an earthquake registering 3.5 on the Richter scale the epicentre of which was only two miles away under St. George's Hill. Everything shook, rocked and began to oscillate wildly from side to side. Solid objects appeared to dissolve into jelly and even our bodies took up the harmonics and wobbled uncontrollably like soft custard. For some time afterwards my internal organs continued to tremble independently of each other. A dreadful sensation.

Surprisingly, for the next few days there was a lull in the volcanic activity. It was as if the seismicity had released a build-up of pressure and the volcano was 'resting'.

Our offspring succumbed to the overwhelming temptation to inspect the volcano for themselves and set off with machete and camera to trek through the bush at Long Ground towards the site of the Lang Soufrière vent. They parked the car where the road ran out and toiled through thick undergrowth up the mountainside towards two steaming vents. They watched in awe as the volcano belched a black plume of ash into the air and took some sensational photographs. Two hours later as the light began to fade and having waded through three "slimy monster" mudflows, they decided to turn back.

The day after their trek on the 21st August, the volcano decided to test our nerves to the limit and at 8.05 a.m. without any warning at all, there was a mighty explosion and a huge mushroom of black ash shot high into the air.

Out of the window in Barclays Bank in Plymouth one of the cashiers saw the massive black cloud rolling slowly and relentlessly down towards the town, and she screamed. Pandemonium broke out. In a panic exodus people raced to cars in a dash to escape the approaching blackness that threatened to engulf the town of Plymouth.

My husband was in town inspecting the damage caused by heavy mudflows in Fort Ghaut and he was driving back to his office in Lover's Lane. It took him only minutes but by the time he reached the compound all the workforce had disappeared, heading north in their vehicles, headlights on and wipers going, trying to out-run the gritty volcanic rain that was turning day into night behind them.

The choking ash eclipsed the sun and Plymouth was plunged into instant midnight. My husband was caught in his car, ash hammering on the roof, trapped in the pitch darkness and breathing through a handkerchief he could only sit and wait. After several minutes the dense blanket of black ash moved away on the easterly wind towards the sea and the sky began to clear *"Like dawn lifting"* he said, leaving behind an astonishing scene. A thick deposit of grey ash lay over everything and an acrid stench irritated eyes and throat.

At our villa in Old Towne we watched in awe as in the distance Plymouth was eclipsed. We caught the edges of the raining ash but experienced only a dusting of grey talc which covered trees, buildings and roads like stone snow.

I collected a sample of the ash. It was soft and warm but heavy, and it set like concrete when wet. I took a photograph of the volcano and the ominous charcoal cloud as it rained west, trailing ash out across the sea. I watched as the helicopter thundered overhead, returning to the ship, reportedly for a hose-down after ash had clogged some vital parts.

HMS *Southampton* had been pulling away from Plymouth on her way to Barbados when the volcano erupted. The marines on board, all thirty-two of them, had been heading off to Antigua for rest and relaxation.

As the day progressed rumour spread that the order to evacuate Plymouth was imminent. Lorries transported beds from Glendon Hospital in Plymouth to St. John's school in the north.

The gossip on the street was that the hundreds of residents from Plymouth and the south would be accommodated in the 'tent city' at Gerald's Bottom and in Salem Secondary School.

Most of the shops in Plymouth had closed and the workers who had fled during the early morning eruption had not returned.

Another rumour on the street said that the Military Defence Force base in Antigua known as Camp Lightfoot was being prepared for a total off-island evacuation. On the radio Rose Willock spoke soothingly and played gospel music.

The rumours were correct. At 4.15 p.m. on the 21st August the Governor and Chief Minister made an emergency broadcast. The Governor informed us that they were *"Proposing to evacuate all areas south of a line below Richmond Hill"* which included Plymouth.

This decision was the result of a meeting at which the scientists had said the magma was less than 1 km below the dome and there was *"A 50% chance of an eruption of some type"* with the possibility of lava flows. The scientists said they could no longer guarantee to be able to give a six hour warning before an eruption.

They were evacuating themselves, moving the Montserrat Volcano Observatory out of Plymouth into the Vue Pointe Hotel, a few yards down the road from our villa.

The shelters were to open at 6.00 p.m. and a curfew was to be put in place between 10.00 p.m. and 6.00 a.m. The Governor said *"I will be signing an emergency order shortly"* and he finished by telling us that he was himself 'relocating' from Government House in Plymouth. Until further notice the Governor's office and residence will be Olveston House. Olveston House is the island home of George Martin who has owned Air Studios, a recording business in Montserrat, for many years.

The Chief Minister urged us to *"Bear each other up, reach out, lend a helping hand to those in need"* and concluded with *"God Bless"*.

As well as tent city, schools and churches throughout the north have been taken over as emergency shelters and the term *'relocation'* has now officially replaced the more emotive word *'evacuation'*.

Frightening though it was for those caught in it, the eruption on the morning of 21st August was described by the scientists as a phreatic eruption, different and less dangerous than an explosive, magmatic eruption. Apparently a phreatic eruption occurs when there is interaction between hot rock or magma and groundwater. The water is flashed into steam which expands rapidly and fractures the surrounding rock venting it high into the air as pulverised ash.

The more serious and potentially deadly explosive magmatic eruption is when magma containing large quantities of water and volatile substances reaches the surface, and the dissolved volatiles are released forming bubbles which expand rapidly, breaking the magma into fragments, sometimes many metres in diameter.

As you can see we are all slowly learning volcanology, the hard way, by personal experience.

At 5.00 a.m. on the morning of Wednesday 23rd August the phone rang. A distraught colleague of my husband was calling from his home in Richmond Hill. He had just been ordered to evacuate and told to head for the safety of the north, beyond Belham Valley. He didn't have anywhere to go and he asked if he could come to us.

The volcano had become very active overnight and the scientists said there was an 80% chance of an eruption without warning. Police and marines stationed themselves along the roads to make sure that everyone in the danger areas left.

By 7.00 a.m. we were making breakfast for eight evacuees who had arrived at our villa in search of a safe haven. All clutched overnight bags and looked dazed with confusion and concern. One, not knowing what else to do, had also brought his three dogs with him.

Within four hours we were informed that all British wives, families and non-essential personnel were being strongly advised to leave Montserrat for Antigua. It was made very clear to us that this time we were not expected to refuse.

My daughter, my son and myself, quickly gathered up our overnight bags. At the last moment my husband was instructed to accompany us to investigate a potential off-island evacuation to Camp Lightfoot on Antigua.

We left our friend and his dogs in charge of the villa, and headed for the airport with the other evacuees. At the airport the noise was deafening. There was chaos as the crush of people heaved forward and shouted for attention at the little LIAT desk. It seemed as if everyone in Montserrat had turned up at the airport and was clamouring to get out.

The milling throng rocked backwards and forwards and with each passing minute more and more people arrived. While waiting for a plane to take us out, my family sat on their suitcases outside in the sunshine and passed the time playing cards with the Governor's son who was being evacuated with us.

The Governor's Office had chartered small planes for the British staff and eventually six of us squeezed into one, leaving the bedlam of the airport behind. As we took off for Antigua we looked up at the volcano, a mile or so behind the airport, but all we could see was cloud covering the summit. It looked innocent enough and it was hard to believe it was a threat to Montserrat.

Fifteen minutes flying time and we were met at Antigua by a member of staff from the British High Commission, whisked through Immigration and Customs and driven to the exclusive Blue

Waters Hotel in time for a pot of tea and a piece of cake. The contrast was incredibly unnerving.

We arrived in Antigua at the end of August as refugees in transit, ill equipped for a stay in one of the island's most prestigious hotels. We did not expect to stay for long and quite thought we would be 'processed' on to the UK within a matter of hours. As a consequence we had brought the barest of essentials in our overnight bags. I had two T-shirts, two pairs of shorts, swimming costume and a toothbrush.

W.H. Bramble airport, waiting to evacuate August 1995

3 - SEPTEMBER 1995

DANGEROUS HURRICANE LUIS

It quickly became apparent that our stay in Antigua would be longer than the two days we had anticipated. In Montserrat the volcano began a series of startling phreatic eruptions with dramatic thunder and lightning crashing around inside the gritty ash of the eruptive column. An ash venting on Sunday 3rd September shot high into the air and the accompanying pyrotechnics lasted for over ninety minutes.

We were told we could only return to Montserrat once the activity had settled down again, but in the meantime we decided to make the most of our enforced stay in Antigua. This popular Caribbean holiday destination boasts a silky-sand beach for every day of the year and has the added attraction of duty-free shopping. We reasoned that it would be a shocking waste not to take full advantage of these temptations while we had the opportunity. So after a shopping trip into the bustling town of St. John's we returned with clothes more suitable to the ambience of the Blue Waters Hotel, casual but elegant, and turned ourselves from refugees into tourists.

Some of our fellow evacuees decided to return to the UK, including our daughter who was returning to University, but there remained a hard core of eight of us wanting and waiting to return to Montserrat at the earliest opportunity.

My husband had returned to Montserrat but he managed to hitch a ride on an RAF C130 Hercules to say goodbye to our daughter. For the short journey between Montserrat and Antigua he was strapped to a large metal pallet in the noisy womb of the plane bunched together with forty Montserratians who were fleeing from the volcano.

Our son remained at the Blue Waters Hotel with me, and he spent his time sampling the recreational delights of Antigua with the Governor's son. They were invited on board the RAF Hercules and on their return they informed me, grinning from ear to ear, that bracing themselves on the flight deck while 'greasing the wings' and doing 2G's was *"a great rush!"*

Early on Sunday 3rd September I was sitting on my bed in the Blue Waters Hotel listening to ZJB Radio Montserrat, hoping to get an up-date on the volcano, when the broadcast was interrupted with an important weather bulletin.

A hurricane watch had been advised for Antigua, Barbuda, Montserrat, St. Kitts and Nevis. In the confusion of recent events I had almost forgotten that we were still in the hurricane season.

I looked outside and the sky was a brilliant blue, the sea looked calm and coolly inviting and the sun blazed down in delicious warmth. It was hard to believe something very nasty was apparently brewing to the east of Antigua.

The Miami Weather Centre was tracking what had begun as a baby tropical wave formed in the hurricane nursery off the West coast of Africa. Conditions were perfect for a rapid acceleration of growth and over a few days the warm sea fed the insatiable appetite of the system until it grew into a tropical depression.

As it moved slowly west towards the Caribbean islands the tropical depression quickly graduated to tropical storm status and was awarded the name *"Luis"*.

The spinning winds increased still further and Luis matured into a full-blown hurricane. The winds gathered even more speed over the warm sea of open Atlantic until finally the vast, awe-inspiring system was accorded the ultimate distinction *"Dangerous Hurricane Luis"* and alarmingly it was heading straight for Antigua and Montserrat.

A hurricane surveillance aircraft was sent out from Puerto Rico to inspect the monster. The crew brought their plane back to Antigua and found themselves billeted at the Blue Waters Hotel with us. They told us that they had rarely seen such a vast disturbance out in the ocean, it was *"a whopper"*. It would take twenty four to thirty hours to pass over Antigua and unless the plotted course changed dramatically overnight this dangerous hurricane appeared to be aiming directly for Montserrat.

First the volcano and now this huge hurricane *"a double whammy"* commented a very subdued radio announcer.

At first the Blue Waters Hotel did not seem to be taking the advancing hurricane particularly seriously. The Manager reminded me that they had weathered Hurricane Hugo in September 1989 and assured me that the worst we would get were strong winds and heavy rain for a few hours *"coming from the northeast"*. He insisted that our suite on the end of the south-east facing block was well protected.

I was not convinced. I squirreled away some yoghurts, bananas and bread rolls from the breakfast table. *"A form of kleptomania"* said my son. *"Contingency planning!"* I retorted.

I begged a roll of sticky tape from the front Reception Desk and we decorated the window, a wall of plate glass, with huge diagonal stripes to prevent splintering glass from flying around.

The two boys dragged in the patio furniture and pushed everything against the back wall of the lounge, well away from the glass wall. They pillaged the hotel games room and returned triumphantly clutching a box of Monopoly. We filled the bath with water, packed away our clothes and sealed them into plastic bags. We were ready for anything.

As the hurricane crept closer on the morning of Monday 4th September the Manager informed guests that a buffet lunch would be provided before facilities closed down at 2.00 p.m. The hotel planned to re-open twenty four hours later during the afternoon of Tuesday 5th September. They gave us two night candles, a beef sandwich and told us to stay in our rooms until the hurricane had passed.

The sea brought the first sign. Throughout the morning it had been gently, slowly, quietly changing. First, subtle little furrows appeared and before long whitecaps laced the surface, popping and rippling in the stiffening breeze. Soon the growing waves formed large undulating rollers that burst with a crash against the shore.

The tall coconut palms began to lean with the strengthening wind, their fronds rustling, alternately fluttering free or straining tensely as the gusts caught. In the next room an RAF policeman settled down and prepared to read his way through a book while the RAF Hercules disappeared off to ride out the hurricane in the US. By 3.00 p.m. we had holed up in our suite and the boys had begun a game of Monopoly.

The phone lines and electricity went down almost immediately. As the afternoon progressed the wind increased bringing with it heavy rain. Watching through the window our visibility was reduced to a few metres and our view of the now foaming, crashing sea was restricted by a seemingly solid wall of thick grey mist. The palm trees were swinging and writhing, whipped almost horizontal by the buffeting wind.

As the hours passed the storm grew more ferocious. We had to shout to each other above the noise in order to make ourselves heard. The changing air pressure hurt our ears and we put in earplugs and opened a small window on the opposite side to the wind direction.

I abandoned the bedroom at 1.30 a.m. when the corner of the roof began to lift. Rain hammered down and water was already pouring through like a river from the enclosed balcony outside. The stairs from the bedroom became a waterfall that streamed into the lounge, backing up and swilling inches deep around our feet.

The boys climbed onto the couch and I paddled into the tiny kitchen and climbed up onto the work surface and stretched out with a pillow. In the inky blackness the whole building was vibrating. It shuddered and groaned with the onslaught of Dangerous Hurricane Luis. Glass in the windows was splattered with seaweed and flexed and bent under the pressure. A solar panel complete with corrugated cover had been wrenched from a neighbouring roof and wedged itself outside our door, crashing and banging, adding to the already deafening noise.

Coconuts, ripped from the savaged palms, smashed like grenades into the walls. My perch in the kitchen became saturated with water seeping in from the adjacent window and from somewhere above my head. At 4.30 a.m. I waded my way back into the lounge to join the boys.

At 7.30 a.m. there was the briefest of respites when the furious wind seemed to slow and pause for a few minutes. We were on the wall of the eye of the hurricane and so did not experience that extraordinary silence and blue sky which accompanies the passage of the 'eye'. Then suddenly, abruptly, the wind direction changed completely and came screaming in from the opposite direction.

Our vulnerable suite took the full brunt. The winds, stronger than ever and gusting to 140 mph, slammed into our wall. A loud crash came from the kitchen as a piece of wood demolished the window and ripped out the frame. Glass, frame and wood smacked into my recent bed. Thank God I had moved into the lounge. It took all the strength they could muster for the two boys to pull the kitchen door closed against the wind and stinging rain.

The boys were fascinated by the power and destructive force of the hurricane and from time to time peered through the window saying *"Cool!" "Wow!" "Awesome!"* and occasionally shouting over their shoulder to me *"Hey! ... Come look at this!"*

They had just sloshed back to the couch when there was another terrific bang, like an explosion, and in rapid succession the side window in the lounge blew in and the complete wall of glass on the opposite side blasted out like a massive champagne cork. So much for our attempts with the sticky tape.

With one wall totally missing and the side window out, the room was instantly exposed to the fierce wind and driving rain.

It was an astonishing sight to see everything in the room whisked into the air, blown around and then disappear out into the wild world. Books, papers and the Monopoly game with a million bank notes, whirled dizzily and vanished.

My son tried to grab a chair as it slid towards the gaping hole where the wall should have been, but as he lifted it into the air the wind plucked it from his arms and sucked it out into the storm. We pressed ourselves against the back wall and for a few moments just watched in stunned amazement. Then the roof began to pop ominously and we beat a hasty retreat.

The communicating door to the adjacent suite was locked, but with three good kicks it gave way, and we tumbled in to join a surprised, and naked, RAF policeman. Under the circumstances he was extremely gracious and welcomed us in before disappearing off to the bathroom to make himself respectable.

Although it was flooded his room had escaped severe damage and we spent the next seven hours sitting on his bed, eating our beef sandwiches, and chatting, while the hurricane blew itself out and on its way up the Caribbean chain.

As the winds diminished we emerged to inspect the damage and discovered that the Blue Waters Hotel as we had known it no longer existed. It had been completely devastated. Parts of the hotel had simply disappeared. Roofs were off, windows and walls blown out, palm trees uprooted and tossed into the swimming pool. Rooms were flooded and the grounds were a sodden, muddy quagmire. Fallen trees thick with impenetrable foliage blocked the roads out.

We were isolated and trapped unable to get out of the area. There was no phone, no water, no power and very little food. The hotel was a disaster area and sixty guests were stranded inside.

Mercifully for Montserrat the hurricane had veered away at the last minute and the island escaped with only heavy rain and strong winds that caused mountainous seas, damage to the jetty, a few tents down, and a couple of roofs lost. But Antigua and Barbuda had taken the full impact, suffering terribly as a consequence. As it carved a destructive path north Dangerous Hurricane Luis also decimated the island of St. Maarten.

The airport was closed for two days, the perimeter fence down and the control tower damaged and exposed to the elements.

In Antigua things began to deteriorate rapidly. A curfew was imposed to try and stop the looting. At the Blue Waters Hotel with no immediate help forthcoming the guests turned mutinous. For two nights the boys and I camped out as best we could in rooms slightly less destroyed than our own. Scavenging, I found some rice in one wrecked and abandoned suite, re-connected a gas cylinder and managed to make them a sort of meal.

We had to use the swimming pool, green and thick with debris and the roots of a fallen palm, to wash the crockery. The trapped water around the site began to smell offensively. It became evident that if we wished to escape we would have to help ourselves.

We heard that the RAF Hercules was returning from Washington, calling in to Antigua, and would be leaving for

Montserrat during the afternoon of 7th September. We decided that it would be better to return to Montserrat and the volcano than to remain under hurricane aftermath conditions at the Blue Waters Hotel.

At last, late on the morning of the 7th, the road from the hotel was partly cleared and it was possible to get through. We persuaded the Under Manager at the hotel to lend us his battered old car. We packed our bags and paid one of the workmen to drive us to the airport. It was a tortuous trip. He had to try all the back roads, weaving around fallen trees, driving over twisted power lines, corrugated sheeting and an assortment of hurricane garbage. The island looked as if it had been blasted by a meteorite. At one point the engine stalled and we spent an agonising few minutes wondering whether it would cough back into life again.

We finally reached the airport only to find that most of Antigua had been camped out there for two days, waiting for the planes to begin flying. A mass of tired, dishevelled, disgruntled people heaved around the empty airline desks.

The RAF Hercules had indeed arrived and we found the crew, only to discover that the aircraft needed refuelling, and the fuel at Antigua was suspected of being contaminated with water. The crew decided to *"sit and wait for it to settle"*, which meant waiting until the following day and sleeping rough at the airport.

We were sitting on our suitcases trying to come to terms with this news when we were spotted in the crowd by an Antiguan friend. She pushed her way through the melee to talk to us. She had connections with LIAT and informed us that an Otter aircraft with about twenty passengers was about to take off for Montserrat, the first flight to leave Antigua since before Hurricane Luis. We leapt at the chance to get on board. Fortunately I had cash in my bag and a surreptitious exchange of cash for tickets took place and by some extraordinary miracle we were suddenly being hustled, running, through a deserted Departure lounge out onto the airport apron and bundled into the waiting Otter. The door was closed behind us.

As we throbbed down the runway, wobbled a little uncertainly, then lifted off, the boys began to sing *"Show Me The Way To Go Home"* and generously handed out miniatures of rum, whisky and gin to the other passengers. The atmosphere on board was magic. It was a great relief to have left Antigua behind and fifteen minutes later, as the runway of Montserrat came into sight, a spontaneous loud cheer went up.

The Governor walked across to greet us as we disembarked. In his official car he had brought a cooler full of ice-cold beer. We thought we were in heaven. He took us to his home for a supper of pizza and apple pie, and we celebrated with a glass of champagne. As the cork popped we heard an accompanying loud 'boom' from outside. We went into the garden and watched as the volcano blew a vacuum bag of dust 6,000 ft. into the air, which drifted slowly north with the prevailing wind. *"A welcome home from the volcano!"* said the Governor.

On the 11th September permission was granted to return to the evacuated areas, with the exception of Long Ground. The shops and offices re-opened and people returned to their homes to clear up after the mess of Dangerous Hurricane Luis. The hospital moved out of St. John's school in the north back into the old Glendon Hospital in Plymouth.

The following day we managed to get our son away from Montserrat on a flight to the UK, via Barbados and St. Lucia, and back to University.

I was looking forward to a period of quiet rest when I heard that another hurricane was on its way. It seemed unbelievable. But it was true, Hurricane Marilyn was following Luis and was anticipated to pass within seventy miles of Montserrat. With sighs of resignation we battened down for another hurricane and boxed torch, candles, matches, water, charcoal and some tins of food. Overnight torrential rain lashed the island and strong winds tore at the buildings.

The following morning we emerged from the safety of the bedroom to find severe flooding across Montserrat. It was impossible to get into Plymouth and the airport was closed. The phone and current were still off from Hurricane Luis and now, with the passage of Hurricane Marilyn, we had no water. Things looked bleak.

Her Majesty The Queen sent a message to the people of Montserrat saying how saddened she was to learn that the island had experienced two natural disasters. Her Majesty was referring to the volcanic eruption and Hurricane Luis but by the time her message was broadcast we had experienced a third natural disaster - Hurricane Marilyn!

We started the slow, messy job of clearing up and Montserratians who had fled to neighbouring islands to escape the volcano only to find themselves caught in the two hurricanes began to return home.

We all believed that with the advice of the scientists it would be possible to manage the volcano and we could carry on a normal existence. The schools re-opened after their use as evacuation shelters and we were lulled into a false sense of security.

However the volcano had no intention of being managed, and after a weekend of high seismicity with a swarm of over 1200 earthquakes, a rumour began to circulate on the 26th September that *"something that shouldn't be up there"* had begun to appear at the surface inside English's Crater in the Soufrière Hills.

It was a deformation on the dome. A 'carbuncle' of rocky brown spoil had appeared at the base of the old Castle Peak dome inside the crater and was growing in size. Boulders 4 ft. across were being 'popped' out of the crater, one having gone through the roof of the Cable and Wireless Station beside the steps on Chances Peak.

Despite the continuing phreatic eruptions and the deformation at Castle Peak the message from the authorities at the end of September was one of 'no change' although we were advised to *"keep listening to the radio and be vigilant"*.

4 - OCTOBER 1995

THE GOVERNOR'S OFFICE

I have offered my services to the Governor's Office as a part-time, temporary, Girl Friday to help out during the volcanic crisis.

There is a perception that the Governorship of a Dependent Territory is a nice road into retirement for a career diplomat in the British Foreign and Commonwealth Office. All that is required of him (or her) is to be a safe pair of hands on the tiller.

Under normal circumstances the Governor would live out the three-year term of office in relative comfort and without crisis, then with much pomp and ceremony depart forever to the UK to collect a 'gong' for meritorious service to the Crown and to retire gracefully with a Civil Service pension.

The Governor represents Her Majesty The Queen and the image on island is of a fatherly figure, benignly supervising all matters relating to the British Crown.

On official occasions such as the Queen's Birthday Parade the Governor is expected to appear in public in full dress colonial uniform, which means tropical whites and pith helmet complete with a plume of white swan feathers.

Until recently Government House in Plymouth acted as both official residence and Governor's Office. But a newly built office now sits at the bottom of the garden of Government House. It is a small cream and green candy box of a building with a white corrugated roof. Hermetically sealed, it is refrigerated to such an extent that the hot tropical air smacks into you with debilitating force as you emerge from the air-conditioned coolness of the office.

The Governor has a Personal Assistant and two Staff Officers on contract from FCO London to help him. Four local staff are also employed, including 'Sammy' Solomon the policeman who has driven the Governor's official vehicle for many years.

When I reported for duty to the Governor's Office I expected to be employed to perform sundry casual, repetitive and boring little duties, like helping to answer the phone which has been ringing almost continuously since the onset of volcanic activity, or doing some filing and perhaps making the occasional cup of coffee.

However, by persistent digging the Staff Officer gleaned that in my dim and distant past I had gained a book-keeping qualification and to my utter astonishment I was immediately appointed 'Accountant' handed all the invoices, ledgers and cheque book, pushed into a rather nice air-conditioned office and placed in front of a computer. After the initial fright it was really quite exhilarating and flattering.

Sue, the warm-hearted and gentle PA, filtered all calls to the Governor's Office and tried to deal with most of them. After a volcanic 'ashin' the calls were guaranteed to come in fast and furious as 'concerned members of the public' wanted to know what was happening and believed that only the Governor could tell them. Phreatic eruptions and earthquakes have occurred on an almost daily basis during October. On Friday 6th October after a particularly heavy ash fall overnight, callers were ringing to find out where they could acquire ash masks.

Then there were the more general enquiries. For instance the old lady living in a tiny wooden hut by Belham Bridge, who called the Governor's Office wanting to know where she could get compensation because her chicken had been run over by a car. And the Rastafarian who rang, having heard that there were grants available to farmers to replant crops after the devastation of the two recent hurricanes. The gravely sympathetic PA was required to use all her tact and diplomacy when explaining to the young Rasta that the Governor would not feel comfortable in dispensing funds to cover the replanting of a lost marijuana crop.

On one occasion two irate young men turned up at the office demanding to see the Governor. It turned out they were employed as 'body movers' by the morgue and wished to speak to the Governor over a recently disputed invoice. The two had been called out to handle a decomposing body that had washed up on the shore at Rendezvous Bay after the passage of Hurricane Luis. It was thought to be the body of a yachtsman who lost radio contact during the early hours of the hurricane. His position had put him somewhere off rocky, uninhabited, Redonda, a few nautical miles northwest of Montserrat. The 'body movers' had sent in a bill for EC$7,000 for their services, which the PA thought somewhat excessive for moving a body the short distance from the bay to the morgue. She suggested they go away and recalculate their fee. In order to justify the charge the men launched into a graphic and grisly description of their duties, saying that the body was in such a dreadful state they required *"several men"* to complete the task, and hence the apparently high cost. In the end, it was left up to the Governor to negotiate a compromise.

Back at our villa the insurance assessor brought in to calculate the hurricane damage had given the go-ahead for remedial work to take place. Alfred, employed by the landlord's agent as a general construction manager, arrived with his team of workmen to replace roof shingles, re-paint walls and repair fixtures and fittings.

The team comprised of Lennie (known as 'Washy' to his mates), Lucas the local stud who always wore a bright blue woolly hat, and Pastor Thomas, odd-jobbing from his normal duties as Holy Man in the Church of God of Prophecy.

At first they tried hard to be invisible. Lucas, tired from the previous night's gymnastics, chose to paint the bits by the floor, so that he could lie down and rest while he worked. Pastor Thomas took upon himself the task of painting the cane furniture on the open gallery.

When they talked together I couldn't understand a word, but I did understand when Pastor Thomas complained it was hard work and boring.

The Pastor is a political person and when I discovered on the 17th October that the first Legislative Council meeting since July was being broadcast live by ZJB Radio Montserrat, I moved the radio alongside him so that he could enjoy the cut and thrust of the debate.

It was immediately evident that the Pastor was a strong supporter of the eloquent Opposition Member, lawyer David Brandt, known on island as 'The Heavy Roller'. The Pastor began shouting down Chief Minister Reuben Meade (known as 'Twisty'). Some say he acquired this nickname because of his unusual running style as a youngster, but unkind political opponents maintain it more accurately reflects his recent governmental tactics.

The Pastor's paintbrush was soon flying along the bamboo as he yelled at the radio *"We not talking politics - we talking issues man!"* as the two protagonists battled over a question on Government ownership of shares in the Rice Mill. Pastor Thomas joined in with shouts of *"Talk to me! Talk to me!"*

Alongside Alfred and his workmen Philip the electrician arrived to reconnect the 'current' to an assortment of malfunctioning items, including the fan in the bedroom and the lights on the drive. He had just settled down to a long day of work when 'Mr. Pest' turned up to put down rat bait and fumigate the villa.

A local company is contracted to visit on a monthly basis to spray the whole villa in an effort to keep cockroaches and ants and other undesirable creepies outside. 'Mr. Pest' primes a small tank containing a cocktail of chemicals, puts on protective breathing apparatus, and then strides through the rooms spraying a toxic ribbon of wet fluid along the edges of the floor in a seamless line. He is very thorough, going into cupboards and outside around the perimeter of the patio. The smell is disgusting and I worry that we are doing more harm to ourselves and the environment than any creepy could ever achieve. However on this occasion his visit was welcomed since he had come especially to place rat bait.

The evening prior to his visit my husband and I had been comfortably digesting our evening meal when we saw a huge rat with the girth of a good-sized cat strolling backwards and forwards on the patio outside. We watched in horror as the beast made a great effort to nose open the tightly shut patio doors in an attempt to get inside the house.

As a deterrent 'Mr. Pest' has placed cubes of what appear to be bright blue wax at strategic points around the inside of the villa, under the settee, under the bed and under the fridge. Outside he sprinkled green pellets into saucers and put them around the patio. Lennie explained to me that rats try to enter the house after heavy rain. He said it was something to do with them getting flooded out of their nests. Lennie urged me to dispose of any rat carcass I might come across as rapidly as possible *"Before dem swell up an' burs"* he warned me ominously. The stench of a burst dead rat was, he assured me, absolutely and disgustingly foul. It brings a new significance to the well-known expression *"to smell a rat"*.

The rains bring other unwanted creatures. After Hurricane Luis an unidentified 'worm' new to the island appeared in Montserrat. It was a large and very hairy caterpillar about three inches long with a voracious appetite. Specimens were gathered up and sent off-island for identification and shortly afterwards the result came back. It was something called a Dasheen Horn Worm a native of Africa, presumably picked up by the winds and carried over 3,000 miles across the Atlantic before being deposited here in Montserrat. Apparently a similar thing happened after Hurricane Hugo in 1989 when a swarm of big, green, locusts invaded the island.

We have been having an excess of stormy weather during October. Tropical Storm Noel didn't trouble us very much but Tropical Storm Pablo howled through bringing heavy rain and thunderstorms. Then on Tuesday 24th October Tropical Storm Sebastian swept across the island bringing violent thunderstorms and yet more rain. The damage caused was worse than we had experienced with Hurricane Marilyn.

The land was totally saturated. Everywhere was badly flooded including the basement at Government House, the new Government Headquarters and most of the schools. Landslips blocked roads with fallen trees and boulders up to 10 ft. across. The airport was closed due to poor visibility, schools were also closed and the Chief Minister sent all Government employees home. Most Montserratians prefer to stay at home when it rains. The wearing of black plastic bin bags and shower caps became the fashionable order of the day for the few people who were obliged to venture out.

We all knew the rain would irritate the volcano as the water percolated down into the hot rock. The scientists confirmed that Castle Peak dome is now growing an additional carbuncle, and so on the 5th October at 4.30 p.m. it was decided to move the patients from the hospital in Plymouth and the elderly from Margetson Memorial Home, back up to the safety of the north. At the same time the decision was made to move the Kinsale schoolchildren out of their village in the southwest to take their lessons in the Plymouth school. The explanation being that the authorities *"couldn't come up with adequate contingency plans for rapid removal of children in an emergency"*.

Around midnight that night after an evening of strong smells, a big phreatic eruption with a heavy ashfall engulfed Amersham and the surrounding areas for about an hour. A friend living on the slopes of the volcano above Plymouth told me it was *"Much, much worse than Ash Monday"*. Ash Monday is the name given to the early morning eruption of the 21st August that blacked out Plymouth and trapped my husband in his car.

The Chief Minister declared a National Prayer Day for the 11th October, and we were granted a public holiday. We were encouraged to go to church for Thanksgiving Services. We obviously didn't pray hard enough because the following day we had an unprecedented four ash eruptions in five hours and a new vent opened up on the eastern hillside.

With one eye on the volcano we tried to carry on normally. There was a Reception at Government House in Plymouth on the 6th October to say farewell and thank you to the crew of both HMS *Southampton* and *'RFA Oakleaf'*. We all did our best to studiously ignore the very strong smell of sulphur in the air.

But as far as we were concerned the social event of the month was the wedding of our friends Mike and Marife on the 14th October. Mike and Marife were determined to be married at St. Patrick's Roman Catholic Church in Plymouth, regardless of the volcano.

About fifty guests were invited including the Chief Minister. Mike's father, the Dutch Ambassador in Uruguay, was the 'bride-giver' while Marife's sister arrived from the Philippines to be a bridesmaid. Her journey halfway around the globe taking an exhausting thirty-six hours.

The volcano tried to create a diversion by opening up yet another new vent in Long Ground and vomiting an ashy plume just one hour before the ceremony.

The chauffeur of the wedding car had been about to collect the bride for delivery to the church. He watched in consternation as the dark cloud approached. Jumping into the pristine white car he quickly drove it out of town and out of range of the ashfall.

St. Patrick's Church stands on the edge of town in George Street where the road rises up towards the Soufrière Hills. On the other side of the road the gorge of Fort Ghaut falls away to a depth of 100 ft. as it travels down through Plymouth to the sea.

Taking six long years the church was originally built in 1848 but was damaged by two hurricanes in 1899 and 1928. It is a large, rectangular, grey stone-faced building. White walls inside, and a high vaulted wooden roof supported by arched columns give a clean airy feeling. The wooden doors are left open during services so that fresh morning air can circulate freely through the church.

Small and fragile, Marife looked beautiful. Wearing traditional bridal white with a short dress under an elaborately sequinned satin over-skirt, she floated down the aisle on the arm of Mike's father, the top of her dark head straining level with the shoulder of her blocky bride-giver. The three bridesmaids wore full-length creations in vivid magenta that fluffed and billowed prettily in the tropical breeze.

The smallest bridesmaid led the procession down the beribboned aisle, scattering rose petals from a basket on her arm onto the stone floor ahead. A shy pageboy followed, balancing the satin pillow for the rings on his palms. The wedding march was a slow waltz and the children had some difficulty keeping time. Their short legs required them to pause slightly between beats, giving the assembled congregation the disconcerting impression that the bridal retinue was performing an unconventional 'goose-step' as it approached the waiting groom.

Father Larry officiated, using the microphone to add a thundering resonance to his naturally powerful Irish voice. His loquacious homily included references to Jesus turning the water into wine at the wedding feast, how no-one should be alone, and God making woman from man's rib to keep him company!

Just as Father Larry was at full steam we heard a loud 'boom' from outside. We pretended to ignore it, but the Chief Minister tiptoed out and came back to indicate that the volcano had just sent another ash plume high into the air. The smell was quickly evident but fortunately the wind direction had changed since early morning and the cloud of raining ash drifted out to sea and we were spared the indignity of an ashy photo-call.

October ended with a bang, literally. On the 29th October, five days after the heavy rain which accompanied Tropical Storm Sebastian, we experienced several large earthquakes at around 10.00 p.m. which shook the foundations of the villa. We were out dining with friends at the time, and were initially unsure whether the movement of the walls was due in part to the effects of the powerful homemade rice and raisin wine.

The scientists told us that these earthquakes were more of the rock breaking volcano-tectonics, which were probably caused by magma forcing its way up towards the surface.

Experience has shown us that high seismicity usually precedes an event at the volcano and although we received no other indication of activity it was not a great surprise when the following day, at 1.10 p.m. on the 30th October, the volcano once again turned day into night over the capital of Plymouth, depositing several centimetres of ash over the town, including the Hospital, the Governor's Office and Government House.

My husband and I were at home at the time, preparing to return to Plymouth for the afternoon. We heard three loud 'pops' closely followed by a rumble and then the sound of dogs barking and people shouting.

We went outside and looked towards town and saw an enormous black cloud rising higher and higher into the air. A small white cloud in the brilliant blue sky had been sitting like a cap on top of the mountain of Chances Peak, and the eruption had punched a hole through the centre as the black and grey ash column writhed and rolled upwards.

It was an awe-inspiring sight. The wind was negligible and the column kept on rising, still pumping out black gritty ash at the bottom, rolling in on itself, curling and twisting until it reached a height of 12,000 ft. The base of the cloud then began to slide stealthily down the hillside to choke the town before drifting, very slowly, out over the ocean.

It was the worst eruption to date and was a very frightening experience for those caught in it, particularly the schoolchildren, many of whom were severely scared.

To all of us in Montserrat it seems self-evident that the volcano is getting worse not better.

5 - NOVEMBER 1995

VOLCANIC ACTIVITY INCREASES

During the first week of November the volcano was very active with several new vents opening up in the moat of English's Crater around the Castle Peak dome.

We suffered five ash falls over Plymouth and surrounding areas in less than a week. A police football match being held on the Sturges Park recreation ground on the northwest edge of Plymouth broke up in disarray when the players ran for cover as ash began to fall over the pitch. Perhaps the first match in football history to be halted by an erupting volcano.

For a few days Plymouth looked like a ghost town with wind-blown ash fogging the air. The schools were closed for two days while the Fire Brigade attempted to hose the ash from buildings and streets. Shopkeepers, hurrying pedestrians and speeding drivers wore masks, scarves and glasses to protect lungs, hair and eyes. Some comics lightened the indignity and frustration of looking like alien bandits by painting red noses and cat's whiskers on their masks. A few completely missed the point of wearing a mask. I watched with amused incredulity as one obsessive smoker cut a small circular hole in his white face-mask for his cigarette, just so he could continue to smoke while driving through town.

At 3.30 a.m. one morning in early November, after returning from a late night dinner party, I was hot and unable to sleep. I went outside for a breath of fresh air. It was very still and a full moon bathed the landscape in a white, ethereal light. From force of habit I looked towards Chances Peak, and at that precise moment the volcano belched. Silently, it spewed convoluting ash slowly into the air expanding into the celestial night like an atomic bomb. Lightning flashes zigzagged brightly through the dense mass. It was a mesmerising sight, made all the more painfully exquisite viewed alone and under the eerie magic of a full moon.

During this time the iguanas disappeared from our garden. They emerged a few days later to climb the flamboyant tree and stretch out on the branches. Normally they soak up the sun on our warm stone walls or on the grass, but now they seemed to want to be off the ground.

There was also odd behaviour from a pair of bananaquits. With single-minded determination these two small, yellow and black birds began to build a nest in the lampshade over the patio table, trailing strands of dried grass as they flew backwards and forwards. Sadly it was a doomed enterprise as they dropped most of the construction material onto the table below.

Alfred continued to supervise remedial work at our villa, and one day he arrived with a Rastafarian namesake to clean and seal the terra-cotta tiles of the gallery.

'Rasta' Alfred keeps his long dreadlocks firmly under control inside a bulging green felt beret that bobs up and down on the back of his head as he works. A gentle young man, he lives in rural Trant's, the peaceful farmland on the east coast adjacent to the airport.

The old sugar estate at Trant's is one of my favourite places in Montserrat. The derelict two-storey plantation house with its flight of stone entrance steps still retains most of its cladding of cedar shingles. The roof is part shingle and part rusty-red corrugated sheeting. The occasional donkey, goat or bull grazes the flat green pasture surrounding the ruins of the house. Half-hidden by the embrace of unruly bushes lie the lumpy remains of abandoned machinery. Flywheels, gear wheels and steam engines stamped '*Made in England*' and imported to crush the juices from the sugar cane. Dating back two hundred years the original round stone mill and tall chimney still stand, almost completely intact.

Part of Trant's is due to be incorporated into current plans for a proposed airport extension, and since the adjacent area has long been linked to Arawak and Carib settlements, an archaeological team from the University of Maine in the United States spent last summer excavating the site. Rasta Alfred considered it a wonderful privilege to be allowed to join the 'dig' and he showed me his treasured photographs.

The oldest artefacts found were carbon dated to 480 BC and belonged to the Amerindians of the Saladoid tribe who appeared to have lived in Montserrat for at least 800 years. Rasta Alfred was proudest of the photograph that showed the remains of a skeleton, lying on its side with knees drawn up, which he said was the body of a prince.

The team found seven skeletons and took the bones of four of them, including the prince, back to the Carnegie Museum of Natural History for further investigation.

Rasta Alfred firmly believes, along with many Montserratians, that the volcano is *"Actin' up"* because the bones have been disturbed and if the bones of the prince are brought back to Montserrat where they belong then the volcano will *"Go back to sleep"*.

Rasta Alfred and I had several interesting conversations while he worked on polishing the patio. He enjoys talking. During one conversation he told me that he didn't understand why 'ganja' was illegal. He listed what were, in his opinion, the many therapeutic and medicinal benefits of marijuana. It was, he asserted, especially good for reducing high blood pressure. In a curiously understandable logic Rasta Alfred maintained that the police were doing a disservice to society by arresting and fining users of 'ganja'. He argued they were making matters worse because the only way to pay a fine was to sell more 'ganja', therefore the police and the Judge were obviously compounding the problem.

In his advice to me he also recommended eucalyptus tea as 'healthy', but it was easy to make it too strong he warned, and that was dangerous. In response I offered him a cup of Earl Grey to try, but he declined.

The MVO have brought some specialist equipment onto the island to monitor the mountain. In layman's terms these instruments measure the 'bulgability' or swelling of the mountain. Using Electronic Distance Measuring (EDM) techniques and the Global Positioning System (GPS) satellite the scientists have discovered that a significant deformation took place during the early part of November. This information, together with visual observation of the crater and the earthquake patterns recorded on the seismic drums at the MVO, gives the scientists a *"fairly accurate"* picture of events within the volcano.

With flippant good humour the young scientists at the MVO have created their own names for the seismic signals that are recorded on the drums. An escalation in activity where the graph shows high peaks in a regular pattern they call *"the BD's"* or *"the bonking donkeys"*. But the signals that really alarm them because they imply something big is about to happen they dub the *"OL's"*, or *"Oh Hell"*!'

On the 29th November, Simon Young from the MVO decided to climb Chances Peak to get a closer look at the volcanic activity. Although he was wearing a mask he was overcome by carbon dioxide and was reportedly *"feeling a bit funny"* for several hours. We have been informed that the gas and acid emissions are high, but as yet we have no specific measurements for SO_2 release.

Like everyone else in Montserrat we have been working long hours over evenings and weekends and at the end of November we decided we needed a 'stress-buster break' before Christmas. So we hastily arranged a weekend in St. Maarten leaving on the 6.45 a.m. LIAT 'red-eye' 30th November.

Old Plantation House at Trant's November 1995

6 - DECEMBER 1995

FIRST PYROCLASTIC FLOW

The island of St. Maarten had recovered extraordinarily well from the ravages of Hurricane Luis in September. We stayed in Philipsburg the capital of the Dutch half of the island. The hotel was in the throbbing heart of tourist tinsel-town, straddling a sandy beach and the sea at the rear, with a mile of humming, colourful, wall-to-wall duty-free shops at the front. For a sun-worshipping jewellery junkie like me it was perfect paradise.

I was shopping for Christmas presents and for our daughter's 21st birthday, to be celebrated on Christmas Eve in Montserrat. I started early and finished late. In and out, up and down, I browsed every glitzy Aladdin's Cave before homing in on Philipsburg's best buys.

I had been advised by a seasoned friend to wait until the cruise ships had departed for the day before starting my bargaining. Beginning at around 50% of the marked price I worked slowly, but obviously reluctantly, towards a mutually agreeable hand-shaking deal. My friend suggested I would gain a psychological advantage by letting it be known, fairly near the beginning of negotiations, that I was not a tourist on a spending spree but a down-islander from Montserrat, visiting St. Maarten to escape the volcano for a couple of days rest and relaxation.

The final triumphant clincher, which she advised I keep until we reached uncompromising stalemate, was the Hurricane Luis bonding experience. Since parts of St. Maarten were still without electricity and the scattered evidence of splintered boats, ripped roofs and wrecked houses was everywhere evident, the shared trauma of Hurricane Luis was a potent uniting force.

We were away from Montserrat for two nights and not wishing to miss the volcano updates we had taken a radio. On the evening of 1st December we switched on and to our surprise heard the Governor speaking. He was announcing that Plymouth and all areas south and east of the capital were being evacuated.

We hung with horror on every word and listened intently as he explained that this second evacuation of Plymouth announced at 4.00 p.m. had been advised by the scientists as a precaution following the previous few days of increased activity.

Residents were being given forty-eight hours to gather together possessions and move *"in an orderly and phased manner"* out of the area. It was not necessary at this stage to move the residential pockets of Richmond Hill, Fox's Bay, Cork Hill and Isles Bay north, beyond the 'safe' line of Belham Valley, and therefore these areas were allowed to remain occupied.

This news depressed us dreadfully and we were keen to return to Montserrat as quickly as possible. It was therefore very frustrating to arrive at St. Maarten airport the following morning for our return to Montserrat (*avec* bulging bags of Gouda and French bread, not to mention the Christmas presents) to discover that LIAT had summarily cancelled the flight.

Although the initials represent Leeward Islands Air Transport some say that it's really an acronym for Leave Island Any Time, or Late If AT all.

However the obliging LIAT Manager somehow organised two seats on a 'full' plane going to Antigua, where another charming LIAT official conjured two seats on an apparently 'full' Dash 8 plane into Montserrat.

We were accompanied on the second leg of our journey by a clutch of 'snowbirds'. Those rich people who have their main homes in North America but like to overwinter in the Caribbean, leaving before the hurricane season begins. Several geriatrics from Canada were travelling to Montserrat, as they had done for many years. When they had left their beloved Montserrat last year it had been a peaceful paradise, now they were returning to an island on volcanic Red-Alert, with an evacuated capital and a shortage of food. They did not seem to comprehend the crisis at all.

After we landed in Montserrat we had to wait for several minutes while the most elderly of the group was carefully guided, wheezing and almost incapacitated by arthritis, down the steps of the plane.

She saw the volcano, shrouded in cloud beyond the airport and I heard her say to her companion *"I'm quite looking forward to it. I've heard it's just a bit of ash and steam"*. I worried that the stressful reality of the situation, and inhaling the ash, might prove too much for her obviously fragile health. She didn't know that the capital of Plymouth had just been evacuated and her winter villa was now on the front line of the no-go zone.

I thought perhaps Immigration or Customs might hand out maps and advisory leaflets about the volcanic activity to arriving passengers, but they seemed much more interested in sorting through my duty-frees.

We were away for just a short weekend and yet in our absence a 'dusk to dawn' curfew and a pass system had been introduced in the evacuated zone, and police were manning makeshift barriers on the road from the airport to the south-east and Harris, and on the Cork Hill road on the outskirts of Plymouth. This effectively restricted entry into Plymouth and the villages close to the flanks of the volcano. It was in part to reduce the possibility of empty properties being burgled, but also to monitor movement in and out of the exclusion area.

Within Plymouth itself the rice factory, Monlec power station and the port still functioned. Farmers are being allowed free access to feed and water their animals and to tend their crops. An estimated 4,000 people have been moved away from the volcano.

The airport closed at dusk and we had heard that the growing dome of the volcano, described as looking like a BBQ pit glowing red, could be seen from the airport at night. Dusk was just sliding in when we arrived back and we debated whether to wait and watch the volcano then take the long route home round the north, or leave immediately and drive through the central corridor through the village of Harris before the curfew came into effect.

The police barrier guarding the east coast road was unmanned, so we decided to take a chance on the central corridor, wishing to see the evacuated zone for ourselves.

It was the most unnerving experience. We drove for half an hour through a deserted landscape, grey with light ash, empty villages, not a soul in sight, not a sound anywhere. Not even the familiar chirp of the little treefrog broke the silence. It was eerie, disturbing and very unreal.

The whole of the population had seemingly vanished into thin air.

The volcano bubbled and coughed under heavy cloud cover to our left as we climbed up into the hills of Harris before plunging down George Street into Plymouth on the other side. We took a right turn down Lovers Lane, past the Public Works Department, coming up to the wrong side of the police barrier at the Delta Service Station just as the 6.00 p.m. curfew came into effect.

Tall spines were growing out of the volcanic lava domes within English's Crater. The domes themselves are multiplying, growing rapidly, and joining. The scientists are worried that the spines (some growing at a phenomenal rate of fifteen metres per day) could become unstable, breaking off to fall back into the dome, or that the domes themselves might collapse. The wall of English's Crater, they assured us, would contain the growing domes and confine any activity, but the open horseshoe above Tar River on the east is an area of high risk, since any disturbed lava might spill out through this breach spreading over the surrounding countryside.

Their caution was justified. On the 5th December we had our first, although apparently small, pyroclastic flow within English's Crater, and to our alarm, on the 21st December reports circulated that we had experienced the first magmatic eruption of the volcano.

We had been told that the second evacuation from Plymouth would be a long one, estimated at least three months. We were on Red Alert now and would have to drop to High Orange', then wait for one month, before reoccupation of Plymouth could even be considered.

A booklet entitled *"A Resident's Guide to Evacuation Procedures in a Volcanic Emergency"* is being distributed. The suggested list to 'walk with' comprises two weeks supply of clothing, toiletries, medical supplies, as much food as possible, a two day supply of drinking water, passport and important papers, plates, cups and forks, and if possible pillows, sheets and blankets.

The situation for the 4,000 evacuees leaving their homes in the south has changed little since the first major evacuation at the end of August, when we were sent away to Antigua. Once again people found themselves cramped into inadequate accommodation in church halls and schools, or tents pitched in schoolyards.

With more heavy rain during the month the cesspits, now coping with large numbers, soon began to overflow and 'dump holes' were hurriedly dug at Little Bay to take the raw sewage. The old 'honey truck' which had the job of emptying the pits, lumbered backwards and forwards on an almost hourly basis.

The flat campground of Gerald's with its trench latrines was left empty in case it was needed urgently for the estimated 2,000 people who remained south of the safe line, in the 'grey' area between Belham Valley and Plymouth.

Many people moved in with family and friends in the north, or rented their own alternative accommodation but some hesitated, then refused to move, determined to stay in their homes in the south for as long as possible. They did not wish to go into shelters simply as 'a precaution'. Life in the shelters, especially at Christmas, was quite unacceptable to them. They believed the volcano would not harm them and they believed they could 'get out fast' if it became obvious that the volcano was escalating dangerously.

Over a period of a few days, shops, offices and banks moved out of the capital of Plymouth. Some made ad hoc arrangements to operate in, or around, Salem village. Since it was a well-established community having the advantage of being just north of Belham Valley, Salem became the 'new' capital of Montserrat.

Plymouth Central Post Office relocated to the veranda of a small house down a narrow track in Salem. Banks moved into garages or rooms in homes occupied by the managers. Osborne's grocery store took over a room at the Vue Pointe Hotel. Government offices rented any property available, and the Treasury moved into a villa opposite us. Cargo containers parked on vacant lots became hardware, electrical, and liquor stores. The noise of hammering filled the air as shopkeepers hastily built plywood huts on common land, or converted villas into office space. Suddenly our neighbourhood was no longer on the fringe of island activity but very much inside it.

The Public Works Department tried to squeeze the entire compound into a three-bedroom single-storey house at Cork Hill.

Civil Servants were encouraged to take leave. Some worked from home converting spare bedrooms into offices. I found myself acting as secretary, receptionist and message-taker to a constant stream of callers using our villa as an extension to the PWD departmental office.

Frequent ash falls made conditions around Cork Hill and Fox's Bay very unpleasant, but Salem and Old Towne escaped with only a light dusting from time to time.

The Governor's Residence and Office rented a twenty-four acre estate in Olveston called *'Camelot'*. It is a five-bedroom luxury villa belonging to the McChesney family and by converting the bedrooms into offices the complex serves the Governor's purposes well. The large reception room, with its grand piano, made a good venue for the Carol Concert and other official functions.

Christmas is special in Montserrat. Montserratians from around the world return to spend Christmas on the island among family and friends. Normally the carnival atmosphere lasts for almost two weeks culminating in Festival Day. The popular Masqueraders come onto the streets to perform their traditional Christmas entertainment, playing from village to village accepting gifts. Several men make up the Masquerade dancing troupe, wearing masks with tall head-dresses, and costumes made from a colourful rainbow of ribbons. The 'Captain' keeps the dancers and the crowd in order cracking a long whip, while his First Mate, a young Mischief, a Queen and four or five others, perform traditional dances to the music of accompanying minstrels. The four musicians emphasise the rhythm with drums and a shak-shak. The performance seems powerfully African, but there is also a flavour of Mummers and Morris dancing incorporated into what has become a unique expression of Montserrat folk culture.

All the festivities had to be scaled down this year, or even cancelled. The Churches are full of 'shelterees' and services were restricted. The relocation was ordered on the day of the Calypso Eliminations, one of the most popular and important Christmas competitions and the traditional street fair was reduced to two days and had to be held in Salem. But in spite of all the difficulties there was still a joyful Christmas spirit in the air and the choirs visited our homes to sing carols and hymns.

Our son and daughter arrived in Montserrat from the UK on the 17th December, and we organised a big Christmas Eve party. We invited a colourful cross-section of the community to join us in celebrating our daughter's 21st birthday. It was also a way of bringing a little enjoyment and convivial company to many who had been working long, stressful hours. We strung fairy lights around the gallery, inflated a plastic Santa and set him on the back of a big whale in the swimming pool. We made vast quantities of sandwiches, pastries, dips, and nibbles and loaded a table until it groaned with the weight.

Pastor Thomas arranged for a steel pan player to provide the music for our Christmas Eve birthday party, and early in the evening he brought Stanley and his two drums (the bottoms of old oil drums hammered concave and 'tuned').

Stanley, known as 'Pope' or 'Killman' to his friends, was so nervous and shy he was shaking. His full-time job is as gardener on the McChesney Estate where he has worked for over thirty years. He has been playing the pans for slightly longer. Pastor Thomas explained that to overcome his shyness Stanley tended to resort to help from the rum bottle, a habit that has to be firmly discouraged, although the Pastor did reluctantly admit that Stanley often played better *"When de wine in he head"*.

Pastor Thomas left Stanley to our care, warning him to behave and stay off the liquor for the night. Our son took pity on the terrified Stanley and fed him two chicken legs and completely disregarding the Pastor's advice, a couple of beers and several rums. For the rest of the evening we had a smiling, relaxed, pan-player, well lubricated but not legless, who behaved like a gentleman and made music like an angel.

Halfway through the party the Governor arrived, dressed as Father Christmas, carrying the birthday cake for our daughter. He made his entrance to the strains of 'Happy Birthday' played by Stanley on his pans. The cake was a sticky pink and white number creation I had produced from several dusty cake-mix packets bought at the supermarket in town.

My friend Pauline had gone to great trouble to sculpt a posy of sugar-paste flowers to decorate the cake. The posy kept melting in the heat and we had to put it in the freezer several times to try and harden the limp petals.

Our son kept the bar lively by mixing some amazing cocktails. Tequila Sunrise, Screwdriver, Fluffy Duck, Daiquiri and Dizzy Blond. And his own special concoction called Volcano Blaster which left his friend Angus with a cobalt-coloured tongue and no recollection of Christmas Day.

Simon arrived late to the party having been on duty at the MVO and warned us to make the most of the evening. Six domes were growing in the crater at the volcano and a spine, shaped like a church, had just entered the record books as the fastest growing and tallest in history. He said there was no knowing what would happen when the spine became unstable and it was being closely monitored.

On Christmas Day the spine fell, dropping back into the growing lava dome and creating a cascade of glowing rocks, but not the dreaded pyroclastic flow that had been anticipated.

At 6.30 a.m. on the 28th December, the Governor and Chief Minister informed the public that after a scientific review which had been held on Boxing Day, the state of alert had been stepped down from Red to High Orange. They continued by saying that if there was no change during the next five days, then a phased return to the evacuated zone, including Plymouth, would commence on the 1st January, one month after the evacuation.

The anticipated return was announced in a joint statement by the Governor and Chief Minister on New Year's Day, the morning of 1st January 1996. The Governor as Head of the Civil Service said he expected all civil servants to be back in Plymouth, and working, by Wednesday 3rd January.

It was good news to those who had been spending Christmas in the shelters. Dr. Ambeh and Lloyd Lynch at the Observatory were confident that the scientists *"Could give twenty-four hours' notice of any change"* also maintaining that observations had shown *"The spines are collapsing without creating damage"* which implies the gases are not high.

There is a rumour, however, that the scientists are disagreeing between themselves and the Governor is relying more and more on advice from the *"Three Wise Men"* senior scientists in London.

7 - JANUARY 1996

BUS-TRAINS AND TROPICAL IGLOOS

Traditionally New Year's Day is the Grand Finale of the festive season in Montserrat. Normally *"Wan ton ah people"* would have been on the streets of Plymouth.

Crowds of boisterous, happy revellers traditionally dressed in pyjamas or old clothes singing and dancing and having fun from 6.00 a.m. until sunset. Although evacuation from Plymouth disrupted Festival Day, the news release on the 1st January that residents could return to their homes in the south was cause for celebration in itself.

However, the volcano continued to be very active with three of the five 'crisis periods' to date occurring during January. We were told that on these occasions seismic activity increased to *"near repetitive levels"* before climaxing in eruption signals, resulting in heavy falls of ash over Plymouth and surrounding areas.

These 'repetitive events' were small hybrid earthquakes which registered on the seismic drums at the MVO but were not felt by us. On the 13th January alone there were 1,000 of these earthquake events. But the highest recorded number in one twenty-four hour period was on the last day of January when after several days of gradually increasing magnitude and frequency the hybrid events were reported to be swarming at six to seven per minute and over 8,500 were counted.

On the 20th January a spine fifteen metres wide emerged from the dome and grew at a rapid rate of one metre per hour to a height of twenty-five metres before the base began to crack and it collapsed back into the lava dome in a shower of ash.

A constant haze of gases from the volcano streaked out across the flanks of the Soufrière Hills and were funnelled down into Plymouth where they settled in a smelly blue mist of sulphur dioxide over the town. A wide brown swathe of dead vegetation marks the hillside passage of the sulphides, chlorides and fluorides that are being pumped out in a noxious cocktail across the countryside of Montserrat.

It took a few days to move everything back into Plymouth after the Christmas evacuation. For those people fortunate enough to be working in air-conditioned offices the fumes from the volcano and the re-mobilised ash gusting through the streets with the wind did not create too much of a problem.

However for the majority of shops, offices and homes without this luxury life has become intolerable. The ash in the air infiltrated everywhere and was an ever-present frustration. A grey gritty residue covered everything, inside and out.

In my husband's office in Plymouth the aluminium louvers covering the mesh screen of his windows are warped and distorted with age and are of minimal use in stopping the intrusive ash. He taped plastic sheeting over the window to keep ash invasion to a minimum and works under electric light.

With no air-conditioning and no ceiling fan he struggles to keep the hot office bearable with two desk fans. It is, he says grimly, *"Like working in the black hole of Calcutta"*. The frequent strong sulphurous smells drifting in from the volcano add to his discomfort.

The MVO are using a small helicopter chartered from St. Lucia in an attempt to observe and chart the mountain's activity. Alex, the current pilot, keeps the helicopter on a handkerchief of grass beside the Vue Pointe Hotel and as he putters in to land he cruises parallel with the cliff-face beyond our garden. He is a source of constant entertainment to us. We watch in admiration and respect as he manipulates the little whirly-bird.

He managed to land inside the crater beside the smoking lava dome so that Simon from the MVO could collect some rock samples for analysis. Simon usually inspects the volcano by climbing the steps up to Chances Peak. He prides himself on being able to reach the top in twenty-eight minutes flat. Coming down is much quicker he says, *"Especially if the volcano is raining rocks from a phreatic eruption at the time!"*

Simon left Montserrat at the end of January. He says he's so exhausted he plans to sleep for a fortnight, but he will be returning from time to time to monitor the volcano.

On a clear day the lava dome, steaming like a dumpling of fresh cowpat, is visible from several parts of the island including Harris, Plymouth, Richmond Hill and Fox's Bay and 'Volcano watching' has become a spectator sport in Montserrat. One evening at around 6.00 p.m. shortly after sunset we drove up to Guadeloupe Corner on the Harris road for a closer view of the glowing cone. We watched as rocks tumbled down the slopes of the hot lava dome leaving behind rivulets of red embers that glowed in the night. The sight was fascinating.

ZJB Radio Montserrat continues to be our chief source of information about the volcano with two daily up-dates from the MVO about activity, one in the morning at 7.15 a.m. and the other at 7.30 p.m. The scientists are now saying they can only give us six hours warning of a major eruption.

Occasionally speeches by the Governor and Chief Minister present the official position. Those in authority are busy with 'contingency planning' for the population of Montserrat, having purchased school buses ('bus-trains'), plastic covered tunnels ('tropical igloos') and twenty metal-clad factory shells for emergency accommodation and storage.

On the 7th January our son and daughter were due to fly from Montserrat to Antigua to catch their UK flight home and back to University. However, a storm closed the airport and as a result their departure was delayed for four days.

Not that they minded this inconvenience since between storms the weather remained a pleasant 80°F and provided relaxing warmth with good tanning possibilities. Having a tan in January in the UK is something of a status symbol it seems.

The wet and warm conditions encouraged the small biting 'no-see-ums' to breed and they were drawn to me like a magnet, homing in to feast from my succulent flesh and causing me to erupt in a pebble-dash of itchy blobs. I have done everything I can to deter the invisible vampires, whose appetite is greatest at dawn and dusk. I have lit pungent green-snake Pyrethrum coils and dotted them around the house, almost asphyxiating the family. I have drenched myself liberally with 'Off' insect repellent until I smell quite disgusting. I have covered myself from head to toe like an Egyptian mummy. My next-door neighbour has proved to be equally tasty bait and she has resorted to wearing tights, sending an SOS to England for several pairs.

A new housekeeper joined me during the month, supplied by the agents who let our property. It is part of the agreement. My new housekeeper is Shirley, also known as Debbie to family and friends. She arrived from Guyana six years ago to act as a nurse/companion to an elderly Montserratian gentleman, then she met Sonny and fell in love. They married last Boxing Day. Shirley was enjoying her honeymoon in Antigua when she was told that the old gentleman she had been nursing had passed away. People said he was devastated when she left and he missed her so much *"He jus' leh go"*.

Shirley is a big, warm-hearted girl, with the vital statistics of a cuddly rubber ball. She was very nervous when she presented herself on the first morning and confessed that this was the first housekeeping job she had ever done. She trained as a nurse when she lived in Guyana. She is extremely thorough and efficient and works at such a cracking pace I worry that she will collapse from exhaustion.

Shirley says that the old folk who were moved to the safety of the north are still there and are feeling the cold at night because the area is so exposed. There has been an increase in the death announcements on ZJB Radio Montserrat during January. These announcements are a regular feature and are broadcast at around 7.30 p.m. just before, or just after, the evening volcano up-date.

The broadcasts start with sombre funeral music from such a well-used tape that it slips slightly as it plays, then the announcer says the name of the deceased person, any nicknames, age, location of death, and location of normal residence. The announcement continues with, *"Left to mourn are...."*, and each and every relative including nephews and nieces, and friends, not only in Montserrat but from around the world get a mention in the long list. Finally comes the detailed information about the funeral, when and where it is to be held, and at what time, with instructions for mourners concerning the 'collection points' for the bus to church. If there is more than one death announcement, which happens occasionally, and if the person is a popular local figure with many relatives and friends, the broadcast can take some considerable time.

One morning in late January the Pastor from the Seventh Day Adventist Church arrived on my doorstep. He was organising the annual *"In-gathering"* of funds for the church, normally held during late December but delayed this year because of the volcano. He wanted to arrange for the Seventh Day Adventist choir to bless our house and serenade us. Their motto is *'People helping People'* and they do a great deal of charity work both here in Montserrat and around the world. During our first evacuation Caribbean church members sent Montserrat a container full of clothes and food for distribution. They also kindly loaned their 'big tent' used for their Saturday holy services, to other denominations on Sunday.

The Minister returned on the evening of 30th January with his choir, and fifteen people pressed on to our front porch and sang 'Amazing Grace' so beautifully that it brought tears to my eyes.

In the group I recognised Caleb, Chief Mechanic and Supervisor from the Public Works Department. Caleb is presently supervising the repair of two of the four buses that have just been delivered to Montserrat to assist in the evacuation of people during times of relocation. They were purchased second-hand from Florida with British Emergency Aid funds. The yellow ex-school buses are twelve years old, with 100,000 miles on the clock. They have been christened 'bus-trains' because they are so long.

Very early one morning while the roads were deserted, the bus-trains were taken out on a trial run to see how well they performed. There has been speculation that they were too long to get round some of Montserrat's tight bends. The back of the empty bus did grind ominously on the ground as it tackled a couple of our steep hills, but it was argued that provided the rear third of the seats were left unoccupied this problem would be overcome. The Education

Department is intending to use the bus-trains to transport the school children.

The quality of life has deteriorated dramatically on the island during January. The uncertainty is affecting everyone and at least two Plymouth businesses have relocated to Antigua during the month. Many good friends have left Montserrat permanently and we miss them greatly.

8 - FEBRUARY 1996

ACID RAIN DAMAGING VEGETATION

HMS *Brave* arrived early in February for a fleeting visit, having taken over West Indies Guard Ship duties in the Caribbean. Marines took further soundings at Little Bay for the proposed evacuation jetty and the Lynx helicopter was used for emergency aid duties, such as accessing Lawyer's Mountain.

Radio transmitters have been purchased to be sited on Lawyer's Mountain in an effort to boost transmissions during periods of evacuation. Previously radio transmissions to the north and to the airport had been lost due to hills obstructing the signal and it was hoped the new transmitters would solve the problem.

Although the site selected was accessible by foot it was impossible to take construction materials up the mountain. There were some interesting debates as to how the transmitters could be successfully installed. One ingenious solution proposed that the equipment should be placed inside four Portaloos on the ground, which could then be swung under the Lynx helicopter, flown up the mountain, and deposited on the site.

Montserrat remained on High Orange alert throughout February while the volcano burped and popped with varying degrees of excitement. Much of the time the top of the mountain was shrouded in cloud cover, but occasionally this would clear and the scientists, and sightseers, were treated to a full view of the activity. Groups of people began hiking up to the crater rim to see the volcano for themselves.

Several warnings have been issued on the radio instructing people to avoid the dangerous area close to the volcano. Normally the terrific heat, cracking sounds of rocks breaking, toxic fumes and very unpleasant conditions in the Soufrière Hills puts off all but the most masochistic and determined trekkers. However Alex, on one of his helicopter observation flights, was astonished to see a group of German tourists boiling eggs and picnicking beside English's crater.

Helicopter flights up into the hills to look at the volcano are considered well worth the charge of US$130. The Soufrière Hills is a mountain giving birth, and we are beginning to experience a sense of privilege as we witness the diversity of the labour pangs.

The volcano-tectonic earthquakes, commonly referred to simply as 'VT's', are caused by fracture or slippage of rock under the ground which occurs suddenly, sometimes in small swarms, but are brief. Their location can be pin-pointed very accurately by the instruments at the MVO. On the 11th February a swarm of forty VT's registering 2.2 to 3.5 on the Richter Scale were located beneath Windy Hill, a short distance away from us. We were shaken awake at 4.00 a.m. by the VT swarm which was accompanied by a loud roaring noise.

Hybrid earthquakes have a lower frequency than the VT's. They are usually smaller and are repeated at regular intervals. These can also occur in swarms, as on 31st January when we had 8,500. These indicate movement of gas or fluid in the volcano and are associated with dome growth.

Other types of earthquake activity include 'tremors' or 'broadband tremors', so-called because of the visual pattern displayed on the drums at the MVO. These suggest movement of gas or magma within the volcano and are associated with periods of steam and gas venting. Tremor episodes can last for several hours (on 13th February the instruments recorded broadband tremor for over eight hours). They are usually followed by earthquake swarms.

However by far the most frequent signals at the MVO during February were those caused by rock falls. Boulders tumbling down from the top and sides of the growing dome. These cause 'Rock-fall Signals' and produce ash falls. It is apparently sometimes difficult to distinguish between 'cold' rockfalls from the surface of the dome and small pyroclastic flow signals which occur where the dome is hottest and most active. Large pyroclastic flows, however, can cause very strong seismic signals on all instruments for several minutes.

Mudflows have their own seismic signature and several of these were registered during February. Viewed from the helicopter these mudflows are impressive. Very hot mud gushing from a vent in the dome, travelling at 30 mph, fifty feet wide and twenty feet deep following the natural line of the ghauts down into the valleys.

Fort Ghaut through Plymouth was filled several times by mudflows and had to be 'dug out' with heavy earth-moving equipment before the deposits spilled out and over-topped the two bridges in town.

Up in the hills above Plymouth the size of the lava dome has been increasing at a rapid rate. Sometimes the growth is vertical, sometimes it is concentrated on the southeast side, and sometimes the area of growth switches unpredictably to the northwest side. By the middle of the month the dome was as high as the original old Castle Peak and the razor-edge cusp of the crater rim began to break away. Two tall spines, bearing an evil resemblance to devil horns, sprang up overnight through the dome.

There were periods of vigorous steaming from old phreatic vents. This de-gassing of the magma was apparently a good sign indicating that pressure was not building up within the volcano. But with the absence of wind during February the gases pressed down through Plymouth and blanketed the town, causing mounting public concern about hazards to health.

Eyes feel as if they have grit in them. Those wearing contact lenses suffer in particular. We have been given assurances that the emissions are not a health risk and we were told *"the mountain is venting itself"*.

The drinking water and springs have been tested and proved safe, but residents are warned to avoid using any water that has been collected in galvanised tanks.

On the evening of the 9th February we had acid rain formed by sulphur dioxide and hydrogen sulphide combining with the showers. I woke the following morning to discover to my dismay that the crimson velvet hibiscus blooms and other plants in our beautiful garden had been effectively drenched with dilute sulphuric acid. The petals and leaves were burned and shrivelled with large yellow stains and brown blotches.

Montserrat's own *"Soca King of the World"* decided to leave the island for a short period to promote his new album in Ghana. Alphonsus 'Arrow' Cassell is one of the island's most famous sons and he lives in Fox's Bay. He began his musical career as a popular Calypsonian and then developed his own distinctive Soca style.

Just before Christmas Arrow recorded several Calypso, house music, rap and dance-hall reggae numbers, calling the album PHAT. One of the numbers, *"Ah jus' can't run away"* has become so popular here that it should be adopted as the Montserrat national ballad.

The lyrics express Arrow's determination to stay in Montserrat despite the activity at the volcano for as long as he possibly can *"As long as Fox's Bay still down der, ... I'll be holding on"* he sings and *"As long as Runaway Ghaut still have water, ... I'll be holding on"*.

I found I couldn't hold on any longer to my itching lumps and bumps and when they began to meld together into one huge pink dome, I thought it was about time I made an appointment with Dagenham Clinic in Plymouth.

Dr. Ronnie Cooper is a big bear of a man with a deep and mellow voice. He took one look at me and my itching bumps and delved wildly into the heap of papers surrounding him on the floor of his office. His desk was piled high with an assortment of books and papers and balancing precariously on top was a bag of fresh eggs, payment perhaps from his previous patient.

"Urticaria" he rumbled triumphantly handing me a leaflet. He prescribed anti-histamines and recommended a visit to the hospital pathology laboratory for urine and blood tests. He counted out the little pills and put them into a brown envelope and instructed me to return the following day.

The 'old' Glendon Hospital in Plymouth was originally the Nurses Home but was refurbished as a hospital after the devastation of Hurricane Hugo in 1989. Although the patients have been moved to the safety of St. Johns in the north the laboratory facilities are still in Plymouth. The immaculate 'new' Glendon Hospital with state-of-the-art equipment had been receiving the finishing touches from the building contractors when the volcano erupted and has not yet been completed and opened.

Plymouth was bustling with beige-clad schoolchildren on their way to lessons when I drove into town. One of the yellow 'bus-trains' was being used to shuttle children down the straight, wide, Cork Hill Road. It brought traffic to a standstill outside the school while it disgorged its cargo.

I wanted to call in to the supermarket for some shopping before arriving at the hospital. It was empty of customers and it was a bonus to be able to park directly beside the entrance steps. Inside a young Indian boy unloaded two plastic trays of fresh baked bread, just delivered. Several local girls filled shelves and dusted volcanic ash off packets and cans with lazy indifference. Two earnest Indian gentlemen stood in the office area at the front of the store, and said *"Good-morning"* as I pushed my trolley past.

Normally Thursday is the day for fresh vegetables, but I picked at the tired remnants left in the boxes and came across some nice stumpy, locally grown cucumbers, which have been hard to find for several weeks. I ignored the mushy over-ripe tomatoes and mouldy potatoes nestled in the bottom. On inspection the cheese I wanted showed an expiry date of two months previous, I hesitated before finally deciding not to purchase. These little irritations are quite normal.

As I loaded the groceries into the car I glanced up at the volcano. Unusually the top was clear and silhouetted against the bright blue sky. The morning up-date at 7.15 a.m. had mentioned stronger broadband tremors with long-period events and *"vigorous steaming"*. Thick grey smoke billowed out in great gusts creating a dusty plume that stretched across Montserrat out over the sea to the horizon. It would probably reach Mexico by mid-day I thought.

The entrance to the 'old' Glendon Hospital is down a narrow road off George Street in Plymouth. I had to stop the car while a wandering goat meandered across the road and headed into the bushy undergrowth. His rope had been coiled neatly around his neck and tucked in securely to stop it accidentally unwinding.

The hospital car park is an apron of ancient tarmac with invading bush and scrub kept low with a machete. Casually dumped containers, large and rusting, litter the area. Old equipment taken out for disposal and abandoned. An iron bath lay on its side across the footpath and a huge drying machine, stainless steel belly visible through the swinging open porthole of its door, rested awkwardly against the wall of one of the hospital buildings. Faded signs point the way to *'Clinic'*, *'Maternity'* and *'Casualty'*.

The hospital complex was very quiet. No other cars but mine. The whole area had a neglected appearance with the feeling that it had grown and spread over many years without plan, pattern or forethought, patched together as need dictated. I walked between two deserted buildings in search of Pathology.

Two Montserratian ladies were sitting on a bench on the narrow stoop of a small square building to my left. Pasted on the wall behind them were posters primarily concerned with sex, Aids and school children. This was the Pathology Laboratory. A small, traditional, Montserratian building, constructed from concrete blocks with a tin roof. The original red paint on the corrugated roof had long since been stripped by the weather and now it was a tired grey with only faint blushes here and there to indicate its former brilliance. The walls had once been painted cream but now reflected the pepper and salt of old age. A stout and gnarled tamarind tree leaned protectively over the little place.

I looked through the open doorway into the cramped interior. The room measured less than two metres square. Two desks, both occupied, a chair with flat trays for arms, and a narrow cot screened by two shower curtains yellow with age, and a hat stand, completed the quick inventory.

A young girl was sitting at the desk just inside the door doing something with a rack of blood samples in small test tubes. At the other desk a slim white-coated young woman with sensationally long flame-coloured fingernails was sorting through four cardboard boxes. They contained swabs, needles, syringes, cotton wool and, rather incongruously I thought, a large old-fashioned alarm clock.

The young girl silently pointed across the dusty compound to another peeling building. I gathered I had to pay in advance for hospital services and I was being directed to the Cashier. The kind ladies still sitting on the bench on the stoop gently gestured me down the path.

I peered through the only open door I could see and gingerly stepped inside. An L-shaped counter confronted me, almost filling the tiny room. A cubicle had been constructed across one part of it and from the safety of her glass booth a stylish young lady scrutinised me. She was wearing a fashionably tight, bright canary-yellow jacket, hugely padded at the shoulders. Her dark hair was a work of art. It was combed flat to her head and plaited to form a tight, neat, crown, surrounding her pretty face. She studied me suspiciously and questioned me closely.

"You live here?" she asked. *"How long you live here?"* she demanded to know. *"You English?"* she frowned. My responses must have been satisfactory, because she then mentally totted up the cost of my laboratory work, and requested a very reasonable EC$28.

I mountain-watched as I returned to the Pathology Laboratory. The view of the volcano from the path was probably the best in Plymouth. I felt I could almost touch the steaming cauldron. The steep ravine of Gages Wall was tucked into the mountain directly ahead. I couldn't help thinking that if the wall should fail and collapse as a result of the pressure of dome growth pushing from behind, then George Street would become a river of molten lava slithering down the hillside into Plymouth. Suddenly the hospital seemed very vulnerable.

When I returned to the Pathology Laboratory the sophisticated lady in the white coat looked up from sorting her boxes and with a flick of a fabulous fingernail she beckoned me inside. She was extremely elegant, and dignified, and superior, and I felt humble. She motioned me into the strange chair with two arm flaps, and seeing the brown paper bag clutched in my hand she asked politely, *"Is that a sample?"* and I nodded dumbly. *"When did you have breakfast?"* she wanted to know, and *"Is it labelled?"*

She reached across her desk for one of the cardboard shoeboxes and held it out for me to place my specimen inside. Beside the small hospital samples already rolling about in the box, my generous jar took on the enormity of a bucket. I blushed, pink with embarrassment.

"Arm out, sleeve up, clench your fist!" Obeying the order I stretched my arm along the top of her desk. She pulled out a narrow

rubber tube from another shoebox and with a deft twist and tug had stopped the circulation above my elbow.

As she leaned forward to take my blood, I turned my head to look out of the open doorway, and found five pairs of eyes staring back at me. On the stoop outside, clustered around the entrance, two men and three women had materialised quietly from nowhere and were watching me closely, and studying my reaction to the 'sticking' with undisguised curiosity. They smiled at me in silent encouragement. I hoped they hadn't seen my sample.

I was dismissed with a wad of cotton wool to press over the puncture wound. Outside in the shade of the Tamarind tree a mother was giving her little girl a biscuit from a picnic box and a juice to drink. It looked as if they expected to be around the hospital for most of the day. The complex was still eerily empty.

On the street people are saying that the hospital patients are to be brought back into Plymouth from the north any day now. But we have heard a conflicting rumour that says the activity at the volcano is increasing and there could be another evacuation of Plymouth at any time. As February draws to close we dither with uncertainty and really don't know what to expect.

Plymouth 1996

9 - MARCH 1996

HELICOPTER LANDS INSIDE CRATER

On the 1ˢᵗ March, two days after my visit to the Pathology Laboratory, the patients were moved back into old Glendon Hospital in Plymouth after an evacuation of five months in the north.

It was difficult to understand why this decision had been taken until we learned that four eye surgeons were arriving in Montserrat on the 2ⁿᵈ March, and over a period of four weeks they were to perform essential cataract operations on sixty-five patients. In order to do this successfully they required the operating theatre in Plymouth.

The facilities for patients at St. John's primary school in the north were inadequate for the surgeons, with wards and departments in various classrooms and the operating theatre located about half a mile away in a converted clinic. Casualty and X-ray were in a nearby nursery school and the hospital's only ambulance had to be used to convey patients between the various buildings.

At the beginning of March we were informed that no evacuation of Plymouth or the south was envisaged for three to six months. However the lava dome of the volcano was growing three times faster than predicted at an average of 10 ft. per day, and a gravitational collapse was a possibility. The good news was that the dome was confined inside the crater and although the system was larger than at first thought, the magma coming up appeared to be degassing freely. Monitoring continued on a twenty-four hour basis.

Simon returned to the MVO after his brief break in the UK. He informed us he had tested the temperature of the dome "*By dangling his pyrometer out of the helicopter*" and it had registered an incinerating 700°C.

The scientists have cut an alternative path up to the crater rim to save the effort (and reduce the danger) of climbing the 2,000 steps of Chances Peak, and to be closer to the growth area of the dome that threatens Plymouth. The trail goes up the north-western side of the Soufrière Hills, through Farrell's and takes about thirty minutes to climb.

At a Red Cross drinks and nibbles evening at Government House, a friend who enjoys rambling and who has only recently arrived in Montserrat, told me that she had been invited to accompany a small group on what she thought was to be an innocent and gentle hike to enjoy the views in the Soufrière Hills around the volcano. It turned out to be hard work and very scary.

The group set off from Farrell's and walked in the general direction of the steaming hills. Having passed a field of marijuana they continued climbing for some time until they found themselves scrambling along on a narrow ledge of a path directly beside the crater edge. When my unsuspecting friend realised how close she was to the growing dome of the volcano, she told me she *"nearly freaked"*.

These 'unofficial tours' have been eroding the path the MVO cut for scientific observations into the crater and are very dangerous. The police know the identity of those involved in leading the treks and have spoken to them, but they continue undeterred, and so now trespass and warning signs have been erected beside the path.

The Red Cross function was an annual fund-raising event, but was not as well attended as usual.

The volcano gave out a smelly little pop just before we all arrived and since the evening was alfresco we had to suffer the malodorous 'scent' of sulphur.

The cakes and sandwiches for the evening had been prepared and supplied by the Red Cross 'stitch and bitch' volunteers. These well-intentioned ladies meet weekly in one another's homes to paint, sew, chat and gossip and generally support the work of the Red Cross in Montserrat. There are a hard-core handful of on-island members, but during the winter months 'snowbirds' arrive to swell the numbers.

At EC$25 per ticket the fund-raising at Government House was designed to encourage the visiting 'snowbirds' to part with their money, but also to thank them for their support before they flew home for the summer.

Since the average age of those attending the Red Cross fund-raiser was around seventy-five the musical entertainment provided by Cutter and his steel pan players was more for atmosphere than action. Cutter had set up the band at the edge of the garden and in the background gloom we noticed our old friend Stanley, swaying to the music of his mates. Stanley had *"de wine in he head"* in excess and Cutter, as Captain, had refused to let him play with the band, removing Stanley's pan from its hanger and hiding it.

Stanley saw us across the terrace and grinned and waved in enthusiastic greeting. He obviously made up his mind to speak to us and with great effort pulled himself together and lurched cautiously in our general direction. Most of the guests were pressing around the bar area and so he successfully navigated the intervening space without incident. He threw his arms around our shoulders in a gesture of camaraderie and as a support mechanism in his attempt to remain vertical. Disconcertingly, his eyes appeared to be looking in different directions, and he had a nasty cut above the left one. He was very, very, pleased to see us.

He confided that 'dem' had threatened to lock him up if he didn't behave, so we thought it wise to remove him, discreetly, from the limelight of the terrace. In time to the rhythm of the music we undulated as a trio towards the band, and gently steered Stanley into the shadows behind the drums. When we released him he folded neatly for the night.

The First Prize in the raffle was a helicopter flight around the volcano, donated by the pilot who has arrived to replace Alex. We have nicknamed him 'Kamikaze Jim'. If Alex was impressive, then Jim is fearless. His last job was piloting a helo in the Arctic chasing polar bears at zero height so that scientists could tranquillise them for monitoring. Before that he had been flying missions in Cambodia. Monitoring a live volcano in the Caribbean must seem light relief to him.

On the 14th March Jim was commissioned to fly an official visitor and his wife from the Vue Pointe Hotel to the airport in order to catch their LIAT flight to Antigua. It happened that my husband and I were saying farewell to the couple at the time, and Jim invited us to join the trip at very short notice. An exhilarating adventure when all I had planned for the afternoon had been the ironing. I squeezed into the back of the helo beside our departing friends while my husband sat in front with Jim in the bug-eye bubble.

Jim planned to take off, circle over the crater, fly to the airport, then fly back up to Chances Peak to pick up two scientists who had been collecting samples, returning to land beside the Vue Pointe Hotel. Jim gave us a quick in-flight safety check about kicking in windows and the location of the fire extinguisher, and we put on headsets so that he could talk to us.

The rotors slowly began to turn, getting faster and faster, until after a few minutes we gently rose up from the ground, swinging away over the sea to turn in a huge arc back over Plymouth and up the flanks of the Soufrière Hills.

To our delight the cloud that had been pressing in on the mountain and the volcano abruptly cleared as we soared towards the dome, and the whole area was bathed in sharp sunshine. It was sensational. I felt like a bird. Jim kept up a running commentary through the headsets as we hopped, skirted, dipped and dived around the outside of the crater, then cautiously buzzed in to look through the horseshoe opening above Tar River Valley, the sides towering above us.

No words can begin to describe the feeling. A colossal steaming bank of grey and brown rocks, an incredible stench of sulphur, thick white smoke and grey gases, tumbling blocks of stone and smaller scree pressing against the sides of the crater wall. Gages Wall, the part of English's Crater that kept the growing dome from spilling down Gages Valley and Fort Ghaut into Plymouth, looked slender with scree piling up less than fifty feet from the top. A huge muddle of growing, glowing, hot magmatic dome rose high above it. It was, to appropriate an Americanism, 'awesome' in the extreme.

After a few minutes of flying right around the outside of the crater and above the dome, we thumped across to the airport. Jim, in communication with the airport tower, informed them he was *"Four by one"* he explained it meant four people on board and fuel for one hour. We landed on the apron and our guests walked across to the airport building to check in for their LIAT flight.

We had to hesitate for a few minutes while the helo cooled down and then we rose, clattering, up into the air again and flew directly towards Chances Peak, the highest point on the island and close to the seat of the volcanic activity.

We left the fertile green fields around the airport and as we got closer to Chances Peak the blitzed landscape beneath us began to turn grey and grim. A devastated area of charred tree stumps and volcanic ash. It was bleak and forbidding. An international photographer, covering the volcano in Montserrat after an assignment in Cambodia, had told me that this particular area around the volcano looked as if it had been napalmed. It was, he said, *"Like a war zone without the bullets"*.

We saw the two scientists as small dark specks standing beside the remnants of the Cable and Wireless tower on top of the grey moonscape of Chances Peak, and we dropped like a settling seagull on a tiny patch between the tower and the ruins of the Cable and Wireless concrete shelter, about 3 ft. from the top of the Chances Peak steps.

The two MVO men quickly scrambled in next to me, dropping their breathing masks into my lap. We were up and away almost immediately, heading south down across Galway's Soufrière with the afternoon sun reflecting brightly on the light buff and white rocks of the ravine, steam rising gently from the meandering sulphurous yellow stream below us.

We were flying at 60 mph, a mere hundred feet or so above the ground, twisting and turning for better views. My internal organs protested at the gymnastics, but I pretended we were chasing polar bears, while sternly telling myself that it would be unforgivable to throw up in Jim's helo.

Then, to my utter astonishment, I heard Jim say, *"Let's see if we can land inside the crater!"* and we were off, rising up the outside of the crater and bobbing over the crater rim *"Just testing the uplift"*.

Deciding it was OK, Jim sidled carefully, slowly, cautiously into the crater, low and slow, along the vast sides of the steaming, rocky mound of the growing dome, until he came alongside Castle Peak.

On a minuscule scrap of the original old peak Jim brought the helo tenderly down.

It was indescribable. We were inside the womb of the volcano surrounded by high domes of steaming loose rock.

To our immediate right, about 20 ft. away, a hot rocky mound with protrusions as big as houses reached down to the crater wall. White steam, so thick it looked solid, billowed out from it. The whole area steamed and smoked like Dante's Inferno.

Directly in front of us, about 30 ft. away, a new feature had appeared overnight. A vast, smooth molar tooth of rocky spine pushed up through the lava and now split open to reveal its yellow and white marrow. Shafts of sunlight penetrated the steam and cloud and caught the crusty boulders, frothy white with hot sulphur.

It was a unique and humbling experience, and an extraordinary privilege. We took our leave and the little helo swung up and away. That was the last time the helo was able to land inside the crater. On the 19th March seismicity began to increase with high steam emissions and further phreatic eruptions. The inside of the crater became a no-go area for the scientists.

Castle Peak Dome 1996

As a result of growing public fears about an escalation in volcanic activity the Governor, Chief Minister, and Lloyd Lynch from the MVO held a press conference on the 26th March. They attempted to alleviate anxiety by saying that there was no cause for panic and no foreseeable reason why there should be another evacuation from Plymouth in the next six weeks to six months.

The volcano, however, was not listening. The very next day after a night of unseasonably heavy rain, the worst ash cloud so far spread across western Montserrat.

It was early morning and I was eating my cornflakes when without warning a section of the growing dome collapsed sending rocks into Tar River Valley, generating heavy ash high into the air. What appeared to be grey glue dropped from the sky and engulfed Plymouth.

For the rest of the day Sahara sand storm conditions prevailed in the capital. Schools were closed, people wore masks, and vehicles slithered on the treacherously slippery roads around town.

The last two days of March saw the island suffering from the heaviest 'ashin' so far. On the 30th the ash reached as far as Old Towne and fell as fine snow for over thirty minutes. I put on my mask, covered my hair, and shovelled up six buckets of ash around the pool deck and patio and hosed the house down twice.

Everywhere was milky white and the roofs, trees, flowers and grass were thick with a grey dust blanket. I felt I was living in a cement quarry.

Worse was to come. On the 31st March there was another partial dome collapse to the east, and a 'block and ash' flow at 8.43 p.m. travelled for over a kilometre into the Tar River Valley setting trees alight and splitting rocks.

The two heavy ashin's in Plymouth deposited a bed 25 mm thick with the Fire Department desperately trying to keep essential streets and buildings hosed. Tropical smog and hazardous wet ash created frightening conditions. Glendon hospital, I was told, was *"In a terrible mess"*.

The animals seemed to be reflecting our tension and are extremely nervous. One of the iguana's, now very tame, came on to the patio in search of banana skins and other titbits. To my surprise he came through the patio doors, across the lounge and into the kitchen and refused to leave until I had found something for him to eat. It was only limp lettuce but he wolfed it down gratefully, then marched outside and promptly jumped into the ashy black pool and swam around for several minutes. Extraordinary behaviour.

Unusually, a small treefrog invaded my kitchen. Normally treefrogs prefer to hide in plant-pots and bushes but this tiny chap had tried to make his home behind the fruit bowl on my work surface. He was no bigger than my thumbnail but he made me jump every time he hopped out. As Shirley said, *"He leap so high he almos' fly!"*

He also makes a great deal of noise with his high-pitched, persistent, mating call during the warm, wet, evenings. When several treefrogs live in close proximity to the house their strident love-cacophony can be audio-torture through the night.

I was told that at the Public Works Department a treefrog made his home in the wash-room faucet, jumping out whenever anyone went to wash their hands. Unsurprisingly his presence was discouraged, until he finally vacated the faucet and took up residence in the toilet bowl!

Although the month of March has had an undercurrent of tension Montserrat celebrated St. Patrick's Day on 17th with real enthusiasm and a National Holiday was declared for Monday 18th.

There are two reasons why St. Patrick's Day is so important to Montserratians. Not only is it to honour the Irish patron saint (as a result of Irish colonisation the associations are very strong) but it also commemorates an abortive slave uprising that took place in Montserrat in 1768.

In the 18thC Montserrat was settled by many Irish Catholic Plantation owners who had originally arrived from the neighbouring island of St. Kitt's to escape persecution from the Protestants. They celebrated St. Patrick's Day with much feasting and merrymaking. The oppressed African slaves organised a revolt, planning to overwhelm their Irish owners when they were too drunk to fight back.

However, one of the women slaves told her master of the plot and he had the ringleaders caught and killed as a warning to the other slaves.

This year the village of St. Patrick's to the south of Plymouth was the centre for a day of cultural extravaganza. Starting early with a *'Dance and Shout for Freedom'* there was a cricket match and local poetry reading *'Plenty Yac Ya Ya'*. There was also a Celebration of Art at the Vue Pointe Hotel, Irish 'singalongs', Leprechaun night at the Montserrat Springs Hotel, and a Junior Calypso Show.

10 - APRIL 1996

FINAL EVACUATION OF PLYMOUTH

Thanks to extreme volcanic activity stress levels soared during the first two weeks of April.

On the 1st April, after only four weeks in Plymouth, the hospital was instructed to relocate back to the safety of the north. It was hastily moved with patients, beds and equipment evacuated in appalling conditions as ash from the volcano filled the air.

On the 3rd April the volcano became particularly active. I was at home in Old Towne and falling ash had reduced visibility to a few yards. My wooden louvers were tightly shut and I had hung sheets across in an attempt to keep out some of the ash that was swirling in a thick mist outside. The wind was coming from the direction of the volcano and bringing with it a steady shower of powdery ash which deposited itself as grit on every surface in the house.

Dogs were barking and occasionally I could hear muffled explosions coming from the direction of the volcano. Everywhere, inside and out, was covered with a thick layer of fine, pulverised rock. As I padded disconsolately through the house I left behind the white imprint of my feet.

The temperature inside was a stifling 95°F. I was hot and the rooms were dark and I was wearing my ash mask.

I caught sight of myself in a mirror and because the breathing valve in my mask looked like a snout, I closely resembled the Muppet 'Miss Piggy'. Another consignment of ash masks, ordered by the health authority, arrived flat-packed. When unfolded they look like the beak of a duck. So our choice of ash mask seems to be either Miss Piggy or Donald Duck.

Many of the girls have taken to wearing shower caps in an effort to keep their hair clean and free from dust and grit. Some use swimming goggles to protect their eyes. We resemble actors from a biological warfare movie.

As the afternoon of the 3rd April wore on I listened to ZJB Radio Montserrat hoping for news reports about activity at the volcano. A studio discussion on the poor state of West Indies cricket was suddenly interrupted with a request to all customers of the dry cleaning company in Plymouth *"To come and collect your goods as soon as possible"*.

Shortly afterwards another announcement ordered all prison officers to report to the prison in town immediately. I knew at once that an evacuation of Plymouth was imminent, and I was not at all surprised when the Acting Governor, Dr. Howard Fergus (Frank Savage having just left the island for a short break) and Chief Minister Reuben Meade, came on the radio at 3.00 p.m. declaring that the capital Plymouth and all points south were to be evacuated immediately.

"Good day fellow citizens," Dr. Fergus sounded well in command *"the ash emission has been continuous and in addition a fissure has opened up on the eastern flank of the dome"*.

After he had finished speaking the Chief Minister smoothly introduced himself with *"A pleasant good evening and afternoon to all residents of Montserrat"* and went on to explain that the volcano had undergone a significant change in activity at 6.52 a.m. with an explosive event. Further explosive events were to be expected. Everyone was being asked to return to the December 1995 relocation position. Very optimistically the Chief Minister hoped the evacuation of Plymouth would be for *"About a week"*.

Moments after the joint evacuation announcement I heard an explosion from the volcano as a sudden, unexpected, pyroclastic flow of hot ash, gas and rocks, raced down the east side of the volcano, reaching as far as the road to the Tar River Estate House. The vegetation burned and trees were on fire.

The eruption generated an ash plume that rose 20,000 ft. into the air. The airport was closed immediately and people heading for flights out of Montserrat were instructed to turn back. ZJB Radio Montserrat appealed urgently for taxis, cars, anything, to collect people from Long Ground. We were told they were standing beside the road waiting for transport out of the dangerous eastern area.

At 3.35 p.m. Dr. Ambeh came on the radio. He explained that eruptive events had increased. He stressed it was especially important to get people in the east out quickly. He confirmed the surges were *'definitely pyroclastic'*. In his opinion the situation would continue to escalate and it was of paramount importance to get people out rapidly. He returned on air at 4.00 p.m. requesting anyone with transport to *"Please go east to help to evacuate"*. There was a sense of desperate urgency in his voice.

The authorities had been planning to test the new alarm sirens at 4.30 p.m. These have been installed in various areas close to the volcano, including one directly outside my husband's office. Although the island was in the middle of evacuating the south, the police decided to go ahead with the test, but told us not to take any notice.

The sirens are surplus British WW2 issue and had presented quite a problem when they first arrived for installation. They were tested, but immediately burnt out because they had the incorrect frequency for the island. They were sent to Antigua to be rewired and the afternoon of the 3rd April was their first full test. The sirens have to be operated by hand, by a policeman wearing earmuffs. I listened intently at 4.30 p.m. straining to hear the sound of sirens and thought I heard a faint humming coming from the Salem area, but I couldn't be sure.

The activity on the 3rd April put us back on Red Alert with a vengeance and each hour, each day, brought new anxieties. Several significant explosive events on the 3rd, 6th and 8th April, with terrifying pyroclastic flows down the east at Tar River and heavy ashfalls in the north and west, caused alarm and confusion.

We were warned to prepare for a *'climactic event'* within a few days. 4,000 people, almost half the population of Montserrat, have fled from their homes in the south.

All schools closed early for Easter. The aluminium-clad factory shells ordered by the Chief Minister to be used as emergency shelter accommodation had arrived on island incomplete. With inappropriate or missing parts (including only half the required roofing sheets and 240 incorrect windows) it meant erection of the units that were intended to accommodate twenty persons each was delayed, and at the beginning of April no alternative shelter accommodation had been built. So the schools, together with the churches, took in the evacuees again. Twenty-four makeshift shelters housing 1381 people.

The rest of the dislocated community have dispersed into rented accommodation or moved in with friends and relatives. Evacuees are spending an uncomfortable and disrupted Easter in the same cramped and distressing conditions as they had spent Christmas.

The same problems that had beleaguered them at Christmas remain unresolved. The cesspits still overflow, particularly when it rains.

For two days we lost reception from ZJB Radio Montserrat because they were not able to transmit on AM when they relocated out of their studio in Plymouth and we were unable to pick up the FM signals. The only alternative, Gem Radio, took the opportunity to leave Montserrat permanently, setting up their station in Trinidad and Tobago. We had to rely on gossip for information.

Further frustrations became evident. Food rations that had been held ready in containers at Gerald's Park for just such an emergency were distributed. But the rations have been deemed unfit for human consumption after some recipients complained of vomiting and diarrhoea, 'out of date' packages, and 'worms' in biscuits. The NATO ration packs had originated from Hamburg with labelling and instructions in German.

The containers should have been kept in the shade, and it was suggested that exposure to direct sunlight might have produced what is called an oven effect inside them, possibly contributing to a rapid deterioration of the ration packs.

An alternative solution has been proposed, that of giving out food parcels, but this has created fractious queues where people wait two hours in the sun, and tempers easily flare. In addition petrol rationing has been introduced and rumours are circulating that the sale of medicines will soon be restricted. Daily life is very, very difficult.

It was obvious that the third evacuation of Plymouth and the south would be longer than the optimistic one week suggested by the Chief Minister. When questioned about the anticipated length of the third evacuation the scientists have been circumspect and will only commit to *'a long time'*, saying that they are preparing for *'the big one'*.

We are assured that the northern third of Montserrat (beyond Belham River Valley) will remain safe, but might from time to time experience the nuisance of raining ash from eruptions, depending on prevailing wind direction.

Some families have refused to evacuate from their homes a third time and insist on remaining in the danger area. Dr. Ambeh is very concerned and has broadcast several appeals for people to *'come out'*. Rose Willock at ZJB Radio Montserrat has appealed to them by name, urging them to leave before it is too late. There is the attitude *"Me na go 'til me see de lava flo"*.

Dr. Ambeh has stressed that the situation at the volcano is very dangerous, saying it was just a matter of time before there was a pyroclastic flow down Fort Ghaut into Plymouth.

The only people officially allowed through the police barriers into the restricted south are those with 'essential business' in the unsafe area. This includes Port Authority workers and farmers who need to tend animals left behind. However special permission was given for Government Departments, banks and other businesses to retrieve equipment and documents from their hastily abandoned offices in Plymouth.

It took a week for the telephone connections to be re-assigned so many workers were obliged to go into the unsafe zone to make essential phone calls. Even the Governor's Office staff, relocated to the safety of McChesney's Estate in Olveston, had to go into the danger zone when they were required to use the official Satellite Communications Equipment.

Over the Easter weekend businesses and residents were allowed to re-enter the unsafe areas on a pass system. Four hundred passes were issued on the 6th April, the day I witnessed my first pyroclastic flow.

It was extraordinary. We were at St. John's and heading towards the airport. We watched in stunned fascination as a vast, compressed, rolling, tumbling, concertina of searing black and grey ash rushed down Tar River Valley. It boiled everything in its path, popping trees explosively as it sped down the uninhabited eastern slopes of the volcano. Captured on camera it made a sobering shot.

The World's media have begun to arrive in Montserrat, and the aid agencies are close behind. Down the road the Vue Pointe Hotel, with many of their forty available rooms and cottages in use by evacuated friends and family, has taken in some of the visitors.

The hotel is also being used for the relocated MS Osborne's store, the schools examinations centre, Father Larry's Catholic Church services, and as the Casualty Field Station.

The hotel has seen a procession of assorted representatives from an amazing number of organisations, all seemingly known only by their initials. They include a cross-section of the media, BBC, ITN, ABC, CNN, the medical, IRC, PAHO and the mighty FCO, MOD, EU, EMAD, ODA, OACS, CARICOM, UNDP, BDD, DTRS. They came and they went. We have calculated that over forty different scientific experts have visited the island to look at the volcano since the commencement of activity in July 1995, eight months ago.

Short, sharp, heavy showers arrived in the middle of April and helped to refresh the island and wash down the roofs, roads and gardens. Unfortunately it also brought rivers of grey ash pouring down our drive. Twice a day we have to hose and brush through the house.

We are warned of an eruption when we hear the dogs barking, and then people start shouting. Looking up into the hills we see another big black cloud, heavy with ash, heading in our direction. We quickly call to each other and in the few minutes before the darkness of falling ash descends, we run around the house hastily closing windows and doors as tightly as possible. My neighbour Sheila has arranged for large sheets of plywood to be hammered across her front windows to keep out the ash. After each ashin' we pray for rain.

My housekeeper Shirley is an inspiration and an enormous help to me. Although she lives in the far north she comes down into Old Towne each day, and together we broom through, shovel up ash, and hose the decks. Shirley arrived recently dressed as usual in her Sunday best, with the somewhat eccentric accessory of a shower cap over her black curly hair.

Shirley changes clothes when she arrives and has a favourite pair of luminescent green lycra shorts. The figure hugging shorts, together with a tight T-shirt pressing in on huge bosoms, makes the humming, happy Shirley a constant source of pleasure to the numerous workmen who arrive to empty the gutters of ash, check my leaking gas cooker, jemmy the stubbornly locked bedroom door open, replace the door frame, quote for installation of an air-conditioner, etc.

The Rasta gardeners are visiting more frequently. Keeping dreadlocks ash free is a challenge. One Rasta wears a bright red rain hood pulled tight around his face, while his friend prefers to keep his locks tucked up inside a large felt beret which rises an astonishing twelve inches above his forehead.

Alfred came to supervise the roof and gutter cleaning. Buckets of heavy wet ash, like moist grey concrete, were dug out by hand before being dumped. One of the lads discovered, ingeniously, that a Hessian sack provided the ultimate in hair, mouth and eye protection. There was no doubt it was effective, but he did look rather weird, up his ladder, head and shoulders inside a brown Hessian sack with torn T-shirt, baggy shorts, and bare feet protruding from beneath.

Alfred says his work has dropped off alarmingly and he is worried. *"Tween a rock and a hard place"* he complained. He has three boys and is concerned about their safety, their health, and their schooling, which is being interrupted. His brother has already packed up and gone to the US. Since he is in possession of an American Green Card he was allowed to enter the States to work.

Alfred has been experiencing a recurring nightmare in which he sees a gully, or a ghaut, with a mudflow rushing down it and lots of people running along. The mudflow catches the people and sweeps them away. He asked me *"How can you get to the beaches to get off the island if its heavy ash and you can't breathe or travel?"* I have no answer, but I have heard that the total population of

Montserrat could be removed in Chinook helicopters from Gerald's Park in forty-eight hours.

The British Government have come up with a voluntary relocation offer. Under the scheme Montserratians can travel to the UK and the normal Immigration procedures will be waived. They can stay for up to two years provided they pay their own fares and have a sponsor prepared to offer accommodation on arrival.

Alfred has relatives in London, and when I asked him if he was interested in taking up the British Government relocation offer, he said he was biding his time, adopting a 'wait and see' approach.

Within two days of the application forms being available, one hundred and thirteen forms had been handed out, but by the end of April only nine had been returned. It is a very simple form, after the question of nationality the main eligibility criteria is a 'yes' answer to the question *"Were you in Montserrat on 1st April 1996?"*

On the street 'dem say' that no more than twenty families are likely to be interested. It is a big decision to leave Montserrat, and the airfares are very expensive. Lennie went for a form, but as a third country national not married to a Montserratian, he has discovered he does not qualify.

On the morning of the 20th April we woke to find HMS *Brave* swinging at anchor in the sea beyond our cliff. She looked like one of those grey plastic models that come tucked into breakfast cereal which when filled with bicarbonate of soda whiz madly round the bath.

Identified only by the number F94 on her side, she had arrived in the darkness of night. We had seen the port and starboard lights and heard voices, then the rattle of the anchor chain as it was released. It was a goodwill visit for two days, during which time the crew helped islanders, including putting in showers in some of the church shelters.

The Lynx helo thundered over my head while it ferried various crates and boxes from ship to shore in what appeared to be an oversized string shopping bag swung beneath its belly. On one trip the bag was filled with food donated by St. Vincent for distribution to shelterees, and tons of dehydrated packages to replace the contaminated NATO rations. The last duty of the Commander, looking pink and freshly-scrubbed in his white shirt, shorts and bobby socks, was to deliver cakes to the evacuees in the shelters.

The volcano is now a genuine mountain. It dominates the landscape and has been given the nickname *'Twisty's Peak'* in mock deference to Chief Minister Rueben Meade.

The dome has expanded an extraordinary 250% in four weeks and at one point grew at a visible and unbelievable speed of 200 ft. in thirty-six hours. It is currently growing at three cubic metres per second. To put this into perspective and illustrate the point, imagine our volcano in Montserrat as increasing in size at the rate of a small car in less than two seconds.

Soufrière Hills Volcano erupting

11 - MAY 1996

MOTHER'S DAY ERUPTION

It was Sunday morning 12th May and American Mother's Day. A shrill voice calling *"Inside! Inside!"* summoned me to my front door. It was Beryl, a wrinkled walnut of a woman, hoping to sell me some onions, or mangoes, or limes.

Before the evacuation of Plymouth, Beryl used to hawk her wares sitting under the tree opposite Rams Emdee supermarket in town. An ideal place for catching passing shoppers and persuading them to purchase from her assortment of fruits and vegetables. But now Beryl has begun peddling her produce door-to-door, walking many miles a day, with a box of fruit and vegetables balanced on top of a coiled scarf on her head.

She stands beside the gate and screeches at the top of her voice until someone comes out. Then, after a sale and perhaps a drink, she puts the box back on her head and sets off to find her next customer. Beryl is a very persuasive and very persistent hawker and recognises a sucker immediately. I have become a regular, and when pickings are lean elsewhere she will sometimes call on me twice a week. If I am not at home, she will use her coiled scarf as a cushion and doze under a tree until my return. *"Me sit, me wait"* she says.

Over the past few months I have learned Beryl's story. She has lived almost all of her seventy-two years in the village of Harris in Montserrat. As a young girl she worked in the cotton fields of the white plantation owners at Roaches, on the southeast side of the island. In those days Montserrat cotton was famous for its very high quality.

Beryl would set off in the dark from Harris at 3.00 a.m. and walk for three hours through the rising dawn to reach the cotton fields. She would spend all day picking cotton, then just as the light was fading she would start back to Harris with the heavy load of cotton balanced on her head. The final walk up Harris hill was hard, she said. She had no affection for the plantation owners, who paid little but demanded much and lived in great luxury compared to the poverty endured by Beryl and her co-workers.

Beryl was evacuated from Harris last month, on 3rd April, but instead of going into one of the churches or schools with the rest of the homeless evacuees, she has rented a small room behind the Suntex Bakery in Salem together with her daughter Hilary and two others. She needs to earn money for her rent and for water and light, and although evacuated she is still required to pay a fixed charge for water and light on her house in the hills. She confessed to me that she often slips back to her home in the unsafe area of Harris in order to wash and cook and harvest some of the fruit and vegetables from her garden.

When she came to see me on the morning of the 12th May, Beryl set her box on the ground and I picked over and selected a couple of limes, two mangoes and a handful of greens that looked like clover on stringy stems. She said they would be good for me, and instructed me to 'scal' them with some hot water before eating them.

As we stood on the step and bargained I noticed in the distance beyond Beryl the volcano had given off a huge cloud. We watched together as it rose higher and higher, expanding and rolling and filling the sky. Beryl said the volcano had blown two or three plumes into the air the day before, when she was in Harris, and many people had gone into the unsafe area to take photographs. According to Beryl people got rich taking photographs of the volcano.

She was unperturbed as we watched the eruption and the rolling black cloud of ash. "It a go o' da wata" she maintained, assuming it would blow away from us and across the sea. Only she was wrong. It quickly became apparent that the huge eruption was coming straight for us. Having blacked out Harris, Plymouth, Cork Hill, Richmond Hill and Foxes Bay it was rapidly heading for Old Towne, Olveston and Salem.

I hauled Beryl inside and rushed around shutting the louvers. As darkness descended and the volcanic cloud of dust and ash engulfed us, I lit candles. The radio was off air, the electricity was off and the phones went down immediately. As we sat together in the flickering candlelight the ash slammed down on the roof above our heads. We could not hear ourselves speak above the noise.

I didn't know if the ash cloud would pass or whether it was a precursor and the beginning of the final chaos in Montserrat. While Beryl sat placidly in an armchair, ash mask dangling under her chin and a comforting rum in her hand, I taped plastic bin bags across the louvers in an attempt to stop the ash filtering into the house.

After the longest forty-five minutes of my life the hammering on the roof began to ease and dusty daylight slowly returned. As we stared outside we saw everything was mummified in a thick cloak of grey ash, grit and pumice pebbles, and the air was a hot, swirling, brown smog. We gazed around in disbelief. What had been a sunny tropical paradise an hour earlier with green trees and scarlet flowers was now transformed into a ghostly, mantled, moonscape.

I bent down and stroked my hand through the thick layer of fine ash. It was humbling to me to realise that I was the first human to touch this crushed and powdered rock. It had the texture of warm silk, strafed by pieces of pumice, fresh from the pulsating heart of the volcano, millions of years old.

One hour later a second cloud, even more frightening than the first, descended on us. This was the product of a sensational pyroclastic flow that tore down Tar River Valley on the eastern flanks of the volcano and for the first time entered the sea, running across the surface for thirty meters and boiling the water.

Shirley had been out at the airport when the first bubbling avalanche of hot gas, rocks and ash travelling at several hundred miles an hour hit the sea. She told me it spread out and boiled the water *"Like a pan on de hob"*. Shirley said those watching thought the sea itself had erupted and were terrified.

The Governor's Staff Officer happened to be up in the helo in the vicinity of the volcano at the time, and from a birds-eye view watched the elemental power in stunned horror. Someone taking photographs too close to the activity was plucked from the danger area.

Seventeen days after the pyroclastic flow, on the 29th May, Simon (back in Montserrat after a long period away) took the surface temperature of the Tar River deposits. They ranged between 200° and 250°C.

Twenty-five scientists were on-island monitoring the volcano at the time of the pyroclastic flow. Measuring ground deformation, setting-up instruments, taking gas samples etc. and two days before the pyroclastic flow they had confidently reported that the dome was *"Just bubbling away quietly"*.

After the four pyroclastic flows of 12th and 13th May it is no wonder the public has little confidence in the scientific advice. However the MVO insists that even if the volcano goes into a more explosive phase, the northern area beyond Belham Valley is still considered safe. *"The safe areas in the north remain safe"* they keep repeating.

It is hardly encouraging to learn through *'word on the street'* that 10,000 body bags have been delivered to Montserrat. At a rough calculation that is more than one bag per resident. The Chief Minister was obliged to deny the rumour, confirming the arrival of the body bags, but insisting that there are only fifty.

In the meantime we struggle on, attempting the Herculean clean-up, with ash masks, and red eyes, and coughs, and tight chests. We have been advised to stay indoors as much as possible and wear our ash masks. We are constantly being reassured that the ash is not dangerous to inhale it is just *'nuisance value'*.

It took almost two weeks to reduce the perpetual nuisance of the ash to no more than an occasional small inconvenience in Old Towne and Salem. I am suffering from repetitive strain syndrome from all the sweeping, and I have pleaded for a vacuum cleaner, and an air conditioner for our bedroom.

Because the schools are still full of evacuees the children are having their lessons in homes, on balconies, in tents and under trees. An announcement on the radio has advised all students to *"Carry along a dust mask and a duster for cleaning desk, books and chairs"*.

The Rastas continue to come to work in the garden, but they are often invisible, surrounded in a cloud of white mist, feet and ankles coated with grey ash. They are always so sympathetic and considerate and want to know how I feel, frequently asking me *"De ash buggin' ya?"*

In the garden the iguanas scamper across from their holes in the cliff when I offer scraps of food. There are thirteen of them now. They look like grey and wrinkled mini-dinosaurs in grey grass, stirring up grey clouds of ash, as they rush towards me for scraps of mango peel, pawpaw skin and greens.

The Government is distributing a weekly bag of pre-filled groceries through the Emergency Operations Centre. The bags are valued at EC$113 per person, though some dispute this believing it to be closer to half that amount. People in shelters are allocated two bags per week, those relocated but living with relatives or friends receive one bag.

In the bag there might be a tin of corned beef, or sardines, some rice perhaps, or noodles, but no bread. If a boat comes in with supplies from neighbouring islands then the bag might contain a plantain, or dasheen, or a bunch of bananas. Although two meals a day are provided in the shelters people often prefer to cook their own meals, generally on coal-pots in the yard.

It is not possible for the contents of the ration bags to be identical, and this causes some ill-feeling, together with the belief that those in shelters get better rations than the others.

Some complaints are legitimate, from diabetics and those suffering from high blood pressure, or milk allergies, or vegetarians like the Rastas. Other complaints are more a matter of personal preference. One person I know doesn't eat corned beef so she is hoarding her tins and sending them back into the unsafe zone. She says she will use them for sandwiches for the children to take to school *"When all dis is over"*.

There have been suggestions that it would be more appropriate to give money, or coupons, which could be redeemed in the shops, rather than this weekly distribution of bags of food. Many unemployed Montserratians are without money and consequently they cannot pay for services, or medicines, or contribute financially to household costs. In the circumstances these people would appreciate hard cash.

The farmers who have land in the fertile hills of the south are torn between working their crops and harvesting what they can, or abandoning them and staying in shelters in the north. They have no compensation and no alternative fields to work, although the authorities are looking at plots in the north. We have been warned there will be no white potato crop this year and greens are already in short supply.

Farmers with animals are particularly vulnerable. Dogs released to fend for themselves by owners leaving the unsafe area have formed packs and are ravaging livestock. On the night of the 19th May, Kenneth Lee from Parsons found thirty of his animals dead. It was a bitter and cruel blow but all he said about the tragedy was *"What happen, happen, I look at it that way - but it's really hard".*

David Brandt recently called Montserrat *"A suffering and bankrupt nation".* There is certainly a great deal of stress, with the aggravation of the ash, the uncertainty of the volcanic activity and the anticipation of the coming hurricane season adding to the burden.

Some individuals suffer more than most, particularly those in temporary shelter accommodation. One old man said *"Y kyarn res', ya kyarn sleep".* General complaints about the shelters include uncomfortable army cots to sleep on, lack of privacy, crowded conditions, queues for the toilets and shower, noisy nights, families split, primitive cooking and inadequate food storage facilities, and recently an outbreak of chicken pox.

It takes the sludge tanker five trips to empty the Brades shelter cesspits alone. The first 'primrose lorry' purchased to empty the cesspits suffered brake failure, and the second did not have the correct gear ratio for Montserrat's roads, which meant it crawled up the hills and moved very slowly between the shelters and the temporary landfill site. The men employed to carry out this unpleasant task have demanded 'dirty money', compensation to deal with the 'wrigglers and worms'.

In an attempt to improve conditions for the evacuees the Chief Minister has authorised the building of 'family units' housing four to six persons, to be made out of T1-11 plywood with 'crinkly-tin' roofs, for erection on various sites, initially in his constituency of Salem.

By the end of the May, some of the steel-framed aluminium clad shelters were almost complete, although progress was slowed, due in part to lack of funds and in part to lack of cement on island. The 'tropical igloos' (those dome-shaped plastic covered tunnels sent by British Aid) still remain packed, awaiting the construction of foundations.

Major Lynch of the MDF has decided to construct temporary timber accommodation for his men at Gerald's Park. He does not want them under canvas through a hurricane season which is anticipated to be worse than last year. Working from drawings and schedules prepared by my husband the MDF have quickly built several wooden barrack-style de-mountable units for their own use, now called MDF Units.

My husband has transferred much of his office equipment from Plymouth into one of the bedrooms at home and he is using our private car as a mobile office. The contents of his filing cabinet are in boxes in the trunk. It is surprisingly efficient. Since he spends much of his time visiting sites, or at meetings, it is very convenient to have all the files to hand.

Civil Servants have been offered unpaid leave of absence for up to two years if they wish to take up the April UK Immigration package. Their jobs in Montserrat will remain secure until their return. The airline BWIA is offering a special fare of US$599 for a return ticket to England, valid for one year, for those people with official forms. Although two hundred forms have been given out so far, only eleven were returned by the 7th May. Eight single applicants and three families. There has, however, been an increase in persons applying for Naturalisation in Montserrat.

On the 29th May a fissure fifty feet long opened up at the volcano and was venting ash. On the 31st May I was at home and felt the earthquake at 1.15 p.m. Moments later my husband phoned from Cork Hill to warn me that a huge black cloud was passing over him and heading my way, giving me time to close up the house. I phoned Sheila next door to pass on the warning. She said something unprintable and I heartily agreed.

The smell of bad eggs arrived ahead of the cloud. I put on my Miss Piggy ash mask and switched on the radio. It was still transmitting but oblivious to the eruption, relaying the cricket match between BVI and Montserrat.

Then I waited, prepared to sit it out in the black sweatbox of the house. Outside visibility dropped to twenty feet and the air inside and out filled with the now familiar brown swirling fog. There is something quite indescribable about the smell of hot ash as it envelops you.

Was this the big one? I didn't think so. The air was thick with grime but the main black deposit of raining ash passed in about half an hour. I had just mopped the bedroom floor when the phone rang and it was Sheila, warning me that another eruption was coming our way, even bigger than before and crossing over Salem and Olveston and heading well into the safe northern part of the island. It was my turn to say something unprintable, and she heartily agreed.

On the evening up-date the MVO reported, *"Activity was relatively high today"* with sixty rockfall signals and two pyroclastic flows down the east. The ash clouds had risen to between 7,000 and 10,000 ft. Line lengths measured on the monitoring instruments had shortened 8mm over a twenty-four hour period, which roughly translated meant the mountain was 'swelling'.

Twisty's Peak' is 3,100 ft. high having topped Chances Peak (previously Montserrat's highest point) by 88 ft.

12 - JUNE 1996

STRESS MANAGEMENT WORKSHOPS

I was apprehensive as we entered June.

On the street gossip was circulating that there would be a big eruption in June. An astrological prediction based on the fact that Saturn and Earth lined up on the 8th June.

June was a Blue Moon month, meaning there would be two full moons. One on the 2nd and another on the 30th. Believed by some to be another bad omen.

Compounding the unease was the assertion that the Bible proclaimed the arrival of the Anti-Christ on the 6th June 1996, something to do with the numbers 666. Hundreds of people in South East Asia have taken this prediction so seriously they are having their children baptised into the Roman Catholic faith in anticipation.

Fortunately for Montserrat the astrologers were wrong and there was no eruption on the 8th, although the following day the area of growth in the dome of the volcano switched its centre of activity from northeast to northwest.

This placed it alongside Gages Wall which acts as the retaining barrier separating English's Crater from Gages, Fort Ghaut and Plymouth below.

Within a few days Gages Wall had been overtopped and mudflows associated with the rains travelled down into Fort Ghaut and through Plymouth depositing thick silt and filling up Port Plymouth adjacent to the dock.

It was a relief when on the 19th June growth activity moved away from the Gages Wall area, concentrating once more in the north and southwest part of the dome.

The relocation from the south to the north of Montserrat has begun to take on a more permanent appearance. We now anticipate being evacuated for at least six months, throughout the hurricane season.

Government offices have become more firmly established, with Salem and Olveston beginning to function as the new centre of Montserrat.

Building activity has increased in an attempt to adjust to living in the north. Renovation of the temporary hospital in St. John's primary school has commenced. In an effort to reduce the interruption to supplies the Water Authority plans to build a stand-by emergency pumping system at St. Peters. They will also build two extra storage tanks at Fogarthy and Dick Hill. They have also begun to search for alternative water sources and have commenced a series of well-drilling tests beside the golf course at Belham Valley.

The Government electricity generating company, Monlec, are coping well with demand for power. They are providing the island with electricity from containers parked on land in Salem. Two emergency generators hum loudly night and day, giving a reliable service with only the occasional hiccup of a brown-out or cut in current.

The roads in the north, unfamiliar with frequent and heavy traffic use, have deteriorated and large potholes are appearing. Unfortunately the hot-mix asphalt plant normally used to repair the roads is situated in the unsafe south, and alternative methods of repairing the highways has had to be found. Also, additional roads are needed as a matter of urgency to previously isolated areas such as Little Bay.

Sir Nicholas Bonsor arrived from the UK on the 6th June to assess the situation on Montserrat for himself. We have been informed that approximately £5 million has been spent on island by the British Government since the volcanic crisis began in July 1995. Commitments have included MVO equipment, personnel and support helicopter, medical supplies, vehicles, emergency rations, prefabricated shelters, radio and communications equipment.

The list is long but many Montserratians have found it difficult to believe that so much money has been spent with so little obvious evidence, as far as they can see, on island.

Food and utility costs are steadily rising in Montserrat. With the sterling exchange rate at EC$4.15 to £1, a litre carton of Carnation Long Life milk cost EC$4.35, a small tin of HP Baked Beans is EC$2.33 and a 15 oz. can of Hunts Stewed Tomatoes retails at EC$4.15. The only reasonable purchase seems to be a 750 ml bottle of 'Mount Gay' rum at EC$21.95.

The Montserrat Red Cross Society, under the direction of Lystra Osborne, began a fund-raising appeal to build a special, permanent, accommodation unit for the elderly in the safe north. Currently fifty old people are being housed in two Red Cross shelters at St. Peter's and Cavalla Hill.

Managers were appointed to supervise the day-to-day running of shelters and to help solve problems that arise within the shelter community. The Managers are being encouraged to attend a special 'Stress Management Workshop' organised on island. This workshop has been expressly designed to 'help helpers' and others who have the responsibility of supporting the evacuees through their stress.

Slowly people are beginning to drift away from Montserrat. Over three hundred forms for travel to Britain under the special scheme have now been distributed by the Administration Department, and ninety-four have been completed and returned. The approach of school holidays, the coming hurricane season, and the possibility of another six months of evacuation, has encouraged many to leave. Forty-two people have now taken up the UK relocation offer.

In order to establish a more accurate picture of the distribution and personal circumstances of residents on island, the statistical department has undertaken a 'relocation registration' exercise. The Government produced a short questionnaire and sent out an army of enumerators to visit every household on island.

The lady who arrived on my doorstep was intimidating. Big, tough, and not to be messed with. After sternly informing me that the British Government wanted me to answer some questions she licked and ticked her way through two pages that seemed to have no relevance to my own circumstances at all.

Questions such as *"Do you have any valid travel documents?" "Where were they issued?" "When did they expire?" "Do you have diabetes?" "What is your blood group?" "Do you have high blood pressure?" "Have you worked in the last year, if so what did you do?" "What level of education do you have?" "Are you interested in voluntary evacuation?" "Where would you go if given the choice?"*

The annual celebration of the Queen's Official Birthday took place on the 15th June. This is a traditional British Colonial event which normally occurs on the second Saturday in June. It is all very ceremonial but the children in particular love this spectacle.

The day commenced with a colourful parade of uniformed organisations at 8.00 a.m. and later that day the Governor hosted a large and convivial party for several hundred invited guests. The Morning Parade has a strict procedure that is solemnly adhered to as an official ceremonial in honour of the birthday of Her Majesty The Queen. His Excellency the Governor is required to attend in his official white uniform complete with pith helmet and 'chicken feathers' to inspect the parade and take the salute.

On the arrival of His Excellency the Union Flag is 'broken', and a Royal Salute given, during which the band plays part of the British National Anthem. After inspecting the Parade, His Excellency returns to the saluting base and the columns of uniformed participants, including the Montserrat Defence Force, the Royal Montserrat Police Force, Prison Officers, Girl Guides, and Red Cross march past. The Union Flag is then slowly and ceremoniously lowered, the Royal Standard broken and saluted while the band plays the National Anthem again.

At that point Her Majesty is imagined to be present at the ceremony, and while the spectators stand in deference to her notional presence a *Feu-de-joie* precedes the removal of all headgear and three cheers for the Queen. Following this, the Royal Standard is lowered, any medals presented, and the Union Flag raised back up the flagstaff. More Royal Salute and more National Anthem before the celebration is completed and His Excellency leaves the Parade ground, closely followed by the Chief Minister and invited guests.

In twenty years of watching the Queen's Birthday Parade in several different countries I have enjoyed, and occasionally endured, some memorable celebrations.

The basic procedure is always the same but unexpected interruptions make each Parade unique. I remember, for instance, the one when a young policeman inadvertently shot himself in the foot moments before he should have fired the *Feu-de-joie*. I have squirmed as the Union Flag was hoisted upside-down and I have winced as the Royal Standard fluttered to the ground in mid-salute. I have also suffered painful renditions of *"God Save the Queen"* when musicians following the score did so at a careful, personal pace, completely unrelated to each other.

But the memory I particularly treasure was the occasion in the British Virgin Islands when the Governor's Labrador raced up to the performing trumpeter and began howling his own canine accompaniment to the National Anthem, to the spontaneous applause of the spectators.

We were about to leave Montserrat for our mid-contract break and Beryl stopped by the house to wish me a happy holiday and safe journey, counselling me to remain 'kahm' at all times when travelling.

"Ya gotta be kahm" she insisted in her sing-song voice, her small mahogany face wrinkling into a smile. She was wearing a thick long-sleeved dress over a cotton T-shirt, her feet pushed into salmon-coloured plastic mules, and her bare legs were dusty with ash picked up from miles of walking.

On her head she had a large, broad brimmed straw hat, and on top of the hat was balanced a cardboard Carib beer box containing mangoes, limes and bananas.

In the box Beryl had put some tamarind leaves and twigs collected from trees beside the road. She intended to take these back to her room to make bush tea. Rinsing off the leaves and twigs she will plunge them into the boiling water for a few minutes. She pointed to a carton of orange and peach juice I had given her to drink, and told me the brew would taste much the same. She assured me it was excellent for colds and the chest, but cautioned me to use discretion, since too much bush tea is not good.

Beryl collected several pieces of Royal Palm bark that had fallen off the tall trees that line our drive. The green growth at the top of the palm dries out and drops away each month as the tree grows, swells and bursts its bark wrapping. This brown discarded bark is flexible and Beryl uses it to make plaited or woven baskets to sell at EC$83 each in Salem. I gave her a large kitchen knife so that she could cut off the damaged ends and she placed the bark sheets carefully into an oil cloth.

As I watched Beryl trim the palms I noticed one of the iguanas emerging from the undergrowth some distance away. He paused to study a tempting red hibiscus flower and Beryl spotted him. In a flash she had dropped the palm and was off across the grass, running low and fast and with obvious evil intent, knife held high in her hand.

Iguana may be short-sighted and unable to distinguish a yellow china plate from a piece of pawpaw skin (or a finger from a banana), but any movement makes them instantly alert. The iguana glimpsed the advancing Beryl and disappeared at speed over the cliff edge, leaving her grumbling and clucking with disappointment as she watched her anticipated supper vanish.

Iguanas are not such good eating as Mountain Chicken, which is the name used locally for the large frog (Leptodactylus Fallax) found only on the islands of Montserrat and Dominica. The Vue Pointe Hotel does not offer iguana on the menu but is famous for its Mountain Chicken legs, which when lightly braised in garlic butter taste absolutely delicious.

13 - JULY 1996

PART OF THE DOME COLLAPSES

We were somewhere over the Atlantic on our return flight to Montserrat when the daily news for Tuesday 9th July flashed onto the screen in the cabin. A brief announcement bluntly stated that Hurricane Bertha was heading up the Caribbean chain and had just passed through the Leeward Islands, including Montserrat and Antigua.

This was astonishing news. I'd phoned the Foreign Office in London the previous day asking for an up-date on Montserrat and they had told me *'A bit of a depression'* was passing over the area, but otherwise both the weather and the volcano were quiet. They obviously hadn't been informed that the 'depression' was in fact a full-blown hurricane, the first of the season.

Immediately after the news report the Captain's affable voice boomed through the plane. In an amiable and friendly tone he addressed his bewildered passengers. He informed us that we would be arriving in Antigua in about five hours. Fortunately the airport had just re-opened after forty-eight hours of closure. *"A lot of heavy rainfall, a bit of flooding, rather overcast, but otherwise things were looking good in Antigua"* he continued cheerfully, ending with *"Have a nice day and enjoy your flight"*.

I wondered how many of the passengers would have boarded in London had they been aware that a hurricane was sweeping across their holiday destination.

Hurricane Bertha had closely followed Tropical Storm Arthur, whose arrival in the Caribbean so early in the season was not good news. An alphabetical list of twenty-one names had already been assigned to this season's storms. After Arthur and Bertha will come Cesar, Diana, Edouard, Fran, Gustav, and so on until finally Vicky and Wilfred.

Although Hurricane Bertha was described as *'no more than a pussycat'* by comparison to the heavyweight Dangerous Hurricane Luis we had experienced the previous year, she caused four deaths through the Caribbean. A primary school in St. Thomas, being re-built after the devastation of last year's hurricanes, was destroyed once again.

After a bumpy flight, courtesy of the stormy petticoats of Hurricane Bertha, we landed at V.C. Bird International Airport in Antigua just a few hours after it had re-opened. And we sat in the confusion of the Departure Lounge for five hours before LIAT finally confessed to having cancelled the Montserrat leg of our flight.

The LIAT service to Montserrat has become increasingly unreliable. Sometimes they cancel flights at short notice, or the planes leave Antigua for Montserrat, but when the pilot sees the ashy emissions coming from the volcano he refuses to land, swinging the plane round and returning to Antigua.

With great good luck 'Kamikaze Jim' was at Antigua airport re-fuelling the helo and he offered us a ride back to Montserrat.

It was good to return to the island, especially as the unseasonably heavy rains (a record eight inches in June), had cleansed the ash from roads, trees and houses and everywhere looked green and crisp and welcoming.

During the second week of July the temperature was a pleasant 82°F and the breezy east wind cooled the air and took the ashy belches from the volcano out across the sea.

In our absence three baby iguana, twelve inches long and the luminescent green of Shirley's shorts, had been using the open verandah of the house as a nursery, and several small crabs were clattering around the deck beside the pool.

Both iguanas and crabs seemed magnetically attracted to the pool and we frequently have to perform lifeguard duties when they show signs of fatigue during prolonged bouts of swimming. I have created an iguana rescue ramp by laying the mop handle across the deck and dangling the head into the water so they can clamber out at their own convenience. It works marvellously.

One of the iguana youngsters, more independently minded than his brothers, we have named Ignatius. We saw him disappearing under the cooker in the kitchen and discovered he had moved in with us. He emerges abruptly at odd times during the day and night, or when the oven gets too hot for comfort.

The mature iguanas, wrapped in their wrinkled grey parchment coats, spend most of the day stretched out on the branches of the flamboyant tree, lazily inert as they sunbathe. Occasionally they contort into extraordinary positions, bouncing the light twigs and hanging on with their long, prehensile toes, then swinging to reach and eat the delectable crimson flamboyant flowers. Sometimes there are as many as twenty iguanas in the garden.

The iguanas are particularly partial to mango, which they adore above everything else, even more than pawpaw. During early July our mango tree was cropping abundantly, producing palm-sized pebbles of smooth and fragrant fruit. In an early morning ritual the iguanas group beneath the tree, gazing upwards in anticipation, or searching the ground for ripe fruit that might have dropped during the night. If I throw them mango skin they race to the spot and grab the prize, slapping their jaws around the ripe rind, slurping and dribbling in joyful ecstasy.

Living conditions for the evacuees in the shelters has not improved in our absence. But now a voucher system of EC$30 per adult per week has replaced the food rations previously distributed. These vouchers can be used at the various stores to buy food, but it is becoming more difficult to get a good selection of groceries on island, particularly fresh vegetables and meat.

The main grocery outlets on island are Angelo's, Osborne's, Victor's, Rams and Papa's. All have relocated into makeshift accommodation in the north, and all are trying to provide a service under very difficult conditions. For a while Rams Supermarket continued to trade from their premises in Plymouth, delivering phoned orders into the safe zone, while they built a substantial new shop in Salem. Angelo's have built a small plywood hut on a parcel of flat land above the golf course, just across the Belham Valley safe line.

Helping to keep the shops stocked is the little sailboat *'Avontuur'* which brings in fresh, frozen and other cargo from St. Maarten once a week, unless bad weather delays her. The *'Avontuur'* is an old boat, built in Holland over eighty years ago, and with her distinctive sails and cheerful colours she is unique to the waters of the Caribbean and held in great affection. It takes the four-man crew up to twenty hours, using both sail and engine, to cover the one hundred miles between Montserrat and St. Maarten.

In an attempt to obtain fresh produce a few of the expatriate wives have organised regular food-shopping excursions to Antigua to buy fresh meat, cheese, and fruit. They charter a small plane to fly them across to Antigua, where they take a taxi to the Epicurean Supermarket, returning to Montserrat the same day with their purchases.

W.H. Bramble Airport provides the only method of getting to and from Montserrat. If the airport is not functioning then we are stranded. I have been told that John Osborne once tried to organise a ferry between Montserrat and Antigua, but not enough people had shown interest, and he told me the insurance premiums were very high.

Although the majority of evacuees are still in the safe north, many have drifted back to their homes in the unsafe south. It is estimated that approximately six hundred people did not return to the north after they had been allowed back to the danger zone to 'batten-down' their homes for Hurricane Bertha. They prefer to live in their own homes with the danger and uncertainty of the volcano than to suffer as evacuees in the north.

On the 18th July, The Seventh Day Adventist Churches on Island held a day of Prayer and Thanksgiving to commemorate the first anniversary of the commencement of volcanic activity. It was a Thanksgiving for being preserved from what could have been worse dangers. *"The powerful hand of the Almighty holding back what could have been greater devastation and loss of lives"* said the Preacher. Everyone was invited to Gerald's Park at 7.00 p.m. There were many guests and Father Larry joined in, looking refreshed and buoyant after a long break off-island. Was it really a year ago that I was a guest at Government House enjoying a coffee morning with the Governor's wife?

Governor Frank Savage and his wife returned to London during July. They were invited guests of Her Majesty the Queen at a Buckingham Palace Garden Party in London. The Governor has been awarded a CMG in the Queen's Birthday Honours list, and his faithful Staff Officer has received an MBE. Within the corridors of power in London the award of MBE (Member of the Order of the British Empire) is referred to as the *'My Bloody Efforts'* gong, and similarly the CMG. (Companion of the Order of St. Michael and St. George) conferred on Frank Savage, is known as the *'Call Me God'* gong.

The Governor arrived back on island during late July into a period of heightened activity at the volcano. It had begun on the 20th July with a phase of high seismicity that produced 560 volcano-tectonic earthquakes in the space of two hours at a depth of 3 km below the crater. Small pyroclastic flows travelled down the top end of Tar River Valley on the east side of Montserrat near the airport. For the next two days activity was near continuous with rockfalls and associated pyroclastic flows setting fire to trees down the east, while the ash clouds drifted west with the wind and dropped heavy ash over Plymouth as they moved out to sea.

Fortunately for me the wind direction at the time was taking the load away from us and we could watch the activity with some detachment. Beryl, who continued to visit me hawking her vegetables and fruit, particularly liked the white steamy emissions which lazily uncurled and swirled in a hypnotically gentle manner. She says she believes heaven will be like that. She is not, she told me cheerfully and emphatically, at all afraid of dying, and went on to explain why.

Beryl experiences visions and once she 'saw' Jesus who showed her the New Jerusalem. It was very beautiful, full of trees and flowers unknown to her, although she thought some of the bright yellow flowers might have been what I call daffodils. In her vision Beryl had called to her friends to follow her *'qwik, qwik'* into the New Jerusalem, but they took no notice, ignoring her and continuing with their work as if they had not heard. So she left them and ran on ahead to board the train which was just leaving for the New Jerusalem. Beryl is absolutely certain that when she dies she will be going to the New Jerusalem with Jesus.

A new feature, shaped like a windmill, rose up out of the dome to a height of twenty-five metres and according to Glenn (visiting the MVO from Puerto Rico), the increase in activity was directly correlated to the growth of the feature.

On the 25th July we had 100 volcano-tectonic earthquakes in a rush in two minutes. Glenn explained that the overall pattern of the volcano is much the same, but there has been a major change in earthquakes. Dr. Ambeh agrees, stating that an increase in activity does not necessarily mean the volcano is more dangerous. They both believe that the dome is growing passively, with magma being extruded to the surface, de-gassing as it rises.

The de-gassing is good since it means the magma is losing its explosive potential. However, there is a word of caution. Some volcanoes have grown quietly for a time initially and then had an explosive element.

Dr. Ambeh explained the pattern of Montserrat's volcano, which had started with phreatic eruptions for three months, had then entered a new phase as lava began to form the dome. Now the sides have become unstable and started to collapse, producing rockfalls and pyroclastic flows.

The heavy rains are causing destabilisation of the material, as well as creating small phreatic eruptions as the water hits the hot rock. The last few days of July saw a dramatic increase in activity as parts of the destabilised dome collapsed, and pulses of activity that had begun on the 27th continued with increasing intensity.

During the early evening of 29th July we had been to Angelo's hut to buy a few groceries. We were returning home and passing the Vue Pointe Hotel just as Jim landed the helo at 5.30 p.m. Behind us a huge black cloud cracked with thunder and lightning and filled the sky as another dome collapse sent a pyroclastic flow down the east. This had been happening all day and groups of people had been standing around watching as the dense ash clouds moved west, trailing thick deposits across the landscape of Plymouth and St. Patrick's.

John Shepherd, a Seismologist, had been up in the helo with Jim and he could hardly contain his excitement. He explained to us that a huge pyroclastic flow had just entered the sea beyond the airport on the east coast creating a fan-shaped deposit of new land.

"It was" he enthused *"Like a huge digger had pushed all the land into the sea".*

In all his experience he had never witnessed anything like it. Two rolls of film had been quickly used trying to capture the momentous events. He told us the whole of Tar River Valley was stripped. There were no trees any more just blackened trunks floating in the sea. Cattle, observed earlier in the afternoon, had vanished beneath the boiling flow.

John believed that the activity would continue for several days *"Expect more of the same"* he warned, as he went off with Jim for a stiff drink.

The following morning, on the 30th July, I was padding into the kitchen to make an early morning cup of coffee and listening to the 7.00 a.m. BBC World News, when I was surprised to hear Montserrat mentioned.

The news report was commenting on the activity witnessed by John the previous evening, and made the situation sound very dramatic and dangerous. I listened intently as the announcer said the scientists were not sure whether the present eruptions might lead to a violent explosion. And here we are, living only four miles away from this smouldering bomb!

At lunchtime the next day we thought the bomb had exploded. Although we are becoming used to the caprices of our feisty volcano, this time it was different. It was an extraordinary and quite terrifying experience.

I was at home, in the garden. At first no noise, an eerie silence, but something made me look up into the southern sky and in a heart-stopping moment I watched the world turn black.

This was no swirling cloud, no mushroom of convoluting grey ash heading for heaven. The whole southern hemisphere was composed of a black wall which appeared to be completely, stunningly, absolutely, solid, and it was heading inexorably in my direction.

Then suddenly the crashing, brain numbing thunder and flashing zigzags of red and blue lightning started. Someone else had seen it and her screams galvanised me into action. No warning, no sirens, not even enough time to phone neighbours. We had less than two minutes to get inside, close up and hunker down for what I believed was finally 'the big one'.

As usual the current went off immediately, and the phones. ZJB Radio Montserrat had vanished, a steady hiss the only audible evidence of the station. As I lit candles to fight the groping blackness, mud balls the size of marbles pounded down on the timber roof with a deafening roar. A fog of ash filtered into the room and enveloped me, the dry acrid smell of it burning my throat and making breathing difficult, while overhead the thunder continued to roll and crack, vibrating the walls of the house. From the bottom of my heart I pitied anyone caught in the open, anyone trapped in a car, and anyone unable to close up their homes.

I did not know whether the darkness would lift, as it had on previous occasions, or whether this time it would be endless night, slowly burying the island of Montserrat in mud. After thirty minutes of uncertainty, the drumming on the roof slowed, then stopped, and moments later the murkiness began to lift as inky grey replaced the previous blackness. The black wall of ash was moving away towards the north of the island. Slowly the grey turned to an ashy haze and the enormity of the eruption, and the messy devastation it had created, was revealed. Residents living in the far north watched in helpless impotence as the central and southern parts of Montserrat took the full force of the worst eruption so far.

The drama of the moment had passed, but the scene that met my eyes was heartbreaking. What had been lush, green and beautiful had been entirely destroyed. Everything, and I mean everything, was dung-coloured, appearing to have been constructed from silage dropped from the sky. The brown mud solidified into brown concrete. The roof, paths, roads, trees, garden, all made from mud.

Close inspection of muddy shrubs showed holes in the foliage caused by caustic mud missiles hammering home before caking the entire bush.

After passing through Salem, Old Towne and Olveston, and giving just a light ashfall in the Woodlands area, the dense and destructive eruptive column swept off over the sea to drum down in the neighbouring islands of St. Kitts and Nevis.

For three hours we had no information. We did not know what had happened. Then ZJB Radio Montserrat began to transmit. Rose Willock was on air broadcasting again, closely followed by Dr. Ambeh. Dr. Ambeh said he thought part of the dome had collapsed, sending an eruptive column 21,000 ft. into the air. We derived no comfort when he blamed the wind direction for our frightening ordeal, and the fact that too much rain had contributed to the collapse of the dome.

The eruption of the 31st July has left many people badly frightened. A child in Salem had screamed hysterically when she and her sleeping mother had been caught in the ashfall. She is so traumatised by the experience that relatives are taking her away to live in Guyana.

Unofficially, we have been warned that something worse might happen within the next two days. My window shutters are permanently closed and I have hung sheets at the windows to try and keep the airborne ash out.

We are all praying for it to rain, to wash the ash out of the air, but I cannot take another 'ashin' like that. I have started to search for a house further north. Futile I know, since every available property was snapped up months ago when the exodus to the north first began.

14 - AUGUST 1996

KEEP ON SHOVELLING

The terrifying eruptions on the 31st July were the final straw for a large number of residents. About 15% of the dome had collapsed sending an estimated three million cubic metres of lava sweeping a distance of two kilometres down the north-eastern side of the Soufrière Hills and out into the sea. A fan of new land was created, over fifteen metres deep. A vast flat plate of hot, uncompacted, pale grey grit.

An old man told me, with a smile in his voice, that maybe God had decided Montserrat was too small for such a beautiful island and He had decided to make it just a little bit bigger.

But the general feeling is one of mounting apprehension. Several expatriate residents and snowbirds with alternative homes have rapidly packed and departed for good. Many, like us, who work for the Government and have no choice but to remain, are trying to move north, further away from the volcano. But most of the houses available for rent have already been taken and there is little choice.

I contacted all the agents on island and was shown only two possible properties, neither of which met our three simple criteria. The villa needed to be further north than Old Towne. It must be easy to clean, and most important, it must be sealable against invasive grit during an ashin'.

After making a thorough nuisance of myself with the agents, I was finally successful when a charming, small, but beautifully furnished villa in Lime Kiln suddenly became available. It seems the owner (Tony Huffman of the US 'Huffy' bike empire) left Montserrat in a hurry after the eruption of 31st July.

Although not much further north than our Old Towne home, it is protected by surrounding hills and therefore less likely to catch the full force of the north-westerly ash clouds that dump on us with such regularity.

It meets two of our demands. Small enough to be kept clean without requiring three workmen for three days each time the volcano burps, and it is possible to close all the windows tightly during ash fallouts, minimising the internal fog.

Protected by the branches of a huge mahogany tree, it is a traditional single-storey West Indian colonial home with a long wooden balcony facing west across a pretty garden to the sea.

Towards the north, dropping down beyond the swimming pool, a valley of treetops stretches across to the lawns of the McChesney Estate in the distance, now the Governor's Official Residence.

Beyond the high garden wall our neighbour to the south is the recently relocated Economy Bakery. Now working from a family villa they produce mouth-watering smells of fresh bread at 5.00 am.

To our delight we discovered that ZJB Radio Montserrat's tower of strength the delightful Rose Willock, evacuated from her home in Plymouth, was a temporary lodger in the villa directly opposite us.

A short walk down the road is the small bay of Lime Kiln Beach, and I reason that in an extreme emergency this will be where I come to wait for a rescue boat.

Our new villa also has the advantage of secure hurricane shutters, a useful bonus as we enter what is known as the Cape Verde Season, the height of hurricane activity when tropical waves roll off the African coast and head for the Caribbean on an almost daily basis. Hard to believe after Dangerous Hurricane Luis last year, but this hurricane season is predicted to be worse than the last.

We were treated to another major collapse of the dome on the 11th August. Thunder and lightning with pyroclastic flows down the east side into the sea all day. It was the biggest activity to date with one ash column at 5.15 p.m. rising to over 30,000 ft., which drifted west across the Caribbean Sea to land in Colombia, closing an airport.

It was the weekend, there was no electricity and the radio was transmitting only intermittently, mostly messages from Dr. Ambeh updating residents on the situation.

Dr. Ambeh suggested we close all our windows, stay indoors and wear our masks. Free masks are available at last, although the supply is limited, being dispensed on a first-come-first-served basis.

The Sulphur Dioxide (SO_2) measurement in the air around Plymouth is being monitored now, and registered a new high of 1100 tonnes. There followed a week of almost continuous ashin' which filled the air with fine grit that stubbornly remained in the atmosphere. It was distinctly unpleasant, and we all agreed that no matter what the authorities say, exposure and inhalation must surely be unhealthy.

Everyone seems to be suffering. Beryl arrived on my doorstep wheezing and complaining that her chest hurt when she breathed. On occasion I feel, quite literally, like a fish out of water as I try to get my breath.

On the local radio station Dr. Ambeh was asked about the effects of the ash on health, but he avoided giving a direct answer and responded by saying it was *"a question for the medical staff"*.

Our social life is being dictated by the activity at the volcano and is severely disrupted. But we did manage to make the Mexican Night organised by Lou and Shirley down at the Golf Club.

The Golf Club is an old plantation house with thick walls, wooden shutters and a run-down provincial charm. Lou took over at the Golf Club after leaving the beach bar of the Montserrat Springs Hotel, abandoned now in the danger zone of Plymouth. About thirty expatriates whose mean age was around fifty-five attended the 'Mexican Night'. The majority were British Government employees enjoying the convivial camaraderie of an evening out. We exchanged advice on how best to deal with incessant and invasive ash.

We also joined Bill and Marjory at one of their weekly *Waifs and Strays* suppers. When Bill and Marjory began hosting their *waifs and strays* open-house suppers for visitors passing through Montserrat (or people who are living on island alone) word got around rapidly. In no time at all the weekly evenings were packed with expatriate drop-ins who arrived unannounced for some decent food, a drink or two or three, and a chat.

Bill's good intentions looked like getting out of control. He recounted the night when seventeen *"lonely riff-raff looking for a freebie"* materialised at his door, and by the end of the evening they had consumed fifty-six beers and several bottles of wine. That was when Bill decided to take stricter control, and attendance is now by invitation only. But the scientists and other British staff on short visits to Montserrat are regulars.

The Governor's Office is experiencing a busy time. As well as 'crisis management' of an unpredictable volcano, the Governor is involved in the decision whether to hold constitutionally due elections in Montserrat in October.

The present NPP Government with Reuben Meade (as Party Leader and Chief Minister) is reluctant to alter the status quo. One of the main problems envisaged is the sheer difficulty in getting displaced voters to the polls to elect their constituency representatives.

There are two main topics of conversation at the moment, the current state of the volcano and the political issue of elections. Does Montserrat need or want elections at this time? Should the island leave the elections until after the volcano has quietened down, or should a caretaker government be installed?

Already though, there is an air of campaigning around, with many of the politicians doing some official and unofficial canvassing.

The Legislative Council (LegCo) which runs Montserrat is composed of twelve members. The Speaker; seven elected representatives from the various areas; two members nominated by the Chief Minister and the Governor; and two ex-officio members who are the Attorney General and the Financial Secretary. The seven-member Executive Council (ExCo) is formed with the Governor, four Ministers of Government, plus the Attorney General and Financial Secretary.

In order to try and come to some decisions about the issue a Commission has been appointed to solicit the views of the people of Montserrat and to report to Her Majesty's Government.

According to the Governor 50% of the people are unemployed; 5,000 have registered for food vouchers; 2,500 have left to go overseas; 1,400 are in shelters and many more are living in cramped conditions with friends and relatives. Three hundred people have now taken advantage of the British relocation offer.

During August the Governor and Government asked the Public Works Department to enter the restricted area of Plymouth to clear the roof of Government House, empty Fort Ghaut and clear main roads of ash.

It was an understandable request. The Governor believes that the roof of Government House might collapse under the weight of ash unless it is regularly cleared. In Plymouth the ash is lying two feet thick in places but the dock is still in use and access needs to be maintained.

The debris that flows down Fort Ghaut has filled it, and there is a risk of it over-topping the two bridges, causing flooding across the lower half of the town unless it is dug out and removed. With more rains expected, leading inevitably to more mud flows down Fort Ghaut, the Government considers it essential to clear the ghaut to keep a drainage channel to the sea.

It is a hazardous operation. There is a very real danger of flash floods and volcanic activity down the ghaut, but PWD reluctantly agreed to do the work. However, they insisted that a member of the MVO (in radio contact with the Observatory) stayed with the team of men while they worked in the ghaut.

On the 17th August the men reported for ghaut clearance work at 8.30 a.m. and after receiving assurances from the scientist on duty that the volcano was quiet, they entered the ghaut and began excavating out the debris.

Since all other equipment was ineffective, the big D8 bulldozer was requested, but never arrived on site, so at 9.00 a.m. the men were pulled out. An hour later, unexpectedly, a flash flood raced down Fort Ghaut and out to sea. Mercifully the men and machines were not in the ghaut at the time. Corbett, one of the men, voiced their thoughts when he wondered whether God wasn't trying to tell them something.

August ends with the expectation of more rain, but so far no major hurricane threat, and with the scientists very jumpy about the activity at the volcano, which seems to be slowly, inexorably, ratcheting up.

In the meantime all we can do is to regularly hose down our homes to clear the ash, and just *'keep on shovellin'*.

15 - SEPTEMBER 1996

THE MOUNTAIN'S CRASHED

Two days after we moved into our new villa, another dumping of wet mud with accompanying thunder and lightning left a mess that took Alfred and Lennie two days to clean up.

Our pan-playing friend Stanley is in charge of our new garden at Lime Kiln and together we are going to try and grow our own produce. He told me that the garden had been very beautiful before the assault from the ash. Stanley is as expert a gardener as he is a pan player.

There are coconut palms with clusters of fat green nuts, mature mahogany trees, flamboyant trees which recently sported a profusion of stunning scarlet flowers, and productive citrus trees of lime and orange.

"De lime seed hisself" explained Stanley, somewhat puzzled that anything should have propagated without his personal intervention. But the constant falls of ash are ruining the plants and they struggle to survive.

"Dem stap grow tall" says Stanley sadly, shaking his head. Many plants have simply given up the struggle and died.

All agriculture in Montserrat is being severely affected by the gases and ash from the volcano. The prime agricultural land is in the south where the exclusion ban is in force. The animals are still being kept in the unsafe zone because no suitable alternative pasture in the north has yet been organised.

Vegetables are in short supply, although the farmers on the flanks of the Soufrière Hills below Farrell's Wall have been defying the ban and curfew for some time by continuing to work their crops. They see no alternative. It is their livelihood.

It was a great relief when early in September evacuated residents from Harris, Streatham, Molyneaux and Lees (the central corridor villages between Plymouth and the airport) were told they could return to their homes if they wished *"Since the volcano is now better understood"*. The Police Station at Harris was re-opened to give confidence and encourage the return.

The greatest risk from the volcano is perceived to be pyroclastic flows from dome collapses, but these are predominantly down the Tar River Valley further south and east of the central corridor area.

Beryl decided to go back to her home in the hills, but she was uneasy. The noise from the volcano was very loud she said, *"a almos' costan' rorin"*.

The return was short-lived. Abruptly on the 17th September everything suddenly changed, and the central corridor was quickly evacuated and closed once again.

The volcano had been huffing and puffing all day on the 17th September (coincidentally the seventh anniversary of the arrival of Hurricane Hugo in 1989 which devastated Montserrat) and some sort of gravitational collapse of the dome was expected. It had been growing rapidly and bouts of heavy rain had destabilised the cow pat rubble of the lava.

Our son and his girlfriend, on vacation from University, were on island visiting us, and they had just returned from Bill and Marjory's weekly *'Waifs and Strays'* supper, when at 11.30 p.m. the volcano dramatically exploded into the night sky.

It was one more unexpected and terrifying experience for Montserrat residents. In the darkness of the night, with the current off and telephones not functioning because of overload due to the surge of panic calls, it was the stuff of nightmares.

For forty-eight minutes thunder crashed overhead with blinding lightning as the volcano hurled hot boulders and rocks up into the air and sent pyroclastic flows down Tar River Valley.

We learned afterwards that a quarter of the dome had collapsed to the east of Castle Peak, exposing deeper magma still rich in gas which had exploded violently on contact with the air. In a band that stretched from Long Ground in the southeast to the Governor's residence at Olveston in the northwest, rocks, stones, pebbles and gravel rained down on frightened residents.

Seven houses were set alight in the evacuated area of Long Ground. The Tar River Estate House, already badly damaged by previous eruptions, was completely demolished. Flying boulders caused craters in the Long Ground road *"Big enough to seat three men"*.

In the central corridor villages, and also in the Richmond Hill and Cork Hill areas, rocks and stones falling from the sky damaged property and vehicles. Rocks four inches across were projected as far as Isles Bay on the west coast. At Lime Kiln and the Governor's residence we escaped lightly, experiencing only raining gravel.

Woken from sleep, not knowing what was happening, and in fear of their lives, people caught in the explosive activity desperately tried to get north. One distraught woman, barefoot and wearing only a nightdress, was found running along the road, quite terrified. Car windshields were smashed by raining missiles as vehicles tried to make their escape.

At 3.00 a.m. the decision was taken to evacuate two thousand people from Cork Hill and they were hastily put into schools and churches for the rest of the night, although allowed to return to their homes the following day if they wished. Many residents spent the night in cars, parked along the road or on waste ground in the far north.

The morning light revealed the full extent of the night's events. Houses were on fire, boulders, rocks and deep ash littered the Long Ground area, and the delta of new land formed by previous pyroclastic flows had been considerably enlarged.

The eruption column that accompanied the explosive activity shot 37,000 ft. into the air and was caught up into the jet stream, creating havoc with air traffic in the region.

We were told that an Air Canada jet flying over the Caribbean sucked in ash and found its engine overheating as smoke filled the cabin, forcing the plane to make an unscheduled landing.

On the Island of Guadeloupe the airport was temporarily closed as pumice from our volcano fell on the runway. The Guadeloupe authorities claimed that two inches of ash had fallen in some areas of their island.

The unexpected eruption caused chaos in Montserrat. Working evenings and weekends has become the norm as the workload intensifies. Meetings are held at all hours of the day and night.

Contingency planning, emergency response, the big clean-up, road repairs, shelter housing, hospital improvements, school accommodation, jetty construction, the list of work seems endless. My husband's pager is liable to beep insistently at any time of the day or night, and it frequently does, even at 4.00 a.m.

A three-day visit from HMS *Argyll* on the 7th September provided the excuse for an official Reception at the Governor's and we were all invited to attend. A 'mini-tattoo' was performed for our entertainment by four drummers from the ship who, silhouetted by the headlights of several strategically placed vehicles in the drive at McChesney's, played the Union flag down.

It was an electrifying sight, all the more admirable because, although it was not obvious to the other spectators, we knew that at least two of the drummers were thoroughly pickled, bordering on the legless, and we wondered whether they could complete their performance without disgracing themselves. They did!

Our son and his girlfriend managed to make the most of their short holiday with us. The highlight was a forty-five minute trip in the helo with 'Kamikaze Jim' (who took the doors off for better filming) when he went to inspect the damage caused by the explosive eruption of the 17th September.

Although they used words like *'awesome', 'fantastic', 'unbelievable'* to try and express their experience, they said it was quite impossible to convey their feelings adequately. Two days later, Jim took the photographer from the National Geographic on a similar flight, who said in all his experience he'd never seen anything like it.

The potential health risks of exposure to ash have become the single most important issue to worried Montserratians. Dr. Peter Baxter returned to the island briefly to continue his medical assessment. He pinned what we call *"Baxter Badges"* on to workers entering Plymouth (dock employees, rice factory workers, bulldozer drivers) in order to monitor exposure levels.

I wrote to the FCO Medical Unit in London for reassurance and advice and received a reply stating *"To the best of our current knowledge there is not any particular hazard to health from the ash particles...*" and continuing, *"The gas levels also are not felt to be dangerous".*

The Governor, speaking on ZJB Radio Montserrat, has informed us that ash samples have been analysed in the UK and the result has shown 10% free silica is present. A rumour began to circulate that samples had also been analysed by a second laboratory who reported a much higher silica content of 40%.

The scientists are divided in their opinion about the explosive eruption of the 17th September. Richie Robertson, currently Head of the MVO in the absence of Dr. Ambeh, reassured residents that although unusual, the eruption was *"just more of the same"* and did not herald a new level of heightened activity. But others believe the volcano has now entered a new and more dangerous explosive phase.

Ordinary life is becoming increasingly impossible in Montserrat. Fuel is on ration and the food voucher system is suffering from teething troubles and being criticised as disorganised and undignified. Queuing all day in the hot sun for voucher handouts has created the same protesting, angry and frustrated crowd as did the previous food parcel distribution scheme.

The beginning of the new school term has been postponed. Half the island's schools are in the unsafe zone, and those in the north are still occupied by evacuees. Due to start on the 9th September, the new term was delayed while arrangements were made to educate the children in a two-shift system and the 'tropical igloos' (or 'plastic tents' as *The Montserrat Reporter* calls them) were utilised as classrooms. These have proved to be quite unsatisfactory, being too hot for the teachers and pupils. However, forty-five lucky children aged between eleven and sixteen were given an unexpected holiday when the Red Cross and BWIA got together and organised a two week stay in Jamaica for them.

Many Montserratians are facing financial worries. There is mounting concern that compensation will not be paid to householders with damaged property. Insurance companies have been expressing a reluctance to cover both commercial and private properties in Montserrat and have refused volcano risk coverage to new customers. What has become known as the 60-40 arrangement was introduced into renewals, where the policyholder is responsible for 40% of any claim damage and the insurance company 60%.

Some families have taken the difficult, and painful, decision to send wives and children away from Montserrat, many to England. The Security Guard at the Public Works Department has sent his wife to England, and said he would have gone too, but he can't afford the fare. Alfred told me he was ready to pack up and leave even before the eruption of the 17th September, but he still can't quite bring himself to take the step. Like many others, he keeps hoping that things will get better. The volcano is slowly dismembering family life.

16 - OCTOBER 1996

POPULATION DOWN TO 6,500

The decision has been made to hold elections on island next month, on 11th November, Remembrance Day.

So now the island is in the grip of election fever and politics has taken precedence over the volcano as a topic of conversation. The Election Commission has confirmed that despite the volcano alert most people want elections at this time, though interestingly there are some Montserratians who favour a Government of National Unity.

After its explosive eruption on the 17th September the volcano remained relatively well-behaved during October. We still dusted off a fine layer of ash deposit from furniture on a daily basis, and LIAT requested that the airport runway is hosed and wetted before each landing.

Having coined the word *'ashin'* for a heavy ash fall eruption at the volcano, we are now using the expression *'stonin'* for the fall-out that drummed down on us during the explosive eruption in September. We are being warned to expect another 'stonin' similar to (or possibly worse than) those experienced in September.

The MVO responsibility is now being shared between the Trinidad Seismic Research Unit of the University of the West Indies, and the British Geological Survey (BGS) in the UK. So we have two teams attempting to keep an eye on the volcano. They tell us that the viscosity of the lava has undergone a change becoming *"more runny"*, less hard, and is being extruded at a rate of 4 cu. metres per second.

In an attempt to explain to us what was happening in Montserrat, a lecture on the Soufrière Hills Volcano was given at the Vue Pointe Hotel. Two visiting Japanese scientists and Professor Steve Sparks from the UK, together with Richie (Robertson) and Willy (Aspinall) from our own MVO, combined forces to brief the assembled audience.

Two hundred chairs had been placed in the Pelican Room for visitors, but there was a huge amount of public interest and the audience just kept growing. We jammed together like sardines, spilling out of the door.

The Japanese scientists told us that our volcano was behaving in a similar fashion to Mt. Unzen in Japan and they showed slides to illustrate. They believe that Montserrat's volcano is about halfway through its eruptive cycle with more, and worse, to come before it finally *"goes to sleep"* again.

It was an absorbing lecture and in a question and answer session at the end we learned that we could be in for two or more years of activity. We also learned the ominous news that the 'surges' (those hot clouds which accompany pyroclastic flows) can rise up and over hills and are a matter of great concern to the scientists. Finally, and most depressingly, we learned that the only certain fact about a volcano is its unpredictability.

A map of Montserrat showing levels of risk associated with specific areas of the island was officially released on the 9th October. This volcano-zoning map is to familiarise us with the 'zones of safety' and the 'states of alert' should activity at the volcano begin to escalate.

The map has seven zones of safety and six stages of alert. The alert stages move from 'white' at zero, (meaning background seismicity) through 'yellow', 'amber', 'orange', 'red' and finally 'purple', which signifies the highest level of alert indicating continuous explosive eruption.

The island has been divided into seven zones of safety. Zone 'A' is the most hazardous and is the area around the crater, including Long Ground. Zone 'C' incorporates the capital of Plymouth. The safest area in Montserrat is Zone 'G' in the far north of the island.

Our house is relatively safe in Zone F, which covers all areas north of Belham Valley on the west as far as Bunkum Bay. At the moment we are currently on alert level 'Amber' which is described on the map as follows *"Dome forming eruption in progress, periodic gravitationally induced collapses, including pyroclastic flow and rockfall generation"*. I think I should feel reassured. Alert level purple is too dispiriting to even contemplate.

The Governor gave a private briefing to the British Government personnel on island. He told us that because of the activity of the volcano there is a plan to expand the Mission in Montserrat quite considerably over the coming months, with additional staff being sent out from the UK.

We are a bit thin on the ground here, with only eight Technical Co-operation Officers on island and a couple of those are due to leave soon. Glancing round the table, I counted a total of eighteen of us, which included husbands and wives and the Governor himself.

The Governor proposed that we identify somewhere within our homes, preferably under a concrete roof, where we could go if the volcano should erupt violently. He suggested we buy gasoline to store in containers, and fill bins and bottles with water. He also recommended that we keep the ash off our roofs, and away from the vicinity of our houses, by hosing down regularly.

The Governor also informed us that Cable and Wireless were proposing to 'close down' all phone lines during the next eruption, with the exception of about sixty which would be dedicated to emergency officials and Heads of Department.

We were encouraged to ask questions after the meeting, but all remained soberly silent. The only question raised was about the potential health hazard of the ash, with particular reference to the silica content.

As expected the Governor was cautious and diplomatic in his reply. The preliminary results of investigations, he told us, showed a silica content *"On the lower side of the high scale"*, but the proper results would not be available for a few more weeks. As we trooped out of the room we were issued with ash masks, and were promised goggles and hard hats to follow.

Following the *'emergency bag provisions list'* on the back of my official zoning map, I have moved several boxes of supplies into our second bedroom, including powdered milk, corned beef, macaroni, matches, candles, and two days' supply of drinking water. I couldn't manage to find anything that would hold the recommended two weeks supply of water, and I bemoaned the fact that our villa has only showers and no bath, because as every hurricane survivor knows the bath makes an excellent water storage container.

The map also has instructions on what to do in the event of an ashfall or rockfall. We have to stay indoors if possible, and wear a dust mask. And if we happen to be out driving when an eruption occurs, then we have to pull over to the side of the road and leave our hazard lights flashing. We should wear a hard hat if we have one, or keep a large pot or metal container to protect our heads if moving around in a gravel fall. Having digested this last piece of advice, I dutifully searched my cupboards and selected a large stainless steel mixing bowl to protect my head, and pulled out a saucepan for good measure.

Preferring a proper hard hat to a saucepan, I was initially grateful when my canary yellow British Government issue helmet was delivered to me. But it appears to have been designed for a brawny bricklayer, one size fits all, and it swamps me. If I turn my head to the side my hard hat remains facing forward.

As an experiment I put on the complete Government issue 'volcanic eruption protection kit', including hat, goggles and mask, then looked at myself in the mirror, and laughed and laughed until my sides hurt. The hat rests on the bridge of my nose, the goggles cover half my face, and the huge mask (so hot it restricts my breathing) covers not only my nose, but my cheeks, mouth, chin and part of my throat as well. I look like a reject from a chemical contamination cartoon. All I need to complete the outfit is the white overalls and rubber boots.

Vicky looked at her mask and decided to put it to much better use. She found it made an excellent strainer for her homemade guava jelly. *"Far better than using Johnny's socks"* she assured me. Vicky and John have recently arrived for a short three-month contract on island, helping to set up a new and speedier system for delivering British Aid to Montserrat under the present difficult circumstances.

John is a big man, larger than life in every respect, with his size 16 shoes, fluffy grey hair, fluffy grey beard and a unique party trick.

The party trick never fails to amaze, and has made John memorable all around the globe, from Montserrat to Tonga.

Taking a large glass of Tequila, an egg complete with shell, and a small dish of hot sauce, he begins by popping the whole egg into his mouth, crunching it before carefully removing the shell, then in one stinging mouthful the hot sauce follows, and finally, slamming the Tequila glass on the bar, he downs that with an enormous gulp. He calls it a Tequila Omelette.

Eric is also here on a short-term contract. He has been appointed as the island Magistrate, trying to clear the enormous backlog of cases in Montserrat. Eric has spent his career at the Horseferry Road Court in London, and it is his first visit to the Caribbean, which may explain the slightly bemused look on his face shortly after his arrival.

As part of his familiarisation he was shown the cells at Salem Police Station, and described them as *"Horrid! Very horrid!"* He said he wasn't looking forward to *"Doing the Coroner bit of the job"*, but shortly afterwards, when he was summoned to pronounce on a death in Salem, it was not, he confided, as nerve-wracking as he had expected. Although the daughters were grieving and distressed, the old lady herself *"Looked so peaceful"* he said.

We have had more than our fair share of British Government officials visiting during October. One group coming to assess 'the situation' stayed a brief thirty hours, and as well as attending an official Reception in their honour, they went up with Jim in the helo for an overflight of the volcano, visited the Brades shelters, and met the MVO staff.

The twelve shelters at Brades are now completed and house twenty people in each. Unfortunately there is no privacy for the occupants who have tried to screen their personal space with sheets.

Gerald's Park is being prepared in order to take 2,000 evacuees from the Cork Hill area should it become necessary. At present there is an estimated population in Montserrat of 6,500, with 25% of them in temporary shelter accommodation and 4,000 receiving food vouchers. More and more people are taking advantage of the voluntary relocation scheme to the UK, with 524 application forms returned to the Government to date.

It seems an additional 106 Montserratians would like to go on the scheme, but say they cannot afford the fare and have requested financial help from the Government.

Brades Evacuation shelters 1996

I have spent most of my time this month writing thankyou letters on behalf of the Montserrat Red Cross to the families in Jamaica who hosted forty-five of our children last month. They had a wonderful time in Jamaica, and hope to remain together as a group now they have returned, planning to visit the old folk in the shelters to talk to them, read to them, braid the ladies' hair and help the men to shave.

I was also asked if I would volunteer to be 'a body' for the mass casualty simulation exercise on the 14th October. This was designed to test the readiness and effectiveness of the emergency response units on island.

The first my husband knew of the exercise was a beeped message at 4.05 p.m. to phone a particular number. When he responded he was told there was an unconfirmed report of a helicopter down at Trant's, and he was asked to stand-by.

For a dreadful moment he thought perhaps Jim had crashed, but knowing that I had been asked to be 'a body' he realised with enormous relief that it was only a simulation.

I have to report that it turned into a bit of a fiasco, not least because the authorities had great difficulty in reaching key personnel. At 4.05 p.m. many were on their way home from work and not close to their telephones.

The casualty site selected at Trant's could not receive radio messages, and this added to the delay. It was almost two hours before the rescuers arrived, and in the meantime the volunteer bodies killed time by drinking Caribs and playing Backgammon.

One of the rescue policeman said it looked more like an expat picnic party than a disaster area. He offered to resuscitate Jenny but she jumped to her feet claiming a full recovery. Kate was declared dead. The casualties were scooped up and bounced off in the back of a truck to be fixed or bagged as appropriate.

Many valuable lessons were learned during the emergency simulation exercise and as a result key personnel have been issued with FM radio handsets. So now, in the event of a real emergency, everyone should be better prepared to act quickly and efficiently.

October has been a month of preparation for 'the big one'. It is believed there is now gas-rich magma in the volcano that might be reaching the surface. By the 25th October activity at the volcano was increasing again, with the dome as high as before the September explosive eruption. The volcano-tectonic earthquakes are increasing, and there is an SO_2 flux of over 600 tonnes per day, occasionally peaking at 1100. This sounds very scientific to the average Montserratian, but whatever the words used to describe the activity at the volcano, we all recognise that things are not looking good.

17 - NOVEMBER/DECEMBER 1996

NEW GOVERNMENT

The phone rang at 6.00 a.m. on Saturday morning 2nd November. A voice on the other end instructed my sleepy husband to 'stand-by' as the alert level had just been raised from Amber to Orange.

We fell out of bed and turned on the radio, and heard the Governor speaking in his sombre 'official' tone.

"This is the Governor of Montserrat speaking, we are now on Orange alert, I repeat, we are now on Orange alert, and I appeal to all persons in Montserrat to remain calm and to tune in to this station for further advice and information".

Apparently, while we ordinary mortals slept, there was an increase in earthquake activity at the volcano with some of the largest volcano-tectonic earthquakes recorded to date.

What particularly concerned the scientists was that as well as the familiar surface and shallow VT's, there were also much deeper ones, occurring at approximately one every two minutes, at a depth of around 2.5 km beneath the dome. This is a new development and the significance is not clearly understood.

As a result, Richie (currently Head at the MVO) advised the Governor to err on the side of caution and a higher state of alert was declared.

The schools in Cork Hill (Zone E) were closed and residents warned to be prepared to evacuate in a hurry. Zone D residents in Richmond Hill were told they could only occupy their premises during daylight hours. People with nowhere to sleep were being urged to report to the Emergency Operations Centre. The 'tropical igloos' erected at Gerald's looked likely to get some use.

After a few days at Orange alert the pattern of activity at the volcano changed again and on the 19th November the alert level was reduced back down to Amber. Richie explained that although the

VT's had died down, there was vigorous steaming coming from the west side of the dome, which appeared to be growing slowly, with the previously active east seemingly dormant.

Simon returned for a tour of duty, taking over from Richie, and he confirmed they were still concerned about a sudden escalation in activity with the possibility of another explosive eruption. But learning that the height of the dome was estimated to be around 2,400 ft. we laymen relaxed, surmising (incorrectly as it happened) that it would grow quietly until it reached 3,000 ft. or more before erupting again.

Abruptly, volcano-tectonic earthquake activity started again, with one thousand recorded in a period of four days. The SO_2 gas emission was also very high, registering on the COSPEC equipment at an alarming 1500 tonnes. A return to Orange alert was ordered at 4.00 a.m. on 28th November, Thanksgiving Day.

Concern has been mounting over the condition of Galways Wall, which forms the south side of the crater. The growing lava dome seems to be pushing the wall out sideways, and a crack has appeared in it that has been getting steadily bigger.

Heavy rain compounded the problem with debris travelling down White's River to the sea, and the scientists are of the opinion that the wall is weak and unstable and liable to collapse, potentially producing a lateral blast that could cause a tidal wave to the southwest if it entered the sea. Simon's concern about this possibility has earned him the nickname 'Tsunami Simon'.

A partial collapse of the dome on the 11th December left a scar that filled so rapidly it collapsed again eight days later. For ten days the lava extruded at the highest sustained rate yet recorded.

Steve Sparks returned to the island to offer advice and to support Simon and the MVO team. The areas of St. Patrick's and Gingoes were evacuated and the zoning changed from C to A, upgraded because of the possible collapse of Galways Wall. This area is now to be included in the most dangerous part of Montserrat.

Richmond Hill to the west and Farms Village to the east, were also evacuated, and St. George's Hill near Plymouth.

The pass system in use to allow people to go into the unsafe area has been suspended, however the airport remains open, with access to it from the road around the northeast of the island. But LIAT is being very capricious and flights in and out of Montserrat are quite unreliable. And the final frustration, the introduction of petrol rationing once again!

My husband has been made a member of the weekly Committee that meets and discusses policy decisions, and controls and co-ordinates activity with regard to the volcanic crisis.

The new Committee is called the Volcano Executive Group, with the Governor as Chairman. The other Committee members include the Chief Minister, the Head of the Emergency Operations Centre, the Head of Montserrat Defence Force, and the Commissioner of Police.

A great deal of my husband's time has been spent in the ashy environs of the capital of Plymouth, passing through the police barrier on an almost daily basis. He is supervising the dismantling of a building in town for re-erection in the safe north as an accommodation unit. It is a pilot attempt, which if it proves successful will lead to the dismantling and re-erection in the safe zone of several of these buildings.

He took me into Plymouth with him recently (complete with mask, handy hard hat and goggles) for the testing of the sirens that have been installed throughout the danger zone. Plymouth was a deserted ghost town. Abandoned, shrouded in grey, thick with ash, and roads more like river beds. The only sign of life was a big black sow enjoying a mud bath in the wet ash outside the old Post Office.

Observers were positioned in several central areas to listen for the sirens. We had to report to the Commissioner of Police and the Emergency Operations Centre on their effectiveness. We stood in the eerie silence outside the old American University campus in Plymouth and waited.

To the minute, far in the distance, the siren wail started, then stopped. Started again and stopped again. And although we continued to wait for several more minutes the sirens remained stubbornly silent. We learned later that some of the sirens had burned out again, blamed in part on the fluctuating current coming from the two generators in the containers at Salem. Sirens have also been mounted on the police cars, but these have proved less than satisfactory, with two failing to work almost immediately after installation.

At our home in Lime Kiln, except for the occasional smell of sulphur brought by the breeze, we have had pleasant blue skies and warm sunshine. There is absolutely no evidence to show that the volcano has moved into a more dangerous phase, and it is difficult to accept that less than a mile away people were preparing to evacuate their homes yet again.

With no ash at all, either on the ground or in the air, it seemed to me to be *"Just Another Day In Paradise"* to quote the singer Phil Collins. Our garden at the villa was looking beautiful. The flowers that had survived the ashin's of September have begun to blossom. The bougainvillea bushes are especially pretty at this time of the year, with their mauve, purple and pink flowers delicately showy against the brilliant blue background of the sky.

I gave Stanley a selection of English tomato seeds to sow and he was fascinated by their growth. Montserrat tomatoes run close to the ground so Stanley was intrigued when he saw the English seedlings bursting through the potting compost to stand tall and straight. They grew fast and were soon two feet high, young and energetic.

We were not so lucky with the English lettuce seeds. They dislike the tropical heat, and we have consistently failed to keep them alive for longer than a couple of weeks.

The other crops are doing well and we are now harvesting okra and cucumber on a daily basis. The marrow plant has been particularly successful, racing along the ground for some considerable distance, weaving backwards and forwards like a green serpent through the vegetable patch.

Stanley 'scrumps' mangoes and limes from the abundant trees at the Governor's residence and frequently brings me gifts of these. Our own pawpaw tree is heavy with baby fruits, and the banana plant has produced an enormous clutch of small green fingers that we expect to ripen just in time for Christmas.

Beryl still visits me on a weekly basis. Her shrill call to attract my attention sounds like a wild banshee as she makes her way up the drive. Her selection of produce is necessarily limited by how much she can carry, and the market forces of supply and demand have meant her prices are getting higher. Rose, living next door, is a self-confessed fruit freak, and a good customer of Beryl's, so by the time Beryl reaches me, there is often little choice left in the box.

The biggest single event on island in November was the General Election held on Remembrance Day. The result was inconclusive and after two days of closet horse-trading it gave Montserrat a coalition for the first time in its history.

The run-up to the elections was dogged by mud-slinging and dirty tricks campaigns by some of the candidates, including allegations of slashed tyres, threatening phone calls and men dressed up as women disrupting meetings.

With an unprecedented twenty-eight candidates scrambling for seven seats (including a husband and wife standing for different parties in two different constituencies) it was a lively time for island politics. Three parties were represented and ten independents.

In the end there were only three returnees to LegCo and four new faces. Reuben Meade was re-elected but he was the only successful candidate from the previous NPP Government. The newly formed Movement for National Reconstruction (MNR) fared better, with Bertrand Osborne and Mrs. Adelina Tuitt gaining seats. Brunelle Mead of the People's Progressive Alliance narrowly beat the leader of the MNR by only eighteen votes, and joined his party leader John Osborne (who was Chief Minister during the rebuilding of the island after Hurricane Hugo) in the house. Two of the independents were successful, the seasoned politician and professed people's friend, lawyer David Brandt, and the thoughtful young freshman Rupert Weekes.

After much debate, the experienced ex-Opposition Leader Bertrand Osborne was declared the new Chief Minister, with Adelina Tuitt the Minister for Education, Rupert Weekes the Minister of Communications and Works, and ex-Chief Minister Reuben Meade the new Minister for Agriculture. The Opposition is composed of David 'The Heavy Roller' Brandt, John Osborne and Brunelle Mead.

The casualties of the election have included 'Dada' Tuitt, who lost his seat in the east. But he was not too dismayed, leaving

Montserrat to join his wife in the UK on the relocation scheme, just in time for Christmas.

As we enter the New Year of 1997 the mood in Montserrat is one of apprehension, of foreboding. There is a strong sense of anxiety. We are all waiting for something to happen.

Post Office in Plymouth November 1996

18 - JANUARY 1997

OPERATION EXODUS

Several British Government Technical Co-operation Officers have chosen to leave Montserrat. Only five contract personnel remain, including my husband.

The island is under siege from the psychological fall-out caused by the stressful eruption at the Soufrière Hills. Working long hours, available at all hours of the day and night and with no way of escaping from the situation, the island, or each other, many expats working in Montserrat have found themselves stretched beyond their limits.

However we are currently expecting several short-term expats to arrive, professionals in a variety of disciplines, but we reserve judgement as to whether swamping Montserrat with extra bodies will improve effectiveness. New staff means a learning curve for the replacement, which causes extra stress on those workers who had been expecting relief. And bitter experience has taught that the wrong replacement is worse than none at all.

Add to this the constant stream of official and unofficial visitors who require briefing and escorting, and it is no wonder there is high blood pressure, backaches, flu and frustration among officers and ranks on island.

In spite of the unreliability of LIAT, January saw a flurry of visitors descend on Montserrat. There is a belief held by some jaundiced old expats that British Government officials like to visit the Caribbean territories during the first three months of the year because the weather in Britain is so appalling.

The most stressful visitors to have on island are Civil Servants with tight schedules and packed itineraries, those who practise the currently popular 'seagull' management technique. They fly in, dump on you, and fly out.

Under these circumstances the volcano can be an unexpected and powerful ally, as on the morning of the 16th January when a partial collapse of the dome at 5.45 a.m. caused thunder, lightning and pyroclastic flows down the east into the sea and the largest ash column to date which left a heavy ashin' over many parts of the island. A contingent of 'seagull' officials attempting to leave on the early morning red-eye LIAT were well and truly caught out.

TV crews from around the world have also been visiting Montserrat filming the volcano. A Channel 4 team arrived in early January with the intention of staying for two or three weeks and documenting the 'people' side of the crisis. A request to film a Reception at the Governor's Residence was refused, but they were invited into a Volcano Executive Group meeting to illustrate crisis management in action.

They were, I have been told, *"an intrusive nuisance"*. Tripping over chairs and cables, dangling what appeared to be a dead rat on a pole, leaning on committee members to get better positions, and requesting members to repeat what they had said, again, and again, and yet again, because the 'sound man' hadn't caught it. The result was a strained and unproductive meeting and what will probably appear on screen as a wooden and rehearsed performance.

In contrast, the TBS network released a National Geographic special in Montserrat which was shown on Cable TV on the 12th January and we all agreed it was brilliant. Without exception, everyone who watched the programme said it was *'fantastic'*.

And Montserrat's old friend George Martin returned, planning to do a documentary about music in the Caribbean. Recently knighted and now Sir George, he arrived in early January with Martin Productions and a camera team. He will be filming Alphonsus 'Arrow' Cassell performing on the beach at Old Road Bay, a sunset scene, and he has generously invited residents to join in and enjoy a free concert.

The Governor's Office has released the unexpected news that Montserrat is to receive a Royal visit. Apparently HRH The Duke of York, Prince Andrew, accompanied by HMS *Brave* is anticipated to arrive on 11th February and is to stay with the

Governor for three days while he familiarises himself with the crisis, and conditions, in Montserrat.

Stanley is very interested in the forthcoming Royal visit and was keen to talk about it. Occasionally Stanley and I have difficulty in understanding each other, and his natural shyness sometimes makes the language barrier more difficult to cross. One morning, having returned to work after taking the previous afternoon off because his knees hurt, he asked me *"Fus' time kween sun?"*

We were cutting down the large hands of ripe bananas and it was very hot work. I puzzled for a moment over what he had said, put two and two together and made five, nodded obligingly and wandered off into the house to get him an ice cream, an occasional treat. He stared after me bewildered and called *"De duck! De duck!"* I hesitated, and then it dawned on me that Stanley was talking about the Queen, not ice cream. He was asking me if this was my first meeting with the Queen's son, the Duke.

Stanley disappeared for several days after this conversation, and when he reappeared he explained that the Mistress at McChesney's, the Governor's lady, had asked him to work extra hard to make the gardens look lovely for 'de duck' and he was busy planting out flowers and cleaning up. The ash, however, was a constant problem and was frustrating all his efforts.

No sooner had we cleaned and cleared after the heavy ash fall on the 13th January, which was followed by an earthquake that had my tummy wobbling as the villa cracked alarmingly around me, than the ashin' of the 16th January came along, bringing even more of a mess, and the cleaning work had to start again.

But the heaviest ashfall of all arrived without warning at 6.35 p.m. on the 20th January, when we had the largest pyroclastic flow to date with boulders six feet across deposited into the sea beyond the newly formed delta in the east.

After the blue skies and beautiful garden of December, it was disheartening to see such dreadful devastation. The tomato plants lay grey and crushed, our productive vegetable patch in ruins, the bushes stripped of blossom, the bougainvillea petals limp and brown, holes burned into leaves by acid mud.

Each pyroclastic flow, and each new ash plume, seems to be bigger and better than the previous one. The dome collapse of the

20th January sent a plume of ash 30,000 ft. into the air and for fifty minutes dropped wet slurry out of the black sky over our heads to the familiar accompaniment of crashing thunder.

Muddy ash fell everywhere, including the far 'safe' north of the island. In Salem, Old Towne and Olveston it was as if a passing cement truck had gone manic and sprayed sloppy concrete over us. It was a dreadful mess.

Even the neighbouring island of Antigua got our ash, and complained bitterly as a consequence. Naturally, the airport in Montserrat was closed and there were no flights in or out for a couple of days while another big clean-up was in progress.

The big clean-up took almost a week to complete, and during this time gusting ash re-circulating in the air scoured the people and the landscape. I sweated it out in a closed house, still waiting, after five months, for official approval to install an air conditioner into our bedroom. When I went out I had to wear my dust mask and put a scarf around my hair. Stanley refuses to wear a mask, complaining that it is too hot to work in for more than a few minutes. I know exactly what he means.

I feel great pity for the four thousand or so Montserratians further south, especially in Cork Hill and Salem, who are unable to seal their houses against the invasive ash and can only endure until rain rinses the foggy air fresh again.

I am particularly sorry for the cramped shelterees, who would have stifled had they shuttered and closed the church halls against the ash as they have been recommended to do.

Any visit into Plymouth and the Exclusion Zone requires a pass. A slip of paper signed by the Commissioner of Police or his Deputy, granting permission to enter. In large type across the top is printed the warning *"High Risk of Volcanic Action: Persons Enter At Their Own Risk"*, with space for vehicle number, number of persons, reason for pass, and finally date issued with times in and out of the area.

The Public Works Department has a team entering Plymouth on a regular basis now, having been ordered by the authorities to 'dig out' Fort Ghaut yet again.

Although it makes sense to keep the dock working and to try to stop Fort Ghaut overflowing and flooding downtown Plymouth, the men are sceptical about the financial worth of continually digging out lorry loads of debris, knowing that in a matter of days or sometimes hours, the ghaut will refill.

The heavy plant and lorries have to enter the ghaut to do the work, making men and machinery very vulnerable to flash floods and unexpected volcanic activity. The scientists at the MVO have expressed concern about the safety of the men working in the Ghaut, especially after the close encounter last August when an unexpected mudflow raced down Fort Ghaut only minutes after the men had climbed out.

The MVO were proved correct. On the 23rd January the men and equipment were pulled out in haste as the MVO reported a flash flood signal on their instruments.

Public Works Department clear Fort Ghaut January 1997

Our source of information about the volcano comes principally from the brief twice-daily MVO up-dates, and we hang onto every news-bite.

Dr. Ambeh is no longer involved in monitoring the volcano and is returning to his home in the Cameroon in July.

Simon left the island in mid-January after his short tour of duty, handing over the Head Scientist baton to Lloyd from the UWI Seismic Research Unit. Lloyd, with his ponderously slow and thoughtful delivery, explained that during January swarms of volcano-tectonic earthquakes were occurring on an eight-hourly cycle, the strength increasing with each progressive cycle. We are still being warned to expect more and worse from the volcano.

Psychologically you can only remain so long in an acute state of high alert, waiting for the big one, and it is becoming apparent that many people think the scientists are 'crying wolf', and a certain complacency has crept in, especially when the anticipated collapse of Galways Wall did not materialise in December. However, the crack in the wall is still growing and is now reported to be over two feet wide.

Even the rumour that the Government is preparing a plan designed to get everyone off island in the worst-case scenario, is greeted with a shrug. Details of *"Operation Exodus"* are a closely guarded secret and a cause of mild speculation on the street.

People wonder how the authorities intend to do it, since it was to be assumed that in a massive eruption roads would be impassable, the airport would be closed, and the only dock is well and truly in the danger zone. And with ash in the air, any helicopter rescue would be hopeless.

Word is going around that one hundred life jackets have been brought onto the island for use during an emergency off-island evacuation. There have been some amusing suggestions as to who would qualify for a lifejacket, and why.

It is to be hoped that the use of landing craft does not play an integral part in *'Operation Exodus'*. Or that landing craft are essential in supplying services to Montserrat if we are stranded and unable to use the dock in Plymouth before the new temporary jetty at Little Bay in the north has been completed, because so far all attempts to beach a landing craft have ended in embarrassing failure.

The first try was watched over by HMS *Boxer*. The ship steamed up and down like an agitated mother, observing operations from a distance. A landing craft was brought in from Antigua, the *'Lady Mary'*, the plan being that she would come into Little Bay to off-load.

The sea at Little Bay can appear calm but does experience heavy swells, especially during December and January. The Captain of the *'Lady Mary'* was willing to attempt the landing, but after watching the sea and the situation, his crew were not, and in the end they mutinied and refused to even try.

Another attempt was made later, with an expert coxswain flown in from England on board to assist, but that also ended in disaster.

It had been decided that since a small crane was needed to lift an incinerator into position at the hospital, it should be brought in on the landing craft *'Lady Mary'* and unloaded onto the beach at Little Bay. At the same time *'Lady Mary'* would be used to place two sea anchors, one at Little Bay and one at Old Road Bay.

The problems arose, it was explained to me, because the 'cable' attached to the winch hadn't been accurately measured and was too long. As the *'Lady Mary'* neared the shore, the swells caught her side-on and thrust her forward, pushing her against the boulders so that she couldn't float off. For several hours the landing craft struggled in the swell and was hammered by the waves, while crew and onlookers stood by helplessly.

Eventually, equipment brought in to construct the emergency jetty at the far end of Little Bay came to the rescue, and with great difficulty the crane on board *'Lady Mary'* was finally unloaded. Without the weight of the crane the *'Lady Mary'* floated free. But the fiasco was not over. As the *'Lady Mary'* left in the gathering darkness she somehow accidentally sank a local fishing boat moored in the bay.

If we have to evacuate by sea, I think I'll take my chance on the beach at Lime Kiln.

19 - FEBRUARY 1997

VISIT OF HRH PRINCE ANDREW

The highlight of this month has been a flying visit from HRH The Duke of York, Prince Andrew.

"The number two son of the Queen", as the Governor put it when announcing the details on the radio.

This was described as a low-key official visit. So low-key, and so official, that only the small entourage of mainly white males that rotated around Prince Andrew seemed to know the details of his itinerary.

Released on a 'need to know' basis, the Royal commitments were so securely guarded that my husband did not receive his instructions of where to be and when until the day *after* the Duke's departure.

The Royal arrival was such a closely guarded secret that only a handful of watchers were at the airport when Prince Andrew landed on the 11th February. One of them was Stanley, who had been commissioned to play a Caribbean welcome on his steel pans, and who waited in a state of nervous torment for his Royal appointment.

Rowie commented on the lack of publicity and consequent apparent lack of public interest in welcoming Prince Andrew. She had heard on the jungle drums that the Duke was having lunch at the Vue Pointe Hotel on the 12th February, and so she stationed herself outside with her two young boys.

She realised that her little family constituted *"The whole crowd"* and said afterwards it was *"positively embarrassing!"* They were, however, rewarded with a wide grin and a royal wave when the Duke arrived.

The usual hectic official programme had been arranged, with visits to the Emergency Operations Centre, the Montserrat Volcano Observatory and into the evacuated and ashy capital of Plymouth.

The trip into Plymouth with the Governor was brief, but long enough to catch an unexpected foggy ashin' from the volcano which obliged Prince Andrew to put on an ash mask. He talked to the stevedores loading the rice boat, and then stood for some pensive moments in Fort Ghaut, gazing at the evidence of recent mudflows, before being driven back into the safe north.

"Plymouth" the Duke commented later *"was depressing, very depressing!"*

It quickly became obvious that this was not a publicity 'show the flag and support the people' visit. It was a searching personal investigation by Prince Andrew into why British aid had not yet solved the problems in Montserrat.

The Duke asked direct and pertinent questions, and demanded straight answers. He gave some of the British officials supervising the dispersal of British funds on island a very hard time. *"Blunt and abrasive"* one commented wryly.

The tight schedule took the Duke to the opening of the new primary school extension in Salem where the children entertained him, and he crouched down to chat to the kindergarten youngsters. He was also shown round the wooden family units and the relocated hospital.

The most memorable occasion for observers was watching the Duke's interaction with and obvious sympathy for the shelterees. Prince Andrew's attitude to those in the shelters, particularly to the children, was one of enormous sympathy and compassion. He walked and talked with the dispossessed families housed at the Seventh Day Adventist Church in Salem and his spontaneous farewell hug to the shelter manager said it all.

The only publicised event for Montserratians to attend was a Parade at Salem Park at 4.30 p.m. on Wednesday 12th February. The island responded to the invitation with joyful enthusiasm and a happy, cheering, bustling, four thousand Montserratians converged on Salem Park to see Prince Andrew.

We wanted to watch the Parade, but my husband and I had been invited, along with about 150 other guests, to attend an Official Reception in honour of the Duke's visit, to be held at the Governor's residence later that afternoon.

We decided to try and make both functions, although we knew it was going to be a bit of a dash.

The field at Salem where the Parade was being held was a bit muddy. So we parked the car beside the temporary prison at Salem Library and walked. Although this is supposed to be the dry season the weather has been overcast with bursts of heavy showers.

Beryl was sitting under a nearby mahogany tree. Her tight grey curls were strapped down under a red scarf, a brown cotton frock a size too large fell loosely around her tiny frame. Her familiar Carib beer box was beside her, full of fruit, and she was trying to sell her produce to passers-by on their way to the Parade. She rushed over and gave me a tight squeeze of an embrace, and then cajoled me into buying some brown bananas from her box at a dollar each *"Good fah makin' fritters!"* she assured me.

Beryl complained she had a cough and a cold and blamed the ash. I keep giving her ash masks to wear, but like Stanley she refuses to use them, saying they are hot and uncomfortable. She makes 'donkey rub down' bush tea to soothe her chest.

A stream of people dressed in Sunday best were arriving from all over the island. By the time the cavalcade of cars bringing Prince Andrew appeared there was a colourful throng of happy Montserratians all keen to catch a glimpse of the royal visitor and to enjoy the spectacle of the Parade. It had been a long time since the island had any fun, and we were all determined to make the most of it.

Among the watching crowd was the Governor's son who told us cheerfully that he had been evicted from his bedroom above the garage so that the Duke could be accommodated. He had been banished to billet temporarily with a member of the Governor's staff.

Winston the dog had also been exiled from the Governor's house during the Duke's visit, as had the resident fluffy grey cat, because, we understood, the Duke is allergic to cats. The cat had been gathered up and taken, resisting madly, to a friend's house, but had promptly gone into a major sulk and disappeared.

The spectators and participants in the Parade were almost exclusively Montserratian, but the 'chair mob' in the reserved seats on the podium appeared to be predominantly British. Photographers from the *'Sun'* newspaper and *'Hello'* magazine were milling with the crowds, conspicuous in their khaki flak jackets. A very pale, large man, clutching a notebook and sweating profusely in a safari suit was obviously a journalist a long way from home.

The official cameraman from HMS *Boxer* in his navy blue shorts, matching beret and long socks, was allowed special privileges and closely shadowed the Duke as he made his inspection.

There were some wonderful photo opportunities, especially of the children, who marched round the field to the music of the band with obvious enthusiasm. All the uniformed groups were represented in the Parade, including the little Brownies, Girl Guides, Girls Brigade, Prison Officers, and the Royal Montserrat Police Force.

I have been asked many times during the Duke's visit to indicate which white male in the official group is the Duke. To Montserratians unfamiliar with photographs of Prince Andrew he is difficult to recognise. But at the Parade His Royal Highness was easily distinguishable in his crisp white Navy uniform, hands clasped behind his back.

As he reviewed the Montserrat Defence Force the Duke moved along the ranks, occasionally stopping and chatting. Following close behind was the Governor, looking slightly self-conscious in full official regalia of white uniform, complete with white gloves, with the 'chicken feathers' on his pith helmet straining in the wind.

During the proceedings our friend Horatio was presented with a medal, and we all cheered and clapped, and then the greatest honour was bestowed on the Montserrat Defence Force as they received the insignia 'Royal' as a mark of appreciation for all the Defence Force has done during the volcanic crisis, and we cheered and clapped again. Unfortunately two of the uniformed participants were overwhelmed by the occasion and collapsed, having to be carried off the field.

HRH Duke of York at Salem Review February 1997

By the time we returned home after the Parade we had less than half an hour to shower, change, and present ourselves at the Governor's for the Official Reception at 6.00 p.m. The gold-embossed invitation had specified 'dress informal' and we understood the Governor was hoping for some Caribbean colour and so we dressed accordingly.

We arrived a little late, but the guest of honour was still above the garage preparing himself. The Governor was changing into something more casual, and half the invited guests were still missing. Darkness was falling and out in the bay HMS *Boxer,* a silver barracuda in the gathering gloom, was lit up like a Christmas tree.

We walked up the drive with a visiting seismologist who was wearing the ultimate in informality, a red T-shirt and shorts, and we surmised correctly that she had come straight from duty at the Observatory.

As we exchanged candid observations about the Duke's visit, we suddenly realised that our asides could be clearly overheard by the occupant above the garage, and we abruptly dissolved into laughter, which set the tone for the evening.

The Governor's wife was waiting to greet each guest. She must have been exhausted and stressed to the limit, but she didn't show it. She looked sensational in an extravaganza of rippling pink, with pencil pleats that ebbed and flowed and glittered and glowed as she moved.

I thought it best to pace my alcoholic consumption in view of the presence of such an esteemed guest, and I asked Desmond, acting barman for the Governor and famous for his generous libations, for a large ginger ale with a little rum. He must have reversed the quantities, for one sip and my throat caught fire. I understood why Prince Andrew is reputed to drink only water at official functions.

The guest list had been prepared to include all those who had contributed in some way to the volcanic crisis and the result was a marvellous hotchpotch of Montserrat's populace. There was a wonderful party atmosphere, a gathering of familiar faces and good friends.

Father Larry was there *"Feasting"* he said *"on the circulating titbits"* of sausage balls, battered fish bites and pop-pieced quiche. John, the American who had come to Montserrat on holiday and remained to help with the old folk in the shelters, was almost unrecognisably scrubbed and smart. He confessed *"I had to borrow this shirt for the occasion!"*

Stanley was on the terrace, playing gentle pan music on his steel drums to accompany the hum of conversation. He looked almost sober. He saw us and grinned and waved. For this special occasion he was wearing the baseball cap I had given him for Christmas.

Prince Andrew slipped into the room alone and unannounced, and his entrance went almost unnoticed. The Governor wandered in, then wandered out. The Chief Minister arrived and did the same.

The Duke moved alone among the clustered guests, quietly amiable, working the room in a relaxed and unobtrusive manner.

Once again I was asked by several Montserratian friends to identify the Duke, and I found myself trying to describe him while he chatted less than a few feet away. One of the girls circulating drinks on a silver tray asked Jennifer the same question. She had also been serving the previous evening, but still had no idea which one of these males in the entourage was the Duke. I think perhaps he should wear a badge, or a crown, or some other obvious sign of distinctiveness.

I was chatting to Jennifer when I felt pressure against my shoulder and paused, I half-turned to find an outstretched hand reaching to clasp mine. Prince Andrew had silently stepped in beside me to join our small group.

As he shook our hands he asked *"And who are you? What do you do here?"* The conversation that followed was animated, intense, probing and very friendly.

Prince Andrew was full of questions. He wanted to know about aid work on island, detail and cause, and he was very well briefed. He knew about Fort Ghaut. *"Can it be saved?" "What will happen?" "What about the rest of the work?" "What's holding things up?" "Why do you think there are so many delays?"*

If we could have been totally honest with him we would have said *"give the Montserratians qualified professionals they can respect and then let's all get stuck in and work together"*. But we couldn't, and we didn't. Though when Boyd implied 'someone should do something', Prince Andrew responded with *"That's why I'm here!"*

It was time for the official party to leave for dinner, and after helping himself to an orange juice from Desmond, and a brief but animated conversation with 'Kamikaze Jim', Prince Andrew was shepherded away and taken to the Vue Pointe Hotel for his next official engagement.

Stanley phoned me at 8.00 a.m. the following morning. He'd been partying well into the night and he *"Feel like me dyin"* he groaned. He told me he was having dizzy spells, his hands were shaking uncontrollably and he was feeling *"all wobbly"*. Adding finally that he was convinced there was *"Sometin' loose in me head"*.

He informed me he was going to bed, where he stayed for two days. On the third day he managed to get to the 'Indian' doctor, who took his blood pressure, arranged for him to have a blood test at the hospital, and warned him to stay off the drink. *"One drink a day only"* was the order.

The Duke departed just after 4.00 p.m. on the 13th February, having officially declared the first part of the emergency jetty at Little Bay complete, and looking very much more comfortable in his 'Action Man' camouflage fatigues, beret and boots.

146

That evening Rose broadcast an interview she had held with Prince Andrew earlier in the day. It was the most sensitive, understanding, and hopeful talk we have ever heard from an official visiting Montserrat. Prince Andrew's concern for the people in the shelters was evident and his desire to *"go home and do something about it"* was clear. He explained that he was in Montserrat *"At the request of the Queen"* who felt that *"The impetus had gone"* from the early days of the volcanic crisis.

It was a good interview, and an emotional one, and having assured Rose that he was *"Going to speak to the Queen on Monday"* and would be *"Writing a report to the Foreign Office as well"* the Duke left, promising to return to Montserrat soon.

Rose, in her warm and lovely manner, captured the mood in Montserrat by signing off the interview and saying farewell to Prince Andrew with *"May God Go With You"*.

20 - MARCH/APRIL 1997

VOLCANO STRESS SYNDROME

March began hopefully with the alert level down at Amber, but as the month progressed and then moved into April the alert level changed from Amber to Orange to High Orange (which is also referred to as 'Administrative Red') back down to Orange and Amber. But by end April it looked as if it was ready to rise again.

Over eight weeks the seesaw of alert states was supervised by a rotation of four Head Scientists at the MVO. Lloyd handed over to Richie in mid-February, who later handed over to Steve, who subsequently passed the responsibility across to Simon in mid-April.

It was all rather bewildering. Some superstitiously blamed the confusing times on the passing of the Hale Bopp comet and the lunar eclipse on the 23rd March.

It is no surprise to learn that a new medical condition called *'Volcano Stress Syndrome'* is being diagnosed in people working on island. Similar, we have been told, to the post-traumatic stress syndrome experienced by soldiers after the Gulf War.

As if this wasn't alarming enough, our anxieties escalated when we learned that copies of a health report, referred to as the *'Baxter Report 3'* dated October 1996, are unofficially circulating around the island. The contents of the Report are said to be disturbing.

Dr. Ronnie Cooper, as Acting Director of Health, brought the report to our attention. He said that after reading it he was very worried about the long-term health risks to residents, particularly to the dock and rice factory workers still in Plymouth.

The Baxter Report states the ash being emitted by the volcano contains cristobalite and bridymite *"The most toxic forms of silica capable of causing lung fibrosis if inhaled over a long period"* although, according to Ronnie, the damage caused won't become apparent for ten to twenty years.

According to the Report there is also, theoretically, *"An increase in susceptibility to tuberculosis, rheumatoid arthritis, scleroderma and renal disease from exposure to silica"*. And an epidemiological association has been reported between crystalline silica exposure and lung cancer. The Report states, *"High concentrations of fine, respirable ash in the air are known to exacerbate the condition of sufferers from asthma and chronic respiratory diseases"*.

We had no knowledge of the Report, written five months ago, or of any potential health hazards that might be caused by the ash. We had been reassured in August 1996 that ash from the volcano constituted 'nuisance value' only. An urgent meeting of British Technical Co-operation Officers resident on island was arranged, and a collective letter signed by all TCO's has been written to the authorities requesting further information and reassurances.

The worst areas affected by ash are Plymouth, Richmond Hill and Cork Hill. With the introduction of the reduced Amber alert level on 18th February the road barrier into Plymouth has been removed and free access was allowed during the day, although visitors are being urged to wear ash masks.

An MVO up-date on 28th February specifically stated *"The ash levels in Plymouth are very hazardous to health, wear your mask"*. But we are being given mixed messages, since at the same time Richmond Hill residents were given permission to remain overnight in their homes, although conditions were described as *"very ashy"* and consequently unpleasant.

The *'Baxter Report 3'* offers guideline values for cristobalite exposure, but states that these would be readily exceeded if the volcano continues ashing and the weather turns dryer.

"It would be unacceptable for the general population to be repeatedly exposed to such high levels" the Report is quoted as stating.

Forty air samples have been taken and analysed by the Report writers, and the highest readings for both cristobalite and total respirable dust were well above the guideline exposures for a community. One, which particularly concerned Ronnie because of the children, was the result of the sample taken from the Cork Hill Advent School.

While we are digesting the contents of the Baxter Report and trying to come to terms with the implications to health, the volcano is growing at the fastest rate ever recorded.

In six days the volcano increased in height by 100 ft. and on one occasion was said to be extruding at an extraordinary rate of 9 cu. metres per second, double the average amount. At the end of April the total extruded mass was estimated to be 49 million cu. metres.

The sides of the dome, which glow crimson in the night sky on a clear evening, are becoming very steep and have completely filled the moat of English's Crater. The original Castle Peak Dome formed 350 years ago during the last period of volcanic activity in Montserrat was destroyed by a pyroclastic flow on the 3rd February.

It is almost impossible to believe that at this time last year Jim landed his helo on Castle Peak so that we could watch the boiling cowpat of emerging dome.

The mainly expatriate snowbirds of Spanish Pointe, a five-minute drive beyond the airport in the southeast, are being asked to evacuate, or in more socially acceptable terminology, 'relocate', because of fears that pyroclastic flows down the east might be a danger to them. There is a large 'blob' on the dome poised to fall and the scientists are sure it will take a huge part of the dome with it when it goes, causing large pyroclastic flows.

Several of the Spanish Pointe residents have refused to move, maintaining there is nowhere for them to go, and saying that unlike many areas in the safe zone, at least Spanish Pointe does not suffer from ash in the air because the prevailing wind comes from the sea. They further argue that any major increase in volcanic activity will be monitored by the MVO, and residents will be warned if events become critical, and they would then be able to leave the area in time.

The scientists have spent considerable time patiently explaining to Spanish Pointe residents that volcanology is an inexact science, and that the Soufrière Hills Volcano is one of the most dangerous in the world, and pointing out the risks they are taking in remaining in their homes.

The Governor has pleaded with them to leave. But a small group are determined to remain and have written a letter to the Governor accepting responsibility for their own decision.

An anonymous limerick in *The Montserrat Reporter* of 18th April expresses the stalemate thus: *"Solicitous Governor Frank, is loath to go pulling his rank, but if the Pointe labelled Spanish saw its residents vanish, he'd become somewhat less of a crank!"*

The volcano is no respecter of holidays or weekends. At 6.00 a.m. on Easter Monday, 1st April, the phone rang and my husband was ordered to an emergency VEG meeting at 7.30 a.m.

There had been continuous pyroclastic flows throughout the night over Galways Wall to the southwest, with the flow travelling 3.6 km down the White River Valley towards the sea. Trees had ignited, and the popular tourist attraction of Great Alp Falls was filling with volcanic debris. A rapidly eroding gully, or chute, estimated to be at least eighty metres deep had formed in Galways Wall.

The alert level was raised to Orange and entry into Plymouth and the south restricted. The central corridor through Harris to the airport is now closed once again and all traffic has to use the long road round the northern tip of the island.

I remember vividly the 1st April last year when the hospital was relocated to St. John's in the north during a thick white-out ashin' from the volcano, and I was very aware that we were about to experience the first anniversary of the last evacuation from Plymouth and the south. I wondered what the volcano intended as an anniversary present to Montserrat.

It seemed a beautiful morning. The sun was clear and hot, the sky a bright and crisp blue, and the sea a flat calm. The atmosphere was peaceful. It was almost impossible to believe that the volcano, shrouded in cloud a few miles away, was acting up again.

Our son and his girlfriend were due to arrive in Montserrat the following day for a brief holiday, and I was looking forward to seeing them, preparing their bedroom and cleaning the house in anticipation.

The doves were cooing gently to each other, the bananaquits 'yellowbellies' and hummingbirds 'sparrows' were dashing in and out of the bougainvillea that had now recovered from the last heavy ashfall. Recent rains and strong wind had cleansed the garden and the roof, and everywhere looked green and lush and tropical.

Stanley came to work on the garden and told me that the turtles had just arrived at Woodlands beach again, and were laying their eggs in the sand. And as he watered the plants he discovered a toad, six inches across and looking like a piece of lumpy rock, hiding in the moist earth of a patio plant.

While I waited for my husband to return from his meeting, I made several pots of marmalade from our own lemons and 'gooseberry' tree. As I looked out to sea I saw the cruise ship 'Aida', red lips painted on her bow and blue eyes on her hull, gently steaming in towards Old Road Bay. Passengers were being ferried ashore to enjoy a day in Montserrat before continuing their cruise up the Caribbean chain.

The authorities feel that it is vital for Montserrat to try and keep the tourist industry functioning during the volcanic crisis, and the fortnightly visits from the cruise ship 'Aida' are psychologically and economically important to the island, but the Captain had taken the wise precaution of issuing ash masks to all those wanting to go ashore.

Until around 10.00 a.m. the day seemed to be unfolding into a lazy, dreamy, pleasant Easter Monday, then quite abruptly, out of the blue, the volcano began to rain ash. The wind direction changed and brought thick, brown, showering silt north and northwest across Cork Hill, Salem, Old Towne and Olveston.

In an attempt to escape the unexpected ashin', the 'Aida' rapidly upped anchor, leaving her stranded passengers scrambling for cover on the shore. People reported hearing 'detonations' from the active southwest and northeast faces of the growing dome. At approximately 12.30 p.m. a long period earthquake registered on the instruments at the MVO. By 1.00 p.m. another heavy ash cloud was sweeping across the northwest of Montserrat and dumped its load over half the island, including me, and the nervously hesitating *'Aida'*.

Later, as the ship returned to collect her passengers from Old Road Bay, I saw that her red lips had become a mucky brown, her eyes were almost obscured by mud, and her white hull, so pristine on arrival, was now dung-coloured by the slimy volcanic residue clinging to her sides. I don't think she will be calling again for a long time.

Within three hours the volcano had turned my idyllic Garden of Eden into a brown, cement covered, foggy nightmare. Not surprisingly all flights were cancelled from the airport, and we spent the night of the 1st April closed up against the ash, on Administrative Red alert, anxiously waiting for an explosive eruption, our son and his girlfriend stranded in Antigua.

It was a false alarm, which further fuelled the determination of the Spanish Pointe residents to remain in their own homes.

In many areas of the safe zone, including Old Towne and Olveston, another big clean-up began once again, with hoses, shovels, brooms and vacuums. By the following afternoon one LIAT flight had managed to land at W.H. Bramble Airport and on board our son and his girlfriend.

The ash remained in the air for four days, a swirling fog re-circulating with wind and movement. I could taste it, hot and dry, and I could feel it as grit inside my mouth, grinding as I clenched my teeth. People complained of chesty colds and coughs.

The warnings in *'Baxter Report 3'* were discussed on the street in the context of the latest ashin'. Heavy rain and strong winds came to our rescue, and fortunately by the 5th April the island had been washed down. But the penalty was flash flooding, and mud flows down Fort Ghaut and Aymer's Ghaut, which overtopped and spread through the lower part of Plymouth. And tents at Gerald's Park were damaged by the powerfully buffeting wind, some reportedly *'torn to ribbons'*.

Our son, who is at University studying for a degree in photography, spent his time on island taking pictures. He went into Plymouth on a special pass and captured on camera the dusty and derelict capital, and the brooding mountain that is the volcano. He also hiked across to Rendezvous Bay in the north to see his Montserratian friend Kong. And he helped Stanley to collect and prepare several 'drums' to be made into steel pans. Stanley told me the drums had held *'dollar rum'*, which according to my son is the sort of rum that makes you step back with a gasp when the lid comes off. They are ideal as potential 'pans' being new, clean and of several different sizes. They were being sold for EC$40 each and Stanley had come to me asking for help to purchase them, saying he wanted to make a set of pans for the Seventh Day Adventist Church in Cork Hill, which he planned to use to teach the youngsters how to play.

I solicited help from the Governor with the finances, and he generously offered the cash, and Stanley set about converting the 'rum drums' into musical instruments. He worked with meticulous care. I watched fascinated as he first beat the base of each drum into a cone, then divided the surface by pencil into small sections. Each section was then hammered to the sound that satisfied Stanley's ear, and punched round with a nail. Stanley then 'tuned' the pan properly before heating it. The whole process took a great deal of time and effort, and I was very impressed with Stanley's patience and skill.

On the 23rd April the scientists advised that the alert level could go back down to Amber. With an almost malicious glee the volcano promptly began a series of rockfalls, with more rockfall signals in the following twenty-four hours than at any other time this year.

Pyroclastic flows down White's River Valley to the southwest went to within fifty metres of the sea, and volcanic debris filled the valley, sadly completely obliterating the beautiful Great Alp Falls. Regular rockfalls of cold material were also overtopping Gages Wall above Plymouth.

As a result we endured an almost permanent ash plume for several days, which blew northwest leaving, yet again, a trail of heavy ashfall over Old Towne, Salem, Olveston and even Woodlands, before heading out to sea and travelling many hundreds of miles from Montserrat.

The houses, gardens, roofs, roads, trees, bushes, were all thickly blanketed in ash for the second time in three weeks, and very dry conditions for several days exacerbated our discomfort. Lennie, helping to clean up the mess, shook his head and commented dolefully *"Tings na get betta"*.

Again we wondered about the health hazards of inhaling ash. I consider myself very lucky, for the new air conditioner installed in the bedroom keeps at least one room reasonably clean and cool.

Food vouchers are now being issued to people in the shelters as well as evacuated persons. Each shelteree receives EC$100 per adult and EC$30 per child, while each evacuated adult receives EC$120 and each child EC$40. The discrepancy between the two amounts is due to the fact that meat and vegetables are still being delivered to the shelters, for use by the occupants. Too many people are still in emergency shelter accommodation, and the housing needs of Montserratians remains a matter of utmost priority to the Government. Acquisition of suitable land in the north to build on is a serious problem, and this has slowed progress.

Most projects on island require official approval by Her Majesty's Government (HMG) in London before they can be implemented, and this procedure is very convoluted. Individuals brought on island to speed up the process seem unable to break through the red tape and sometimes even appear to contribute to the confusion. As one official put it *"The response mechanism is still too involved"*. This is no comfort to the ordinary Montserratian.

The current Governor, Frank Savage, is due to leave Montserrat in mid-September and his replacement has been named as Anthony (Tony) Abbott, currently the HMG Consul General in Perth, Australia.

My husband's present contract also finishes soon, and we will be leaving for a long, well-deserved vacation. However we will be back. My husband has agreed to return to Montserrat for a further year but in a different capacity, this time working not for the Public Works Department but directly for the British Government as Emergency Projects Co-ordinator (EPCOD).

21 - MAY 1997

LABOUR GOVERNMENT IN UK

We have just learned that in the British General Election the Labour Party has ousted the Conservatives, and Tony Blair is the new Prime Minister.

We wonder how a change of Government in the UK might affect Montserrat, considering the Government of Montserrat is relying heavily on grant-in-aid from the mother country during this time of volcanic crisis.

One of the first acts of the fledgling Labour Government has been to change the name of the Overseas Development Administration to the Department for International Development (DFID), but apart from creating some confusion with the headed notepaper, there seems no other immediate effect.

Our volcano is indifferent to British politics. On the 13th May it sent a huge ash plume high into the sky. The wind was blowing hard due west, fortunately, and the majority of us in the safe zone escaped relatively unscathed from the ashin' cloud as it passed out to sea.

As I watched the plume rise in the southern sky it seemed to me that the activity was coming from a different part of the dome, more to the north and east down Tar River than from the recently experienced 'ashins' of the southwest. I turned on the radio hoping to catch an update.

ZJB Radio Montserrat was playing reggae and didn't appear to have noticed the eruption. After a few minutes, with still no reference to the volcano, the music changed and I was listening to Arrow's new release. The lyrics express the uncertainty and anxiety of living in the shadow of the erupting volcano. *"Jus' like sittin' on a burnin' fuse"* sings the Soca son of Montserrat, but *"Keep the faith"* he urges, and learn to live *"One day at a time".* This recording has replaced Arrow's earlier success *'Ah Just Can't Run Away'* as Montserrat's most popular song, capturing the mood of the island.

Eventually the update came. I heard that activity at the volcano had increased and was beginning to move around inside the dome. On the 15th May the biggest pyroclastic flow since the end of January raced down the eastern flanks of the volcano.

We were told that the volcano had entered a new phase with many long period earthquakes, which implied that gas was near the surface of the dome and 'pressurising' inside. A roaring noise like jet engines, not heard since the phreatic eruptions in late 1995, was noticed. It was considered possible that this could be a precursor to serious, possibly explosive activity, and a potential lateral blast was not ruled out. The GPS data gave the impression that Farrell's Wall was 'bulging' or 'swelling'.

When swarms of hybrids and some volcano-tectonic earthquakes were reported on the 17th May, it was no surprise to us that the scientists advised the authorities to put the island back up to Orange alert. With a collective sigh of resignation we prepared ourselves for more unpredictable action from the volcano.

The MVO was unable to obtain 'visuals' of the volcano until the 19th May, because a cloud cap of ash and steam obscured the dome. When the cloud cover cleared and Jim finally managed to get the helicopter up to inspect the dome, a survey revealed it had grown massively and was now 3250 ft. high with a volume estimated at 60 million cubic metres.

We were told that the steep dome was *"Too high to sustain itself"* and we were warned to anticipate a collapse of some sort at any time.

Regardless of activity taking place at the volcano, our garden in Lime Kiln slowly began to recover from the series of April 'ashins'.

While Larky cleaned the pool and pumped out all the ash debris, Stanley and young Kester tackled the garden with pickaxe and cutlass. Young Kester had come to me asking if I had any odd jobs he could do. He said he was saving for a pair of 'moonboots' he had seen in Arrow's Man Shop in Salem. So Kester has now become a regular visitor to the house, working alongside Stanley in the garden or doing other odd jobs as required.

Big warm-hearted Shirley still calls to see me, even though she is no longer working as my housekeeper. With so many people leaving Montserrat (1,000 have taken up the UK relocation option) Shirley was able to get a job at the temporary hospital in St. John's. She had trained as a nurse in Guyana and was delighted to have managed to get back into the profession.

Shirley told me she had been a nurse at the hospital in Georgetown, Guyana, in August 1985 when President Burnham died. President Burnham is a legend in Guyanese politics. He was Premier in 1964, Prime Minister in 1966 and First President of Guyana in 1980 and since he was only sixty-one in 1985, everyone thought he would remain President for a long, long time. His sudden and untimely death came as a terrible shock.

Shirley described to me in graphic detail what happened that day at the hospital in 1985.

During early summer President Burnham, a heavy smoker, had been advised to have a biopsy on his throat, so it was suggested that he go to Cuba for the operation. However he decided to bring the Cuban surgeon to Georgetown instead.

Shirley, whose cousin was one of the President's bodyguards, was introduced to him as he entered the private wing of the hospital. She watched the President as he walked to the Operating Theatre with his wife, his own doctor and the sister in charge, joking with the staff as he went.

According to Shirley, when they administered the anaesthetic *"Dem ge im to much, it be to strang!"* and the poor man died on the table before the operation had even begun. Shirley says she heard a great wailing coming from the theatre and total panic followed. His doctor started screaming, and the Cuban surgeon frantically tried to revive the President, but without success.

The President was eventually declared dead and taken out of the hospital, not wrapped in a sheet, which was the usual custom, but *"In a sleeping bag in an open vehicle".*

Shirley continued with her eyewitness account, the story getting more and more bizarre. It seems that after the President was embalmed, a huge funeral procession slowly toured the city so that the whole population could publicly mourn his passing. It took over half a day, but unfortunately, along the way, the refrigeration unit broke down and *"De body spoil ... spoil bad!"* Shirley told me mournfully, her big eyes round as buttons, her nose wrinkling with disgust.

They had planned to send the body away to be 'rubberised'. *"Like a statue. Like Bob Marley!"* Shirley explained to me. However there was a rumour that because the corpse had spoiled so bad they *"Tip he in de sea on de way"*.

After two months what was supposed to be the rubberised corpse was returned and laid in a shelter. Shirley says you can go into the shelter and up to the coffin and if you press a button, the lid slides away revealing the dead President. She went to have a look herself, but thinks it's more like a carving than the real thing, and she insists the likeness isn't quite right.

The President's relatives say he was 'burned', cremated, and put under the carved statue of him. Shirley says no-one knows the real truth, but she personally believes he was tipped in the sea.

It was President Burnham who ordered all Guyanese to do a six-month mandatory army training course. Which is how Shirley found herself with ninety-three nurse trainees and doctors on a course in the jungle shortly after her baby was born.

They spent three days getting to the camp by boat, and then lorry, and were expected to learn how to shoot and run up mountains. Shirley shook like a vast jelly as she laughed at the memory. She has always been generously proportioned, even at an early age, and she struggled heroically but unsuccessfully to do what was required of her. She was greatly relieved that the nurses and doctors were treated rather better than the 'pioneers'.

Shirley's husband has got fed-up with ferrying her around Montserrat in his car, and he has been trying to teach her to drive. It has taken some time, but at long last she was ready for the test. One day, when Shirley came round to see me, she was carrying in her hand several sheets of paper. She was preparing herself for the police written examination and she had obtained the questions and answers in advance. All Shirley was required to do to pass her written test was to memorise both questions and answers correctly.

She wanted me to type them out neatly and in order, so that they looked like *"De reel ting"* and she could practice. There were thirty-three questions, and a friend in the Force had thoughtfully supplied the appropriate answers. As I glanced down the list some of the answers surprised me, seeming highly unorthodox and not at all to my understanding of the Highway Code. I was tempted to change them, but Shirley would have none of it. She assured me the answers were absolutely correct.

The first question was innocently basic and relatively simple, *"What is a vehicle?"* it asked. Question five however, *"What is a skid?"* had the interesting answer *"A skid is when a car have on smooth tyres and there is no traction"* and the unambiguous answer to the question that followed *"What can you do to prevent skids?"* was a blunt, uncompromising and eminently sensible *"Avoid driving with smooth tyres!"*

When overtaking another vehicle, the exhortation to *"Blow horn to alert driver"* provided me with an insight into the road etiquette of many West Indians whom I had previously supposed to be expressing impatience with my leisurely driving style. Horn blowing is obviously an integral part of the Montserrat Highway Code.

Question 31 asked *"What should you do in relation to a direction given to you by a police officer in uniform?"* Both Shirley and I were very tempted to say something controversial here, but the recommended answer was probably the wisest if Shirley wanted to pass her test. It sternly advised *"Obey the instruction!"*.

Several days later Shirley phoned me, intoxicated with delight, she had successfully passed her driving test.

My husband and I left Montserrat for our end of tour leave in the middle of May. The PWD office had organised a wonderful leaving party, and after many 'hi-fives', slaps on the back, speeches and kind compliments, they gave my husband a signed Kevin West photograph of the volcano at night. With red lava tumbling down the steep slopes it is very impressive.

My husband reciprocated by presenting each of the ladies with a single beribboned carnation and expressed his deep appreciation of the friendliness and comradeship within the Department over the two years of his contract.

When he returned home after the party he told me that leaving so many good friends would have been very difficult if he had not known he was returning to Montserrat in a few weeks' time.

As we waited for the LIAT flight from Montserrat airport, Sheila and Frank arrived to say goodbye. They have been in Montserrat since the start of the volcanic activity in July 1995. In fact I first met Sheila at the coffee morning at Government House on the day the volcano awoke, and later we became close friends and also neighbours in Old Towne.

The four of us stood together, our backs to the airport building, and looked up at the volcano beyond the little communities of Bethel and Bramble village, and remembered that first sign of activity on 18th July 1995. It had all started with a roaring sound, like a jet engine, with plumes of steam venting from the virgin green hillside high into the air.

It is now a vast mountain dominating the landscape. It was steaming vigorously, and occasional small rockfalls could be seen rolling down the steep sides. The mound towered high above the encircling crater rim, almost overtopping the crater edge above Farrell's Yard.

I shivered slightly, and commented that the volcano seemed very close, very large, and suddenly very sinister.

W.H. Bramble Airport May 1997

22 - JUNE 1997

BLACK WEDNESDAY

It was lunch-time in Montserrat on 25th June when at precisely 12.59 p.m., for a period of twenty minutes, the volcano erupted dramatically and with devastating consequences.

It spewed out millions of tons of white-hot ash, gravel and rocks in a scalding, swirling cauliflower of incandescent gases that raced down the north and northeastern flanks of the volcano. It overwhelmed the countryside, blotting out daylight, and smothering the land in a dense choking fog of black ash which snaked northwards in a suffocating smog to shroud much of the island.

'Black Wednesday' it is being called. Montserrat will never be the same again.

My husband and I returned to the island from our UK leave five days after the eruption. As we scrambled down from the helicopter at Gerald's Park we were greeted by Peter Baxter. He was waiting to climb on board the helicopter to fly to Antigua.

After a brief welcome back hug, he took me aside and told me that my friend Beryl *"The fruit lady"* had returned to her home in the hills of Harris and had been caught in that dramatic and terrifying eruption. She was one of the victims, one of the identified dead.

Felina Celestine, Phillip Robinson, Joseph Greenaway, Hezekiah Riley, Isolyn Lewis, Melville Cuffy, Edith Greenaway. It was a distressing task but they managed to identify some of the bodies recovered. Currently two more remain un-named. Fourteen other people are still missing, presumed dead.

These are the first direct fatalities from the volcano. Another five, including little Mary Chloupek from Spanish Pointe, were badly burned and had to be flown by helicopter to Guadeloupe and Martinique for treatment by the French medical burns unit.

W.H. Bramble Airport 5 km to the northeast of the volcano had a lucky escape. An urgent warning to the airport and on the radio enabled the workers and passengers (including the Governor and his wife who were returning to the island) to evacuate the airport complex and get to the high ground above Trant's just minutes before the first massive eruption.

The Governor's wife told me later she had been listening to the radio while waiting in the car for the Governor, when she heard the order to evacuate, and she called to him. The airport was cleared immediately and in great haste.

As the watchers who had escaped from the airport stood on the elevated ground at Trant's overlooking the runway, a second pulse of pyroclastic flow swept over the airport road they had just travelled, stopping within 50 metres of the terminal building and the southern edge of the runway.

Linda White was at home in Trant's. She heard the warning siren sounding and went outside to look up at the mountain. It was covered in low cloud but did not appear to be unusually active. Linda supposed it was the weekly Wednesday siren practice, but a little early, and returned inside.

It was Linda's immense good fortune that her policeman son, aware of the imminent danger to the area, arrived moments later and grabbed his mother. Together they fled. Linda would undoubtedly have perished if she had remained in her home.

The shocked group, clustered together above Trant's, watched in horror as the flow poured out in a fan across the landscape burning everything in its path, setting fire to buildings, and exploding gas cylinders used for cooking. It buried the central corridor road in fifteen feet of ash. It was an unbelievable sight numbing the senses.

The farmers, who had been working their crops on the slopes at Farrell's Yard, stood no chance of escaping from the blistering volcanic furnace that swept down the hillside and overwhelmed them. Every one of them perished. Beryl had been there too.

It was several hours before the full extent of the damage and destruction caused by the pyroclastic flows was fully understood. Over 4 sq. km of the landscape had been blitzed and left as a charred and smouldering moonscape of grey ash, gravel and rocks. Some of the boulders tossed from the womb of the volcano were an astonishing four metres in diameter.

Here and there, at the extremities of the flow, small pockets of startling green splashed the lunar landscape. Oases untouched by the burning ash, saved by subtle land contours. Beyond the grey boundary of the hot ashy deposits, the green of the fertile fields was a dramatic contrast.

Nine villages, including two churches, were destroyed, and the village of Farms was completely buried under ash. The flow had come down Mosquito Ghaut forking at the northeast turn above Farrell's Yard and separating.

The heavier material in the pyroclastic flow followed the Ghaut down towards Harris, Spanish Pointe and the airport, while a 'rogue' tongue had surged north, crossing the road to Streatham and Windy Hill, before following Dyer's Ghaut west down the Belham River Valley. It stopped 1 km short of Belham Bridge, only 200 ft. from Cork Hill School where the children were gathered. Another kilometre and it would have reached the golf course beside the Vue Point Hotel to enter the sea on the west side of Montserrat at Old Road Bay.

The Royal Montserrat Police Force and the Royal Montserrat Defence Force worked frantically to try and rescue those who were injured or trapped, and to recover any bodies. Search and Rescue teams, together with Jim in his helicopter, and a Lynx loaned by a passing foreign navy ship, brought out over ninety people from the area impacted by the eruption. It was estimated that at least fifty people had been in the Harris area alone. Cut off by the flow, eleven had to be winched to safety, including ninety-year old Ellen from Harris Lookout.

For those who survived and were later rescued, to be caught in the nightmare was a terrifying ordeal. Two friends in Harris village ran for safety, one going in one direction, one another. One survived, the other inadvertently ran into oncoming flow.

Simon Tuitt, from the airport, went up to Harris to help a friend, but as they were leaving he turned to go back to the house for a minute. His friend survived, but Simon is listed as missing.

A family from Spanish Pointe tried to leave by car, thinking they could drive across the layer of hot ash left by the lip of the pyroclastic flow, which cut them off from safety. But the scorching ash burned the tyres, and they had to be plucked from the car roof by the helicopter.

Many suffered burns to feet and legs, including Arthur Meade who found himself engulfed in darkness and trapped in his car at Dyer's. Worried that it might explode at any moment, he jumped from the car, stepping in hot ash, which seared his flesh as it got inside his boots. Using a flashlight grabbed from inside the car, and gasping for breath, he managed to stumble to the safety of Lees.

As the darkness of falling ash cleared, Arthur persuaded a friend to drive him back towards his abandoned car. The engine was still running, but the hot ash had burned away the tyres. However Arthur was determined to rescue his vehicle, and managed to 'rim it' down to Cork Hill and safety. He was later flown to Guadeloupe for treatment to his burned feet.

HMS *Liverpool* was diverted from her WIGS duties and headed towards Montserrat to help. The Caribbean community up and down the islands went on stand-by to assist, and seven nurses were sent from Jamaica to help with the injured at St. John's Hospital.

The question has to be asked *"Why did so many people die?"* and *"Why were so many people in what was effectively an exclusion zone?"*. According to the map this was a dangerous and restricted area.

There is no single, and no simple, explanation. The Volcanic Risk Map is regularly up-dated and on the 6th June it showed Harris and Bethel in Exclusion Zone A, with Streatham and Spanish Pointe in Zone B, and the airport and Lees in the comparative safety of Zone C.

However, during June the map was re-drawn four times and the zones changed as activity increased. With seven zones and six alert levels creating a possible forty-two different options for action, we did not always appreciate, on a day-to-day basis, which areas were becoming increasingly dangerous to occupy. And the eruption of the 25th June *"surprised"* even the scientists who said it was *"Much bigger than expected"*.

Some of those working in the danger area were farmers, returning during the day to tend animals and crops. But some just wanted to go home. They could no longer tolerate life in the shelters and preferred to return to their homes and risk the volcano. A night or two in a shelter, or with friends, is rough but acceptable, but a week, a month or a year, is not.

After almost two years of activity, several evacuations and subsequent returns, we have come to believe that the volcano can to some extent be 'managed' by the authorities as they act on scientific advice. We also firmly believed that sufficient warning could be given if activity escalated and those in the danger area would be able to leave rapidly and safely. The eruption of 25th June has proved to us just how naive and dangerous this simple faith can be.

Before the massive eruption on the 25th June, the airport was closed at least twice as a precaution when it appeared that activity was escalating.

Willy Aspinall, as Chief Scientist at the Montserrat Volcano Observatory, wanted to keep it closed, concerned that the scientists could give less than two minutes warning of a major event. The authorities wished to keep the airport open if possible. So a member of the MVO team was stationed at the airport with radio contact to the Observatory, and roadblocks were placed around the airport.

It seems activity at the volcano had been gradually increasing over the two weeks preceding Black Wednesday. Concern continued to mount when Mosquito Ghaut was affected by pyroclastic flows on the 15th June.

Mosquito Ghaut is the deep valley beyond the crater rim on the north flank of the Soufrière Hills above the fertile Farrell slopes. It turns northeast as Paradise Ghaut to skirt the village of Harris before running as Paradise River into Pea Ghaut and finally, as Farm River, it discharges into the sea beside the southern edge of the airport runway.

A significant flow down Mosquito Ghaut on the 17th June brought material 4 km down the valley, the surge 'scorching' Harris.

Early on the morning of the fateful 25th June, Willy and Keith from the MVO drove through the Exclusion Zone, and saw in the distance some farmers in the fields at Farrell's. At that time there was absolutely no evidence that the day would turn out to be so terrifying.

According to the MVO report, at 11.00 a.m. *"An intense swarm of hybrid earthquakes began and rapidly escalated to repetitive events which merged into continuous tremor after 12.15 p.m. At about 1.00 p.m. major pyroclastic flow activity began in Mosquito Ghaut, which generated an ash cloud to over 30,000 ft. within minutes."*

The top 300 ft. had been blown off the dome reducing it to 3,000 ft. and leaving a 'spoon shaped' hollow with a steep back wall above Mosquito Ghaut. Within hours of the blast new growth had already begun to refill the hollow.

During the last week of June the volcano has been producing eight-hourly cycles of activity, what we refer to as 'rhythmic breathing by the dragon'. Rapid inflation accompanied by earthquakes, followed by deflation accompanied by pyroclastic flows. It is, we are told, magma being supplied to the dome.

With each pyroclastic flow the topography of the island is changing, allowing subsequent flows to travel further and faster than previously.

Access into Plymouth is now completely restricted since pyroclastic flows topped Gages Wall and travelled down Fort Ghaut reaching Webb's Village and, later, St. Patrick's Church and Old Glendon Hospital in the town. The alert level remains at Orange, and residents of Fox's, Weekes, Delvins, St. George's and Cork Hill are being advised not to sleep in their homes and to 'voluntarily' evacuate for the *"Wholly safe"* one third of the island north of Belham Bridge.

On the 27th June, two days after Black Wednesday, explosions from the volcano scattered rock 6 km to the northwest, falling at Fox's Bay and evacuation was considered necessary. Since approximately 1,500 people are involved, this has meant an immediate increase in demand for accommodation in the seventeen shelters in the safe north.

Many displaced people have sought shelter with friends and relatives in preference to the cramped shelters, a few even choosing to sleep in their cars on vacant land. My friends Linda and Harry Green were among those ordered to evacuate from Fox's, and they moved into their unfinished home in Woodlands.

Linda had watched the eruption of 25th June from her balcony at Fox's, on the west side of Montserrat. She had a perfect view. *"It was different, very unusual"* she told me *"Moments before the eruption a dense white cloud rolled rapidly down the hillside, hugging the ground. It wasn't a pyroclastic flow and it wasn't an ash cloud, I don't know what it was."*

In April the shelter population had been calculated to be 220 persons, the number has now risen to 1,220. A young woman, reluctantly moving into the Salem Secondary School shelter, comforted herself with the old West Indian saying *'De wors o' livin betta dan de bes o' dead'*.

After the devastation of the 25th June, the airport, although undamaged, remains closed. The emergency jetty being built at Little Bay, despite its limitations of no lighting, no storage, and only able to take vessels up to 20 ft., has become the alternative access and departure point in Montserrat for all except certain Government officials who are allowed to use the small 'Squirrel' helicopter. This is landing at Gerald's Park and ferrying small groups regularly to Antigua.

A ferry, *'Early Bird II'*, hastily chartered by the British Government, has arrived from Anguilla and runs a service from Little Bay, Montserrat, to Antigua, twice a day. Instead of the fifteen minute LIAT flight between the two islands, it now takes almost two hours to cross the stomach-churning choppy sea. A modest EC$75 each way secures a seat.

Black Wednesday has changed Montserrat. It is a nation bereaved, a nation in shock. Everyone knows someone who died. There is to be a National Day of Mourning on July 8th and Father Larry will speak at the Memorial Service at the St. John's Anglican Church.

I went to the little cemetery at Carr's Bay to pay my respects to those who had died. Seven new mounds of earth lay side by side along the back. Small, colourful wreathes placed on top of the freshly turned soil.

Beryl was not afraid of death. She had a great faith in *'De Lor'*. At one time a Pentecostal, she later joined the Seventh Day Adventists, because, she said, they let you join in the service more.

I remember the premonition she had about her death, and her 'vision' of the New Jerusalem waiting for her. I recall how thrilled she had been when, in her vision, Jesus had told her he had 'a blessing' for her. Now, I like to imagine her running through the beautiful trees and flowers she described in her vision, young again, calling to everyone in her high-pitched sing-song voice to leave everything *"An cum, qwik, qwik!"* as she boards the train for the New Jerusalem.

Beryl 'the fruit lady'

169

23 - JULY 1997

PEOPLE LOSING HEART

A new Volcanic Risk Map was released on 4th July and has been distributed around the island. It has been simplified into three zones and has arrows showing the extent of pyroclastic flow and surge deposits to date.

A thick, black, felt pen line demarcates the Exclusion Zone of southern Montserrat. It begins on the west coast beside 'The Nest' on the beach at Old Road Bay, and follows the contour of Belham River Valley in a more or less straight line across the centre of the island to finish just north of W.H. Bramble Airport on the east coast. Restriction of entry into the Exclusion Zone will be enforced by the erection of permanent steel barriers across the roads.

In one sweep of the pen two-thirds of Montserrat has become a 'no-go' area. It includes the heavily populated Cork Hill community, the Golf Club, the 'snowbirds' retreat of Isles Bay, (where nestles the exclusive villa home of Robert C. Penney III, American millionaire, who incidentally has just generously donated US$200,000 towards the Red Cross home for the elderly).

The second zone drawn on the new map is a narrow band of Montserrat, less than 500 metres in places, running more or less parallel to the Exclusion Zone line. This is now called the Central Zone which must be evacuated at two hours' notice if it becomes necessary.

Included are the expatriate residences in Old Towne, and the local Frith and Flemming areas. My old neighbour Sheila, my friend Jennifer, Sir George Martin, and the Vue Pointe Hotel are all currently within this narrow 'buffer' band, and until recently, so was I.

The areas of Lime Kiln Bay, Olveston and Salem have become the new front line of the safe northern zone which the scientists say is protected from the volcano by the Centre Hills.

It has been generally agreed that 300 ft. above sea level is considered safe from potential surges. Willy has assured us that there will be *"Nothing life threatening beyond this line"*.

But rumours are rife, and there is a great deal of dissatisfaction and confusion on the street. What if the northern zone is not in fact 'safe' and the barriers are pushed back again to include Salem, or even Olveston? What if everyone has to be evacuated off-island? Is there indeed a future for Montserrat?

After having been assured again and again that areas of Montserrat north of Belham Valley were safe, this startling new risk map reveals the vulnerability of Old Towne and Frith. To add to our anxieties heavy rain has been forecast as the height of the hurricane season approaches. We have been warned to expect the added hazard of *"boiling hot mudflows"* down all the ghauts.

On the street they say the politicians are not pulling together, indeed gossip states that the Chief Minister Bertrand Osborne has been asked to step down by a fellow Minister. Some people have called for the British Government to take control, others have suggested suspending Government altogether and allowing a Committee of some sort to run the island during this time of crisis.

People are losing heart. This has been the last straw for many whose confidence was shaken badly on Black Wednesday. It has all proved just too much for many people, particularly those with young children, and a mass exodus of Montserrat has begun.

On the 4th July the ferry was overwhelmed when approximately two hundred people wanting to leave the island arrived at Little Bay hoping to board *'Early Bird II'*.

A second trip was arranged so that all those who wished to leave could do so. A tropical wave was passing over Montserrat at the time and this made sea conditions turbulent. The voyage to Antigua, normally uncomfortable at the best of times, was an ordeal for the passengers who described it variously as *"terrible"*, *"frightening"*, *"and dangerous"*. They were seasick and extremely scared. They also complained that the Captain of the *'Early Bird II'* was *"Unreliable, often drunk and rude"*.

After this experience the authorities quickly replaced *'Early Bird II'* with a more acceptable ferry, the *'MV Deluxe'*. It is a new, air-conditioned vessel which has proved much more acceptable to passengers travelling backwards and forwards between Montserrat and Antigua.

In addition, another vessel has arrived, the *'MV Admiral Bay'*, which is on loan from the St. Vincent Government. Although it takes up to four hours to cross from Montserrat to Antigua the larger vessel is more stable and able to carry cargo as well as passengers and has proved popular.

As well as the two ferries a Bell 212 helicopter began operations on 10th July. Since 'Kamikaze Jim's' small Bell 206 helicopter is still being used on a daily basis by the MVO to monitor the volcano, the new larger helicopter is used primarily to carry passengers, nine at time, backwards and forwards to Antigua, priority being given to Government officials.

The co-pilot of the new helicopter is a Vietnam War veteran who was shot down twice over Vietcong territory. The first time his helicopter went down he did not expect to be rescued, but another helo came in under fire and lifted him out. However, the second helicopter was also hit and 'spiralled' out of the sky leaving the two pilots alive but in enemy territory. Under cover of protective fire, a third helo came to their rescue, and brought them to safety. When he told us his story we wondered whether flying for Montserrat might prove to be a bit tame.

Since W.H. Bramble Airport is no longer in use, Gerald's in the far north has been transformed into the new helipad. One of the plastic covered frames that had been erected at Gerald's for potential evacuees, although torn and damaged by wind and abuse, has been pressed into service as a Customs and Immigration facility and with a couple of tables and some screens it serves the purpose admirably.

Shortly after the 25th June eruption the RMDF and RMPF went into the Exclusion Zone during 'windows of opportunity' to rescue equipment from the airport to be taken to Gerald's.

Shopkeepers such as Rams, Angelo's and Victor's are allowed to enter Plymouth under escort during these windows of opportunity to bring out goods stored in their premises in town, and Barclays Bank are still using their facility in Plymouth as a secure base.

Rams Emdee Supermarket has opened a new shop in Salem. They say their freezers in Plymouth smell so disgusting that they dare not even lift the lids. Angelo's Supermarket has brought out some of their fridges and freezers and intend to move their wooden shed from beside the golf course at Belham (currently in the Exclusion Zone) to Cudjoehead in the north. Victor's, who built a splendid little wooden shop close to Belham Bridge that they were extending and which is now also in the Exclusion Zone, are talking of leaving the island for good and going to St. Maarten.

Petrol is being tankered out from Plymouth during these 'windows of opportunity' and taken to the safe north. Fuel was rationed during early July until the new petrol and diesel emergency storage tanks were filled at Carr's Bay and arrangements were made to transport fuel to Montserrat by ISO tanks.

Difficulty in obtaining fuel for cars has added to the irritations we are already experiencing. We have been instructed to listen to ZJB Radio Montserrat for information, and the broadcast on 11th July was typical.

The morning was set aside for supplying fuel to essential vehicles only. Then vehicles with registration numbers between 3000 and 3999 were instructed to queue at the garage between twelve and four, and finally vehicles with registration numbers between 4000 and 4999 were told to queue between five and nine in the evening.

It is quite normal to spend up to four hours in a queue for fuel in St. Johns while the one nozzle at the petrol station steadily works through the waiting vehicles.

When David went up for fuel, following instructions on the radio (his vehicle registration number being between 1000 and 2000) he queued for an hour and was then informed the station had 'run out'.

The ultimate frustration is endured by those who have used their last drop of petrol to drive up to the station in the north, queued for some considerable time, and are then told that *"the pump is dry, come back tomorrow!"* Tempers are frayed and many motorists have had no choice but to abandon their vehicles beside the road.

Queues are also forming at the banks. A rumour began to circulate that ten of the Barclays Bank staff wanted to resign, and that both Barclays and the Royal Bank of Canada were considering closing down and leaving Montserrat within seven days.

We now hear that the Barclays staff have been persuaded to remain, but in the meantime customers have panicked and are rushing to the banks to take their money out in hard cash. I saw one old lady with such a vast wad of notes she could hardly hold them in her hands as she walked away from the house in Olveston that is currently serving as the temporary premises of the Royal Bank of Canada.

While we are trying to adjust to this muddle, the volcano has remained lively. During the first week of July the pyroclastic flows, under impressive columns of ash, crept further into Plymouth. On the 18th July, the second anniversary of the commencement of activity at the volcano, new dome growth had almost completely filled the spoon-shaped scar formed by the massive 25th June eruption.

The activity on the 18th July, which rained mud on my home at Lime Kiln, took out the island's Cable TV when, allegedly, lightning zapped the aerial on St. George's Hill. Rumour suggests that we will be without TV for several weeks, since it is not possible to reach the area affected to repair the damage.

This month has been a watershed for many, when the very personal decision between 'fight or flight' was made. As one politician put it *"We are a worn out people"*. Hilary, overwhelmed by grief over the death of her mother Beryl last month, has left for Canada to be with her half-sister. Elderly Ellen, rescued from her home by helicopter on the 25th June, has gone to England to be with relatives. Stanley has decided to send his son to Antigua to live with an Aunt.

Resignation from jobs to take up the assisted relocation scheme to the UK has become a popular option. Three policemen resigned during the first week of July (and a fourth was arrested in Antigua and imprisoned for two years for carrying cannabis).

Six nurses have also resigned, and another thirty-one nurses have signed a statement expressing their concerns about the safety of Montserrat and requesting a 'severance package'. Ronnie says we are all suffering from burn-out and need a break.

In an attempt to give the children of Montserrat a much needed holiday, the Red Cross and Montserrat Christian Council managed to arrange for them to stay with families on several Caribbean islands, including Jamaica, Cayman Islands, St. Lucia and Antigua. But this has not stemmed the flow of migrating Montserratians, and by the end of July over one thousand people had left the island.

Many of those who remain in Montserrat are moving out of the Central Zone towards the safer north, not wanting to live with the potential of a two-hour evacuation order, possibly during the middle of the night. Unfortunately, accommodation is scarce and becoming increasingly expensive as demand outstrips supply.

Sheila, due to leave Montserrat on the 4th August, has packed up all her belongings and sent them back to the UK, and moved out of Old Towne into a small villa above Woodlands.

Mary Carmen, the delightful and elegant Mexican wife of one of the Governor's Office staff, has moved for the third time in three months, to a house near McChesney's, but she still gets ashfall and worries what effect this is having on her little two-year old son.

The Governor and his wife have also moved their residence. Although the Governor's Office is still at McChesney's in Olveston, they have leased the villa 'Palmhurst' in Palm Loop on the cliff beyond Woodlands Beach.

The villa has been empty for some time and was up for sale. The narrow drive to the single-storey building is lined with small royal palms. The villa has the advantage of a large reception, dining and lounge area, and an extensive pool deck, both of which are suitable for official functions.

Some of the Government House furniture from Plymouth has been salvaged and brought to Palmhurst, including the dining table, chairs, bookcases and the large, official portrait of the Queen in an ornate gilt frame, which now hangs on the lounge wall.

Jennifer and Boyd have also moved out of their home in Old Towne. They were fortunate to be offered an empty villa just above

Woodlands Beach, owned by friends. 167 steep steps lead from their garden down to the beach.

Father Larry has remained in Old Towne with Carol and Cedric Osborne at the Vue Pointe Hotel. He was sharing the Roman Catholic Church shelter accommodation in Salem with his flock, but he has been persuaded to move into one of the rooms at the hotel as he is suffering from poor health at present. Ash in the air is aggravating problems with his chest, but he is conscientiously wearing his ash mask now. He has managed to get permission to conduct weddings at the Vue Pointe Hotel, as well as the weekly religious services. He still returns to the shelter for his daily lunch, which usually comprises rice, peas and fish. It is put on a plate at mid-day and Father Larry eats it whenever he arrives. *"Equally tasty hot or cold!"* he assures me.

On his second day back on island in his new job as Emergency Projects Co-ordinator, my husband found himself unexpectedly involved in trying to solve the housing crisis for the evacuees in the shelters. To his utter astonishment and disbelief he was instructed to produce, as a matter of urgency within forty-eight hours, a matrix of possible emergency housing solutions to be presented to the Government of Montserrat.

My husband's working brief was to empty the schools of 1,000 people before the end of August, one month's time, for the beginning of the new school term.

Alone, and starting from nothing, he worked through the long night, gathering information from around the globe.

The possible immediate solutions included a generous offer from the Government of St. Maarten, who were prepared to lease to Montserrat their 'container city' of units that had been brought in for emergency use after the devastation of Hurricane Luis in 1995.

The list even included the sourcing of a cruise ship, capable of being off Montserrat within days and able to accommodate and feed several thousand people. Factory shells, portakabins, mobile homes and prefabricated houses were all investigated and sourced, together with costs, delivery times, advantages and disadvantages.

Within the forty-eight hour deadline the results were presented to the Government Ministers. After a long and exhausting meeting where each proposal was thoroughly discussed, the authorities gave the solutions a ranking in order of preference.

It was understandable that the Montserrat Government would wish for permanent constructions as a solution to the re-housing problem. At the top of their list they chose block-built individual housing as their ideal preferred choice. But they were unanimous in their agreement that speed was the essence since the task in hand was to provide for the immediate housing needs of those in uncomfortable shelter accommodation, and to empty the schools ready for the new term next month. The consensus of opinion was that imported prefabricated houses will be the most rapid and acceptable solution.

Land acquisition remains the biggest problem. Much of Montserrat is privately owned and leasing arrangements or compulsory purchase takes time to negotiate. And any solution in the matrix (with the exception of the cruise ship) required extensive infrastructure to include all services, drainage and roads.

The results were appraised by the Montserrat Government and then passed to HMG in London, and on the 9th July, at a Ministerial meeting, the British Government authorised £6.5 million to be spent on emergency housing in Montserrat and by the 21st July a three-man team from the Consultants Brown and Root arrived on island to begin the work.

A flight with 'Kamikaze Jim' in the helicopter brought home to my husband the devastating effects of the eruption on Black Wednesday, 25th June. He told me that the whole topography of southern Montserrat has changed. Flying over the central corridor area between Plymouth and the airport it is at times difficult to distinguish where you are.

Familiar landmarks, and roads, have completely disappeared under a sweeping expanse of grey gravel and rocks. It looks as if a vast mudslide has pushed across the landscape. Here and there the charred ruins of a house can be seen. The bare walls of Harris church remain, and an abandoned car stands trapped in ash, tracks still visible. With the doors of the helo off he was able to take some astonishing photographs.

During the flight my husband had to jump from the hovering helo to check the waterworks on Killiecrankie Hill.

"Just think of it as stepping from a canoe" shouted Jim *"but keep your head down!"* he added, grinning.

As they flew on and inspected the area along the east side of the Soufrière Hills they saw the carcass of a dead cow floating in a swimming pool in one of the villas in Spanish Pointe. Beside the pool several cattle were herded together.

"At least they have water" commented Jim.

A handful of sheep had discovered the empty airport terminal building and moved in, sheltering from the hot sun and nibbling on the remnants of green beside the runway.

Jim brought the helo down on a handkerchief patch of stubbly grass, a short distance away from a doleful donkey whose poor legs were completely stripped of flesh, burned and red raw. Jim had seen the wretched donkey a few days earlier, and had gently led it to safety, and was now regularly bringing it water. He calls the donkey 'Chopper'. 'Chopper' had injured himself when he walked through the white-hot deposits left by the pyroclastic flow.

Harris Church after 25th June 1997 eruption

Nearly one month after the 25th June eruption the pyroclastic flow deposits retain a temperature of 642°C. just five feet below the surface.

Another lucky survivor from the eruption of 25th June is Abraham. Abraham, mentally handicapped, was found inside a house in Streatham on the 7th July, alive but very poorly and with burned feet. Jim had passed over the area many times in his helicopter, searching for people, but Abraham had not thought to seek help and had remained for almost two weeks, alone and injured within the house.

Jim has been helping Kathy from WSPA to gather up stray dogs and cats so that they can be evacuated off-island to new homes in the States. Dr. Swanson, the local vet, has been going into the unsafe zone regularly and taking food and water to animals in Richmond Hill, Fox's Bay and Cork Hill. He estimates that he has been feeding up to sixty animals a day.

A temporary kennels has been built at Brades to accommodate the abandoned animals, but many of the dogs let loose by their owners have banded together in packs and are terrorising the south, killing sheep.

Those animals that survived the pyroclastic flows and are able to fend for themselves are thought to have moved further south rather than north, and it is surmised that in a few years' time there will be wild pigs and cattle roaming the southern hills of Montserrat.

Cockroaches, on the other hand, seem to have vanished completely. I have mixed reactions to this observation. My villa in Lime Kiln was home for vast numbers of the shiny brown scavengers, and a constant battle for supremacy raged between them and 'Mr. Pest' the exterminator. When I returned to the villa after our break in the UK there was no sign of a cockroach, not even one. They seem to have completely disappeared, and I must confess I find this surprisingly disturbing.

24 - AUGUST 1997

PLYMOUTH ON FIRE

August has been a mad, sad month. Emotionally and physically draining. After two years of crisis management in Montserrat, trying to second-guess the volcano, things have begun to fall apart and it seems as if the Law of Chaos now prevails. The situation is spiralling out of control. There is a feeling of panic in Montserrat, and rising hysteria.

On the last day of July the volcano entered a new and frightening phase, identified by the scientists as *"Vulcanian explosions with column collapse"*. During the first two weeks of August we experienced fourteen spectacular 'Vulcanian' explosive eruptions at the Soufrière Hills.

It was observed that the volcano was acting *"like a Swiss watch"* with the inflating and deflating contractions coming at approximately ten hourly intervals. We heard the loud 'boom' each time ash was ejected at speed, before it mixed with the air and writhed and rose like a rapidly expanding freshly shorn sheep fleece into the sky.

The lightest particles went up into the eruptive plume forming a fluffy mushroom that filled the sky and drifted slowly out across the world.

The heavier particles and dense blocks, some up to several metres across, fell back to earth to form pyroclastic flows that spilled down all sides of the volcano.

We experienced the resultant fusillade of debris across the island as far north as St. John's, with the familiar thick residue of ash and mud. But we also experienced a new phenomenon - hailing showers of gravel, stones and clast. At Lime Kiln we were peppered with small two-inch projectiles, but closer to the volcano much larger metre-sized ballistics rained down. A crater 300 metres in diameter appeared within the dome. It was, quite simply, an awesome, powerful spectacle. The mountain seemed to be giving birth.

Colossal pyroclastic flows set Plymouth on fire and choked the town. The dense black clouds swept across the sea to drop ash on the neighbouring islands of Antigua, Nevis, Guadeloupe and St. Maarten, disrupting flights and grounding aircraft and causing concern to all.

With dramatic eruptions, heavy ashfall, mass relocations, businesses closing, strikes, and a scramble to leave the island, Montserrat has reached an all-time low. The confusion has been exacerbated by the coincidental absence at the beginning of August of most of our leaders, including the Governor, Chief Minister and five other senior officials. And changes of scientists at the MVO during August have brought different interpretations and responses to the unfolding volcanic crisis.

At 4.50 p.m. on Holiday Monday 4th August, as activity at the volcano escalated with more vigorous burning flows down Fort Ghaut and across Plymouth, I heard the familiar boom and rumble of another eruption and then the siren wailing at Salem.

With obvious reluctance the Acting Governor, Howard Fergus, advised everyone to evacuate the Central 'buffer' Zone of Old Towne and Frith's for the night.

Buses were sent to bring people out. Most were expected to go into the shelters, but it was reported that out of an anticipated seven hundred evacuees from the Central Zone, only two hundred had sought emergency accommodation.

"*A substantial number are roughing it*" was the official explanation. Many saw the move as purely temporary, a cautious contingency plan, and slept in their cars, fully expecting to return to their homes the following day. And indeed permission was given for residents, including the Vue Pointe Hotel, to return to the Central Zone during daylight hours, but they were expected to move out each night, and immediately when the siren was sounded.

Overnight, our home at Lime Kiln had become vulnerable and was now on the edge of the safety zone. We were described somewhat confusingly as being "*In the southern part of the northern safe zone "*. The air was heavy with re-suspended ash and gritty with gravel and pumice.

With my husband rarely home during early August, I spent much of my time alone, responding to the wail of the siren by hiding in our 'hunker-hole' beneath the pool where we had put beds, water, food, candles, torch, passport and books.

Sometimes the sound of the siren would come too late and I found myself unable to get to the safety of the room before the ashin' cloud engulfed the villa and blackness descended.

Etched into my memory is the morning of the 7th August. I had just been listening to Rose on ZJB Radio Montserrat, broadcasting from a hastily assembled studio in the bedroom of a villa in the hills behind me.

Rose was hosting a live conversation with Chief Minister Bertrand Osborne speaking from London. He was commenting on the talks the delegation had been having with the British Government, saying they had gone very well, with approval for an extra £40 million to Montserrat, in addition to the £6.5 million already allocated to housing.

The Chief Minister was optimistic, hoping for a new airport, rises in pay for the disgruntled Civil Servants (who had just expressed their frustrations with a two-day sickie) and more housing. He finished his interview with Rose by telling her that he and the Governor had been presented to Her Majesty The Queen, who was very concerned about Montserrat, and Her Majesty wished us to know that she was thinking about us and offered her sympathy.

It was moments later that I heard a loud rumble coming from the direction of the volcano. I grabbed my yellow hard hat, goggles and mask, the radio, a torch and some chocolate chip cookies, and being too late to get to the 'hunker bunker' I made a nest in the wardrobe with a couple of cushions and settled down on the floor. I put on my hard hat and my mask and prepared to sit it out, trying to ignore the desire to go to the bathroom that was getting progressively more urgent.

The stonin' that followed was the most intense I have ever experienced. During the deafening bombardment I heard the sound of splintering glass and wondered what had been shattered.

I put my hands over my ears to try and muffle the noise. It was mid-morning, but outside was as black as night, and inside the air quickly clouded to become dry and foggy as invading ash swirled around me in a thickening mist.

As the hammering of the stones on the roof gave way to gravel rain and twilight, I slipped out of the wardrobe for a quick visit to the bathroom. I passed through the kitchen on the way, and remembered that a bottle of champagne was cooling in the fridge. On my way back to the wardrobe I grabbed the bottle, a glass, and as an afterthought, the telephone and the Union Jack.

If this eruption turned out to be 'the biggie', I had some vague plan that I could wave the flag, which I hoped would be visible from the air and sea, and Jim would fly in with his helicopter and rescue me.

As the mud and pumice continued to rain down, I took off my mask and raised a champagne toast to Her Britannic Majesty, thinking of me in London, and it has to be said it was the best champagne I've ever tasted!

I turned up the volume on ZJB Radio Montserrat, to my surprise still on air. Young Shirlian, a trainee learning the art of announcing, was struggling on alone. She put on Elvis Presley, who crooned in a deep and melancholic voice *"God help me to pick up the pieces"*.

I had another glass of champagne and two more chocolate chip cookies. It was an emotional few minutes.

Steve Sparks (MVO call-sign *"Sugar Sugar"*) arrived on the 12th August to take over at the Observatory, and he commenced an official 'overview' of the current situation with a new assessment of potential risks and a prognosis of future volcanic activity.

The Report, officially released to the Government of Montserrat on the 14th August, makes sobering reading. It indicates that during the coming six months the volcano can be expected to be active at the same, or at a slightly elevated, level, with a 1 in 100 chance of *"something critical"* happening, and the possibility of *"grapefruit-sized ballistics"* falling on the crowded community at Salem.

Expressions such as 'safe' and 'unsafe' have been carefully avoided and the term *"comparative safety"* has been substituted instead.

As a direct result of the scientific report, Chief Minister Bertrand Osborne, just returned from his visit to England, made a 'broadcast to the nation' on Saturday 16th August at 2.00 p.m. As far as most Montserratians were concerned this broadcast came out of the blue and was devastating. The whole of Salem, Lime Kiln and south Olveston were instructed to move further north, and several hundred people were given four hours to evacuate all areas south of Nantes River and the Centre Hills.

To my dismay that included me. We were expected to be out of our homes by nightfall. Daytime occupation of the area was permitted, as long as the volcano remains quiet and we have transport to evacuate immediately if necessary, and if we keep our radios tuned to ZJB Radio Montserrat and leave upon hearing the siren at Salem.

This has meant that the busy and bustling commercial centre of Salem, where businesses and offices had so recently relocated from Plymouth, is now firmly placed in the new Exclusion Zone. So is our home in Lime Kiln. We were being slowly pushed further and further north.

Since it was not possible to accommodate on island all those persons to be evacuated, we were informed that a phased, limited, off-island evacuation was about to commence, with the intention of moving long-term shelterees first.

British Aid workers were scrambled into action in the UK and arrived in Antigua to set up a Reception Centre in order to organise onward transit to the UK.

After the broadcast I received a phone call from my husband. He was wholly immersed in the on-going crisis, and hastily ordered me to move out of our Lime Kiln home and find somewhere for the night. *"Just make sure you tell me where I'm to sleep"* he instructed me before hanging up the phone.

I began frantically ringing villa owners and friends in the northern third of Montserrat in a desperate attempt to find alternative accommodation.

Most rental property is in the Exclusion Zone of Old Towne and Olveston, and any available property beyond the new Nantes River cut-off had long gone. Leo, from Brown and Root, heard of my dilemma and very kindly offered me a spare room at the villa they had managed to acquire in Palm Loop.

However, a chance remark by Paula at West Indies Real Estate saying that the Governor's Office were relinquishing the lease on a property they had been renting at Woodlands (half a mile away but just inside the new northern zone) encouraged me to phone the Governor's wife. She was herself busily packing, preparing for their final return to UK in early September, but she was very sympathetic. A few minutes later the Governor himself rang me, and offered us the use of the villa in Woodlands. I considered myself very, very, fortunate.

Most were not so lucky. It was estimated that at least six hundred people remained in the Salem area, unable or unwilling to move out. Against Government orders the Salem bars remained open through the night.

The day after the order to evacuate Salem, on the 17th August, there were some 1,114 people pressed together in inadequate shelter accommodation beyond Nantes River.

At night, as the curfew was imposed, many people slept in cars lining the grassy slopes beside Lawyer's River, while some made space to sleep on office floors, or stayed with friends.

Alfred, like many others, has left for the UK. He had been close to despair, telling me that his boys were having nightmares and waking up screaming. He reached the point where he considered he had no alternative but to leave Montserrat, and in early August he purchased his own tickets, at great expense, for the UK. When he came round with his wife to say farewell on the day he left, he looked very stressed and nervous. Having been a successful businessman in Montserrat, he was now leaving his homeland with a dependant family for an unknown future in London.

Ironically, with the announcement of the off-island evacuation on the 16th August, and the news of negotiations on a 'relocation package' and air fares to those who wished to leave Montserrat, some families who had fled to Antigua in panic, now began to return.

"Flocking back" in the words of one official.

Apparently, they were concerned that they might not be eligible for the package of benefits if they were not resident on island when details were released. Some, who had already paid for their own flights from Antigua to London and were about to leave, even considered cancelling and waiting for more information from the Government.

As a result of this uncertainty, over the weekend of the 16th and 17th August only twenty-seven people left Montserrat, but the returning ferry was heavily over-booked, completely reversing the trend of the previous four weeks.

The fact that Salem is now firmly in the Exclusion Zone has hit businesses very hard, and some are, quite simply, ruined. Many have finally decided to leave the island, including W&W Electronics, the Bakery, Barclays Bank and two insurance companies, and during August Montserrat Building Society suspended trading.

Over 60% of the Society's mortgaged properties are in the Exclusion Zone and house owners are either not able to pay off the mortgage or have simply left the island.

When the Montserrat Building Society froze business people were left unable to access their savings in the company. They did not know what was happening to their money, and this contributed greatly to their frustrations and distress.

At the same time the banks were running out of cash and the Government of Montserrat had to resort to bringing in funds from St. Kitts, by helicopter under armed guard.

After obeying the instruction to leave Lime Kiln on the night of the 16th August, I spent three days driving backwards and forwards during daylight hours collecting and boxing all our belongings.

Once, when the siren sounded as I was packing crates at Lime Kiln, I had to jump in the car and beat a hasty retreat back beyond Nantes River.

On our second day at the new villa, amid the confusion of boxes and belongings, I was asked if I would mind having a 'house-guest' from the Governor's Office for a few days.

It would have been ungracious and churlish to refuse, so I found myself looking after Richard, who had been sent from Barbados to offer Press Officer support to the Governor. Not normally part of his terms of reference, but here on a damage limitation mission to *"Help stop the FCO flak!"*

Somehow we all soldier on despite the difficulties. I came close to the brink of breaking on only one occasion. Within days of taking over the new villa, having carefully unpacked everything and sorted our belongings into the drawers and cupboards, I was informed, indirectly, that the Governor's Office had changed its mind and now wished to retain the villa and renew the lease for the use of their own personnel.

Quite abruptly we were homeless again.

It seemed an impossible predicament, and frantic enquiries confirmed that there were no empty properties available anywhere on island. But by a stroke of great good luck I received a call from my friend Gloria to say that a Canadian 'snowbird' who owns a small villa in Woodlands was prepared to rent it out and was I interested? And so, for the second time in less than a month, I feverishly began to pack, in order to move into our fourth home on Montserrat.

The prisoners held in Salem temporary jail have also been on the move. They have been put in an old sugar mill further north, but with no light and no ventilation. Two days after the move five high security prisoners escaped, frustrated, we were told, at the conditions in which they found themselves. However, on the 20th August, in the middle of a protest rally at the Governor's Office over the management of the volcanic crisis, (primarily rejecting the proposed 'settlement package' which had just been made public) four of the prisoners volunteered to give themselves up, on the condition that they could speak to the Governor in person.

After the Governor promised to look into their grievances, they were re-arrested and led back to the sugar mill.

The fifth prisoner, known as 'Sparrow', is considered the most dangerous, and he decided to 'go his own way' and still remains at large somewhere on the island.

Currently there are twenty-two prison officers, including the Superintendent, and approximately thirty-four prisoners including one female, with ten considered criminally insane.

Plymouth after 25ᵗʰ June 1997 eruption

A young, recent arrival at the Aid Management Office was assigned the task of working out the details of the *"voluntary relocation package"* or *"resettlement grant"* for people wishing to leave Montserrat. The proposal was to be sent for ratification to London.

The plan was to provide financial support for approximately two years. As I understood it, the calculations were initially based on a typical British salary. Over an eighteen-month period the draft proposal suggested that recipients should get EC$40,000 per each head of household, EC$30,000 per spouse or other adult over sixteen, and EC$20,000 for each child under sixteen. Plus fares to the island of choice, Caribbean or UK.

It seemed extraordinarily generous but quite unrealistic, and I seriously doubted whether London would ratify such a package. Put into perspective EC$40,000 is the equivalent of the annual salary of the Director of Public Works in Montserrat, before tax. I had been earning EC$10 (approximately £2.50) per hour when I worked at the Governor's Office, which gave me an annual salary of around EC$18,000. The proposed figures in no way reflected the reality of Montserrat's pay structure.

I imagined what Stanley would do if he were given the equivalent of £25,000 in his pocket and fare paid to Trinidad. It would seem a vast amount of money to him. He would feel like a millionaire. But I was quite certain he would be back in Montserrat within six months, destitute, having spent or more likely given away, every penny.

One morning I asked Stanley what he wanted from the British, and after some thought he said his wish was quite simple. All he wants is to remain in Montserrat with a job, a house, some food, and medical attention.

When the response came from London it was not well received. The resettlement package had been trimmed and was considerably more modest than the one we were told had been requested.

The authorities were prepared to pay for flights to the UK for those that wish them, and those wanting to go to other Caribbean destinations have been offered a six-month average wage settlement of EC$3,820 per adult over eighteen, and EC$950 for each child, plus airfares, and hotel accommodation in Antigua while waiting for seats on a flight.

Anyone with savings of more than EC$16,000 will not be entitled to financial help. Montserratians have described the package as *"Grossly inadequate"*.

Unfortunately, an off-the-cuff remark by Clare Short, Labour Minister for DFID in London, has further incensed the population of Montserrat. Frustrated at what she sees as greed (£40 million in aid for 5,000 people *"Money doesn't grow on trees!"*) she made the indiscreet comment *"They'll be wanting golden elephants next!"*

Many Montserratians are furious with the remark, which has been made much of in the UK national press, being seen as 'offensive' and 'unhelpful'.

British Prime Minister Tony Blair has set up a Commons Select Committee to look into what the British papers are calling *'The Montserrat Affair'* and members will be taking statements and depositions from those involved in the crisis management both here and in London.

Suddenly the international press are much in evidence again. They descended like a plague of locusts and for a short time the island was 'hot' news.

During the third week of August alone over seventy articles about Montserrat appeared in the UK papers. We had visits from Jeremy of *'The Guardian'*, Ben Brown from the BBC, Malcolm Brabant for *'The Times'* and a crew from Sky TV, plus many more, including the less well known such as *'The Dallas Morning News'*.

Ben Brown went into Plymouth to do a report on the ashy capital. It was very interesting watching the satellite BBC World News reporting from Montserrat.

Ben Brown, admitting the ash beneath his feet was *"rather hot"* stated the proposed evacuation was voluntary, adding ominously *"But those who choose to stay are gambling with their lives"*. Not quite the message the authorities had wanted to convey.

Journalists wishing to go into the Exclusion Zone are being warned *"Risk your own lives but not the lives of Montserratians"*.

Somehow the *'Daily Mail'* got our villa phone number, and so did the journalist Malcolm Brabant, and I had to field their enquiries. The *'Daily Mail'* calling from London wanted to know the name of a good hotel and a flight to the island. I laughed out loud, and tried to explain the only hotel was in the danger zone and abandoned, that there was no airport, and they could only reach the island by ferry from Antigua, weather permitting.

Malcolm Brabant wanted to know if we thought the island was about to experience a cataclysmic event, and *"Was there to be a mass off-island evacuation?* Followed by the question *"Was the compensation package generous or mean?"* And finally, straight to the point, he wanted to know *"who had put the package together?"* To his frustration we diplomatically avoided direct answers to his questions.

About two hundred dissenters to the new package decided to march on the office of the Chief Minister on the 21st August, with placards saying *"Bertrand Must Go"*. I could hear the crowd up the hill behind my villa as they waited outside Bertrand Osborne's office.

It was a noisy demonstration, but sounded to me quite good-humoured, with laughter interspersed with the chanting. Three hours the crowd stood there.

I heard David Brandt's voice trying to talk to them, but in the end Bertrand Osborne has decided to stand down as Chief Minister. He resigned, he says, because his fellow Ministers don't have any confidence in him anymore.

"I'm accused of being too pro-British" he commented ruefully.

Some hours later David Brandt was sworn in as the new Chief Minister of Montserrat. His acceptance speech was potent with his customary passion. He assured the population

"I will give my sweat, my tears, my blood and my energy" adding *"let us go forward together with courage and strength"*.

By the 27th August 1,236 persons had registered to leave Montserrat voluntarily, wishing to go to sixteen different country destinations. The majority, almost eighty per cent, said they want to travel to the UK. Antigua at 4% was the next most popular destination.

Three families have specified St. Kitts, eight want to go to USA, three to St. Thomas, one to Scotland, and one to Jamaica. Very few are interested in staying 'in transit' in Antigua.

Laura, my housekeeper in our temporary home, has decided to leave for the UK, taking her little girl Chari away. Laura says she would rather remain in Montserrat, working as a housekeeper until the last day, with her husband and among family and friends, than be sitting in the Rex Halcyon Hotel in Antigua being 'processed' and waiting for space on a British Airways flight to London. *"I want to get straight to England"* she says.

This was the prevailing attitude and might explain why, on Saturday 23rd August, the first day of the voluntary evacuation, when Aid Management Office staff had reserved 130 rooms in hotel accommodation in Antigua and were waiting to welcome the evacuees, only eleven people, and not the anticipated two hundred, disembarked from the ferry. The accompanying minders, together with navy and press, outnumbered the evacuees on a ratio of about 20:1.

The medic from HMS *Liverpool* accompanied the ferry passengers on the first official crossing, handing out anti-nausea tablets and brown paper bags to those on board.

Because of tropical waves in the area the sea was rough, and half-way to Antigua, after observing that brown paper bags do not make very good puke containers, the doctor apparently said "*This is dreadful*" and resorted to swallowing one of his own pills.

He had inadvertently given Mary, an escort to the evacuees, a double dose of nausea tablets and she rolled around in a semi-comatose condition, disembarking "*black and blue with bruises*" and believing she was in Zambia.

She says she was so drugged when she staggered off the ferry in Antigua she remembers nothing about the welcoming reception committee, or the refreshments, or the steel band playing, although she vaguely recalls thinking it was a bit odd to have a steel pan band playing Caribbean music in Zambia.

The total number officially evacuated between 23rd and 28th August amounted to sixty-two persons, one of whom was 'Arrow' our Soca king.

The Governor's canine companion Winston was due to leave Montserrat in late August to be flown to the UK for quarantine in advance of the Governor's own final departure later in September, but in view of the politically sensitive atmosphere around, and the presence of a hungry press, it was thought 'prudent' to cancel the arrangements. As a member of his staff observed "*We have to be so careful, it's like tap-dancing through a minefield*".

It would be very bad publicity to have the Governor's dog photographed as an 'evacuee', even though the dog's departure had been arranged weeks in advance and was entirely coincidental.

On the evening of the 30th August my husband was away at a late meeting, and my FCO houseguest and I were watching the BBC World News at 8.00 p.m.

Suddenly it was abruptly interrupted, with the shocking announcement that Princess Diana had been involved in a car accident in Paris.

According to the brief bulletin her escort, Dodi Al Fayed, had died and so had the driver. Princess Diana and her bodyguard were both injured and had been taken to hospital.

The circumstances surrounding the accident seemed confused. We were told that the car, taking Princess Diana and Dodi from the Ritz Hotel after an evening meal, was being driven at high speed through a tunnel when it apparently crashed into the side wall.

There is some suggestion that it was being 'pursued' by press in cars and on motorcycles. Three hours later, at 11.00 p.m. our time, the news came through that Princess Diana had suffered a heart attack and died from her injuries.

Everyone is in shock. Together with the rest of the world, people in Montserrat are stunned by the tragic news.

My houseguest borrowed a white shirt from my husband and my son's black tie, before reporting for duty at the Governor's Office. He was not sure of the official etiquette required, so he called Barbados for instructions, and to enquire whether there will be an official period of Court Mourning since Princess Diana is not now recognised as a 'Royal' personage after her divorce from Prince Charles.

Officially no-one seems to know quite how to behave, although I have been told there will be a Condolence Book at the Governor's Office for people to sign.

It's a bit battered and dusty. It was found at the back of a cupboard and had apparently been 'waiting' for several years for the death of the Queen Mother, but now to be used for Princess Diana.

Sometimes life is very sad.

25 - SEPTEMBER 1997

NEW GOVERNOR ARRIVES

On Monday 1st September, George Foulkes (Permanent Under-Secretary to DFID) and his entourage of around seven arrived on island in an attempt to mend fences after the notorious 'golden elephant' gaff by Labour Minister Clare Short.

In an effusive greeting he clasped the new Chief Minister David Brandt warmly by the hand and patted him heartily on the shoulder, pausing just short of a full bear hug of an embrace.

The usual whirlwind round trip of Montserrat followed, with a visit to HMS *Liverpool*, which had on board eight prisoners from Montserrat who are being taken to the Cayman Islands jail to serve out their sentences.

A quick tour of the new jetty area at Little Bay, with a brief visit to the fuel storage tanks, and a dash to Davy Hill in pouring rain to see the site of the proposed new housing followed. Afterwards the visitors were shown the hospital at St. John's and the Red Cross shelter at Cavalla Hill.

Much merriment was caused when an old lady, on being introduced to George Foulkes, gazed up at him and bluntly commented *"Aren't you fat!"*

The following day an official Joint Statement was issued from Government House which welcomed *"The categoric assurance given by Her Majesty's Government that it is committed to maintaining a viable community in the north of the island as long as it is safe for people to live there."*

The statement continued that Ms Short *"has today confirmed that essential facilities including health care, education, utilities and internal and external communications will be available for Montserratians who wish to remain on island."*

For those people who do not wish to remain on island, two choices are offered. The first is relocation to the UK with an initial right of entry for two years without restrictions. London is also offering to pay the 'transportation costs' of those needing help to relocate, presumably this translates as 'airfares'.

The second choice on offer is *'A Financial Assistance Package'* for those preferring to stay in the Caribbean. Though the actual amount of 'financial assistance' is yet to be determined. Item 3 on the Joint Statement specifies the preparation of a long-term Sustainable Development Plan for the island.

This is seen on island as a message of hope, and as if to reinforce the message a new ferry, the *'MV Antilles Express'*, started at Little Bay on the same day. This ferry is a catamaran from Guadeloupe which seats two hundred passengers. It will be a great improvement, with the journey from Montserrat to Antigua anticipated to take no more than an hour, and much more stable conditions.

Winston, the Governor's dog, will be one of the first passengers to travel on the new ferry, lovingly boxed for onward transportation to quarantine in the UK.

Friday 5th September turned out to be a very busy day, as a tropical storm heading in our direction was up-graded to hurricane status.

We were busy boarding up for a potential hit from Hurricane Erika when, during Friday afternoon, the Governor unexpectedly announced that the volcano was hotting-up again, and everyone south of Nantes Rives (which includes Salem) had to be out of the area by 8.00 p.m.

It seems the volcano is growing at a very fast rate, six to seven cu. metres per second compared with the average of two to three cu. metres, and it has reached a height of 3,280 ft. with an estimated 160 million cu. metres of 'goop'.

The MVO prognosis states *"The most likely outcome over the next six months remains that the activity will continue at similar or somewhat elevated levels"*.

Steve Sparks on behalf of the MVO has sent a thirteen page additional supplement to his 14th August 'hazard report' to the

Governor. The covering letter stresses concern that the Salem area remains occupied despite pleas to vacate.

With unfortunate timing we had decided to move into our new house that weekend, and I spent Friday with one eye on the volcano, running backwards and forwards between the two properties trying to board both villas against the possible onslaught of Hurricane Erika, while transferring our belongings from the old home to the new one, and hoarding food and water in case it was needed.

With the unpredictability of the volcano we have decided to crate up most of our possessions for shipping to the UK, planning to live spartanly out of four suitcases. So, as well as moving home and battening down the hatches, I managed to pack twenty-one boxes (and the car) for shipping to the UK.

It was on one of my trips between houses that I noticed, as I looked out across the sea, that our beautiful new ferry was disappearing fast over the horizon, and not in the direction of Antigua. Apparently it was intending to ride out the hurricane in Guadeloupe.

Poor Montserrat, our only means of escape had vanished and we were left alone to face the potential of two natural disasters simultaneously. It was a lonely and uncomfortable feeling.

But nature had sympathy for us. Hurricane Erika swept 125 miles to the north-northeast of Montserrat at 6.00 a.m. on Saturday morning, and although the sea was whipped into wild grey waves and the rain lashed down, we were not badly affected.

Tucked up tightly inside our new house, we watched Princess Diana's funeral being broadcast live from London, along with 2.5 billion others worldwide. Our weather outside seemed entirely in accord with the mournful mood.

As predicted the volcano did become active over that weekend, but nothing too violent. It sent several pyroclastic flows down the flanks and there was some damage down Belham Valley. Fortunately for us however, the strong winds circulating around Hurricane Erika took the resultant ash away from Montserrat, dumping it squarely on Antigua.

The Antiguan authorities are not used to dealing with ash from the volcano, and they called Montserrat in consternation, asking for ash masks, and saying they had closed schools, several nightspots and cancelled two American Airlines flights because of our erupting volcano.

A new hazard map has been issued. It is simple and unequivocal. The island has been dissected into three zones. The Exclusion Zone covers two-thirds of south and central Montserrat, from Nantes River in the west to Pelican Ghaut in the east, including Salem, Old Towne, Trant's and the airport.

A very narrow band called the Central Zone runs between Nantes River and Lawyers River and to my stunned amazement it now includes our new home at Woodlands. It also includes the Governor's Offices at McChesney's Estate but this is no consolation to me.

Apparently it is feared that this area could be vulnerable to a northwards-directed pyroclastic flow. It does seem as if each time we try to move away from the reach of the volcano into a 'safe' area, the scientists decide to move the danger zoning to include us again. All of us in the Central Zone have been given instructions to be prepared to leave at very short notice. I am very pleased I have only four suitcases now.

The third and final zone is the safe northern area, beyond Lawyers River, and this is considered suitable for both residential and commercial occupation.

The MVO have taken their own advice and moved from the site they have occupied in Old Towne for almost two years, to a large house in Mongo Hill, just north of the Centre Hills. Unfortunately they are no longer able to see the volcano directly, but they do have more rooms and safer working conditions for the scientists.

His Excellency Governor Frank Savage and his wife left Montserrat for good on the evening of 11th September. We Brits had our own low-key goodbye. Wine, with a traditional Montserrat 'goatwater' at McChesney's.

Only four women present, including the Governor's wife and myself, and the other two are themselves leaving within weeks. We were bombarded by 'thunder-bugs' that got in the drink and the goatwater, and we spent most of the evening flicking black flies off each other.

The official Government of Montserrat farewell to Governor Savage was held on the 10th September, with over one hundred guests, the majority being Montserratians. The three Chief Ministers who have served with the Governor during his term of office each gave a speech.

Reuben 'Twisty' Meade, Chief Minister during the beginning of the volcano crisis, hugged them both warmly as he said his farewell, but hours after their departure he was inciting his Salem constituents to march on the Governor's premises at McChesney's and Palmhurst with a view to occupying them.

He says he was driven into making this gesture by growing discontent about the discrepancies between the housing of expatriates and Montserratians.

On the street it is being claimed that some of the newly arriving unaccompanied males working in the Aid Management Office for the British Government have been allocated luxury villas and vehicles for personal use, paid for by the British Government, in stark contrast to Montserratians many of whom are still in shelters or sharing homes.

Unfortunately there is an element of truth in these allegations. Pre-volcano activity, British expatriates and their families working on island were given a ceiling to their rent allowance and lived, and worked, modestly alongside Montserratian neighbours. With accommodation very scarce, these old rules seem not to apply, and glaring anomalies have arisen, with some of the newly arriving British expatriate unaccompanied males (brought here to help with the volcano crisis) enjoying the splendid comfort of luxurious villas with swimming pools, and air-conditioned transport.

In an attempt to release tension an island stress-busting event was held at Gerald's on the 15th September. It was planned to coincide with a fund-raising spectacular for Montserrat being organised at the Royal Albert Hall in London by Sir George Martin.

We called our evening *'Many Happy Returns'* and we welcomed the return to the island of *'Climax'*, the first band ever to record at Sir George Martin's Air Studios in Montserrat. Performing alongside *'Climax'* were local artistes such as *'The Mighty Ash'* and a recently formed group called *'The Golden Elephants'*. It was a thoroughly wild night with an estimated 2,000 people really enjoying themselves.

Six days later the volcano erupted massively. An eruption similar to that of the terrifying 25th June event created pyroclastic flows down the flanks of the volcano, completely destroying the abandoned Tuitt's Village, and burning the now derelict terminal buildings at the old W.H. Bramble Airport.

These pyros heralded a return to the type of activity experienced at the beginning of August, but without any precursory hybrid warnings.

From the 22nd September a series of very alarming and yet completely awesome Vulcanian explosions began, with two to three a day at roughly nine-hour intervals. The resulting tremendous ash columns rose high into the bright blue sky. Writhing brown and grey and black towers of destruction which drifted malevolently northeast, covering all areas of Montserrat in fall-out.

Vulcanian eruption over our house 1997

On the 21st September, two-inch pumice was falling as far north as St. John's, in the apparently 'safe' northern zone of the island. We have been told that the new explosive activity is due to the gas rich content of the magma. The scientists are not sure why the explosions are continuing, but believe that groundwater from recent heavy rains associated with Hurricane Erika may be involved.

The activity at the volcano has caused a stampede to leave Montserrat. 961 Montserratians have now left on the Government relocation scheme, with over 3,000 'signed up' to go. To my surprise even Shirley has completed the necessary papers. They have asked me for advice and I have tried to be candid. Her husband says he would prefer to go to Birmingham rather than London because *"He doesn't like big cities"*.

What can I say? Personally I think they should remain in Montserrat, or go to the British Virgin Islands, where Shirley has a brother-in-law. It is such a difficult time for Montserrat and her people.

My Montserratian housekeeper Laura and her daughter Chari left for London on the 11th September. Laura admitted to me that she was 'scared', not knowing what she was going to, and with nowhere to live. But she was determined to leave, telling me that she wants Chari (who dreams of becoming a dentist) to have regular schooling. Laura's husband has remained in Montserrat, in one of the wooden family units recently constructed by the Government.

I gave her some clothes, and some advice, but otherwise I feel powerless. All I could suggest was that if she needs assistance in dealing with official UK forms and the accompanying bureaucratic red tape, she should go to the nearest Citizens Advice Bureau and ask for help.

Montserratians are ill-equipped to cope with the profusion of demands the UK will make on them, and they will need all the help they can get. Currently there is no welcome, or advice, being offered to evacuees when they arrive in London, although there are plans for something to be in place by the end of the month. But that will be too late for Laura.

The air is misty with ash the whole time now. It is being blown from trees, buildings and roads and we have to keep the windows tightly closed as we drive. It is like peering through fog and is very depressing to see even the north of Montserrat covered in a grey shroud.

The shelves are bare in Angelo's little wooden supermarket, and he says that no new provisions have been brought to the island for over two weeks. Rams Emdee Supermarket is on the wrong side of the Exclusion Zone, so I cannot shop there. He has been ordered to close and should only supply wholesale to other shops. But the owner of Rams has recently invested a great deal of money building this new supermarket, after his large Plymouth store was finally closed for business. Now he has been instructed to close again, so it is understandable that he is very reluctant to obey the authorities who believe that the presence of an open supermarket in the Exclusion Zone is encouraging people to go back to the unsafe area.

Our new home looks as if it has been sprayed with wet cement, and the steep drive is not negotiable, the wheels of the car cannot get traction on the slippery ash. Again and again we just roll up our sleeves, put on our ash masks, and shovel and hose a way through the ash.

The ritual of cleaning continues, and by the end of September the volcano had produced approximately twenty-five Vulcanian explosions and showed no signs of quitting.

Fortunately our villa is very small and newly built with tight fitting windows. Consequently it is easier to keep the ash out of the living area, and small enough to keep clean when the ash does invade.

Denzil came to install an air-conditioner in the bedroom. Denzil is a big, balding, loose-limbed man, who suffers from asthma, and while he was working at the house he had a mild asthma attack. We called Dr. Perkins to renew Denzil's inhaler prescription and discovered it was identical to one I had brought from the UK. With the immediate relief of the inhaler Denzil quickly recovered and after a rest (and a beer) he was back to normal.

Denzil tells me that his asthma attacks first began when he was fourteen and he endures on average one every six months. Normally they occur at night, and he can feel his heart *"Pounding fit to burst"* he says, and he can't breathe. He has installed a huge air-conditioner in his bedroom and sleeps without a pillow.

As a teenager he found that regular exercise and keeping his weight down helped to reduce the incidence of attacks, and by the time he was in his early twenties he had become one of Montserrat's top runners. He confessed that the volcano is leaving him *"Very stressed out"*. His home is in Salem, in the Exclusion Zone, but the authorities have erected road barriers and ordered the evacuation of Salem with a 6.00 a.m. to 6.00 p.m. curfew imposed.

Denzil says he has nowhere else to go and he is currently sleeping on the floor of his brother's office in Salem, but each night as he returns to the Exclusion Zone and tries to enter, he expects to be refused.

About twenty men have insisted on remaining in Salem despite the curfew, and they play dominoes and drink together each night. Denzil has refused to go into the portakabins at Look Out that have been assigned for the use of Salem residents, referring to them as *"containers"*.

"I'm not an animal to be put wherever the Governor decides I should go!" he told me. I asked him what he would really like and he replied *"A small, self-contained house"*. A house he can occupy alone. He thinks the wooden ones being built by the Government will blow away in a hurricane and he'd prefer his house to be concrete.

Montserrat's new Governor, Tony Abbott, went up to the Salem campus to see for himself the conditions under which the shelterees are living. He is very keen to get the ends together, and has made it a priority to clear the shelters as quickly as possible.

While he was there an argument broke out between two of the inmates over food vouchers and one allegedly attacked the other inflicting a nasty cut. The Governor himself called the ambulance, but it took over an hour to arrive and they say the man lost a lot of blood.

There is such a sense of desperation and defeat in Montserrat this month. Surely things can only get better?

26 - OCTOBER 1997

POPULATION DOWN TO 4,000

The house has been tightly shuttered and the new air conditioning unit installed by Denzil has been working overtime this month and the strong, nauseating smell of sulphur is in the air again.

On the 1st October we had two massive explosive eruptions of the volcano, one at 11.30 a.m. and one at 5.40 p.m. These were followed by a third eruption at 1.00 a.m. the following morning.

On each occasion we were blacked out as mud and pumice rained down and the curtain of ash swept north. Two thousand hard hats were requested for distribution to people in the 'safe' north.

We endured 76 eruptions before they ceased abruptly on the 21stOctober.

After each event we stoically set about trying to hose and shovel the worst of the mess away before the next eruption, but it was a tough and thankless task.

Driving conditions were appalling and extremely hazardous with 'white-out' conditions from re-circulating ash. We prayed for rain, which when it finally came in a thunderous deluge on the 14th October, only served to create a treacherous and muddy skating rink. However it did the job of clearing the air, the foliage, the roofs and the roads again and giving us a brief respite from the ash.

It is fascinating to watch the symbiotic relationship between land and weather. The volcano gives one, two or three great big blows that cover us in thick ash and pumice, and we groan and wear our masks and attempt the big clean-up. Then along comes the rain and cleans us out, washes us down, and helps us to feel fresh again. A few hours later and another 'boom', followed by further dumping of ash, and then if we are lucky the rain comes again. And so it goes on.

Sometimes the gap between an ashin' and a good rain can be several days, and it is during these periods that we get really disheartened, dusty and dejected. The ash blows around in the air and gets into everything including hair, lungs, eyes, and house. Even the sheets on the bed feel gritty.

During October Sir Kenneth Calman's medical report *'Health and Health Services Implications of the Montserrat Crisis'* has been in circulation around the island. The report is critical of the island's healthcare system. It also states somewhat alarmingly *"High levels of volcanic ash containing crystalline silica are present in many occupied parts of the island"* and advises us to wear our masks.

While I was reading the health article published in *'The Montserrat Reporter'*, Salo arrived to work in our garden. A thankless task, but he was attempting to strim some of the longer grass and as a result residual ash was flying up into the air and he was enveloped in a thick cloud.

When I offered him an ash mask he laughed and refused to wear it, assuring me that in his opinion the ash was not a health hazard. But he took the proffered mask, saying he would use it next time he needed to *"Paint the varnish!"* In his opinion inhaling varnish is hazardous, volcanic ash is not.

But most people seem to be heeding the warnings about the dangers of ash inhalation. When I went shopping at Angelo's (having heard that a boat with fresh produce had just arrived) it was interesting to see that all the shoppers had dust masks dangling around their necks as they stampeded towards the fresh lettuce, broccoli and celery.

One of the girls from the MVO has been given the task of travelling around the island after each eruption collecting ash samples for analysis from various areas. I have been 'bagging' my own samples and I now have quite a sizeable collection.

For interest I have been eavesdropping on the scientists' conversations on the short-wave radio. It is quite fun to listen to them when an ashin' is in progress. Voices from around the island give on the spot descriptions of what is happening. Pops might call in from 'Observatory North' saying he can see the 'blow' but nothing has arrived with him. Then Simon's voice comes on air saying that there is light ash falling in Woodlands, and moments later correcting this to say there are small pumice fragments, adding imperturbably *"It's getting pretty dark here now"*.

Another scientist driving on the road clicks in, and I can hear the swish, swish, crunch as his windscreen wipers desperately try to give him vision as he struggles in his car towards MVO North.

"I can't see anything" he reports anxiously *"it's raining mud and ash"*. The others tell him to take care and pull over and wait it out. Then Pops comes back on to say that now he is experiencing fall-out as the cloud moves across the north of the island. *"It's getting dark here now"*.

Apparently the magma being forced up at the volcano now is dark grey and 'blocky'. At almost 200 ft. higher than the old Chances Peak (the highest point in Montserrat before the activity began) the old dome is very unstable and thought likely to collapse at any time, particularly with the new dome pushing out and up. There are currently swarms of volcano-tectonic earthquakes taking place.

The explosions also caused pyroclastic flows to spill down the sides of the Soufrière Hills, enlarging the deltas in the sea at White's and Tar River. The Tar River petticoat now measures 1.5 km from left to right, and extends 800 metres out to sea, and the volume of the fan has been calculated at around 16 million cubic metres.

The unsettled weather that helped to clear the island of ash brought breakers rolling in to the jetty and Little Bay was closed several times. On one occasion nothing could dock for three days, and I watched as a tug pulling a barge chugged up and down for two days off the coast, waiting for an opportunity to off-load its cargo.

The rough seas created problems for the ferry; it broke two of its mooring cables as it attempted to come alongside with over 250 people returning from a day trip to Antigua. The ferry has been offering weekend special price return fares to Antigua and these have been very popular. Many people have taken the opportunity to shop in St. John's, returning to Montserrat laden with bulging bags.

The facilities at Little Bay are very crude, with a makeshift Customs shed and no method of moving baggage from the dock, it has to be hauled by hand by the passengers.

Customs are being accused of stubbornness and insensitivity. On one occasion they made passengers open every single bag. While they waited in the dark in a shuffling queue, the volcano erupted and as ash and pumice rained down on them pandemonium broke out.

Governor Abbott and his wife decided to try out the ferry to Antigua for themselves, since there have been so many complaints. Unfortunately on the return journey, just as the Governor was dozing off, the Captain decided the swells at Port Little Bay were *"Too high to allow docking"* and he turned the boat around and headed back to Antigua, where everyone had to try and find accommodation for the night. Not an auspicious experiment for our new Governor and his wife.

Shortly after her arrival on Montserrat the Governor's wife invited seven of us to join her for afternoon tea. The volcano had been blowing well that morning, and everywhere the air was full of ash. There is only one air-conditioned room at 'Palmhurst' and that is the main bedroom. So, not being one to stand on ceremony, the Governor's wife ushered us into their bedroom where we settled ourselves down for cups of tea and slices of cake.

I was reminded of the coffee morning I had attended at Government House shortly after my arrival in Montserrat on 18th July 1995, the day the volcano rumbled back into life after 350 years of dormancy.

The volcano is driving Montserratians away. In a period of four days at the beginning of October three hundred people left the island. On the 7th October figures showed that 1360 Montserratians had taken up the Voluntary Evacuation offer and relocated, and by the end of the month over 4,000 had registered for relocation. 74% of these have requested the UK as their final destination.

A hasty census of island residents was conducted during October, and it is estimated that the population is now down to 4,000. A drop of 6,000 residents since the volcanic activity began.

But while Montserratians are leaving, the island is being swamped with the arrival of new British Government expatriate personnel. There has been a seemingly constant stream of pubescent young men, nubile young women, and deaf veterans arriving on an almost daily basis, appointed in London for short, unaccompanied, contracts on island.

A head count has given us a total of over fifty recently arriving expats. It isn't always easy to identify the work functions of the new recruits. Individual areas of expertise seem to be very narrow, but the subjects covered are legion and include logistics, statistics, economics, psychiatry, social development, town planning and even one consultant who has been brought to Montserrat to 'allocate' the new housing units at Davy Hill to shelterees.

A high proportion of these new arrivals are quickly showing symptoms indicating they are temperamentally unsuited to the stress of living with an erupting volcano.

Hives, headaches, short tempers, an inability to sustain normal office hours, over-indulgence in alcohol, sexual liaisons with married colleagues, unexplained absences, weekly trips to Antigua, and other similar behavioural patterns have quickly become evident in several of the new staff.

This is not helping to calm the already strained and sensitive relationship that currently exists between the British Government and the people of Montserrat.

It is ironic that DFID have chosen this moment to tell the few Technical Co-operation Officers employed by the British Government since before the eruption in July 1995, (and who have been experiencing the volcano side by side with their Montserratian neighbours for over two years) that they can no longer stay in Montserrat on 'accompanied' status. This means that wives are being ordered to leave the island. If TCO's desire to remain in Montserrat it must be on bachelor status.

This decision is not easy to understand and has created further stress for couples like Bill and Marjory who have given so much help and support to Montserrat over the past few years.

Fortunately for my husband he is no longer affected by DFID decisions and I can stay here with him as long as I wish.

While my husband feels he can still contribute to the crisis in Montserrat, then we shall remain.

But I wonder just how long we can continue to survive this strange and stressful way of life.

We are planning to return to Sussex for Christmas for a couple of weeks of sanity with the family, and to breathe some cold, clean, fresh air.

27 - NOVEMBER 1997

PRINCE ANDREW RETURNS

Looters are entering the Exclusion Zone and breaking into shops and houses in Plymouth. The police launch chugged down the coastline to investigate and caught a boat (registered in Guadeloupe and reported stolen) pulling away from Bunkum Bay.

On board were three men, identified as escaped prisoners from St. Lucia, and a large quantity of items they had taken from shops and homes in Montserrat. The men were arrested and put in a cell at Salem but almost escaped again. They were discovered levering the hinge pins out of the cell door.

The looters are often imaginative, but with limited intelligence. The police arrested a man who was pushing, of all unlikely items, a wheelchair out of Plymouth. The wheelchair was laden with stolen electrical items. The police simply followed the tracks he had left in the ash.

In another incident, an intruder was discovered ransacking the abandoned Police HQ in Plymouth and helping himself to police equipment.

'Dem say' on the street that it is possible to order an item, and it will be stolen, subject to a small 'commission'.

The volcano is behaving badly again and on 5th November 'Starlight' night (Bonfire night to me) the air was full of ash. We were told that the hybrid seismograph readings were 'clipping' and it was implied that *'the big one'* was imminent. We waited apprehensively for our very own fireworks but thankfully the evening passed without incident and we were spared volcanic pyrotechnics.

The 'Three Wise Men' in London who help to advise the Governor on the volcano have stated that it is very dangerous and completely unpredictable. We are being told that the volcano has entered *"a new and dangerous phase"*. It seems that during the October explosive eruptions, the instruments on island recorded the highest seismicity from a volcano ever. A new world record, we were informed.

Residents of Salem who had only just been allowed to return to their homes and businesses, were ordered out of Salem yet again, and unmanned barriers erected. But as before, the young men in Salem are refusing to leave, in spite of repeated attempts to persuade them. They believe they understand the mountain better than the scientists and will know when they are in danger.

Reuben 'Twisty' Meade and John Osborne, both ex-Chief Ministers of Montserrat, walked with the Salem men to Palmhurst, the Governor's home in Palm Loop. The Governor came out to speak to them but refused to discuss specifics with Reuben while he was 'mob-handed' and he requested that Reuben meet him the following day at a more suitable venue, to discuss grievances.

The use of the expression 'mob-handed' stung the Salem men to the core. *"We are not a mob!"* they shouted. The following day *'The Montserrat Reporter'* described it as a *'maladroit remark'* and in one-inch headlines ran the banner *'Governor Abbott Insults Montserrat'*. The subsequent article described the men as *'a bustling crowd'*, *'an agitated crowd'* but certainly not a *'mob'*.

But the Governor has managed to reach a compromise, and it is agreed that people can go back into parts of the southern Exclusion Zone during 'windows of opportunity' so that they can collect their belongings, furniture etc.

Labour and transport will be provided and entry into the Exclusion Zone will be strictly controlled and carefully supervised, with only ten persons a trip. Also the controversial food voucher system has been scrapped, and now needy families will be given cheques to spend how they wish.

The night before the demonstration the Governor hosted a small dinner party at Palmhurst. It was to say farewell to Frank Hooper, outgoing Commissioner of Police. The guests included the Attorney General, Head of Administration and one or two of Frank's friends. The meal was simple, potato soup, pork with stuffing, roast potatoes, broccoli and carrots. For dessert we had peppermint and chocolate chip ice. It was a rather stiff and formal affair, and I was told afterwards that all the laughter seemed to be coming from our end of the table.

By contrast we attended a very relaxed and informal buffet lunch on 22nd November as guests of Chief Minister David 'Heavy Roller' Brandt, in the presence of HRH Duke of York. Prince Andrew had taken time out of a personal holiday to call into Montserrat for two days, as he had promised to do during his first Official visit earlier this year.

There were twenty-seven guests at the buffet lunch, including Father Larry (who delivered a very emotional Grace), Sister Ann, Carol and Cedric Osborne, local architect Alfred Dyer, local builder King Lee, Frankie Michael as head of Emergency Operations Centre, and Horatio Tuitt (newly appointed to the Emergency Department).

There was a noticeable absence of politicians, with none present except the Chief Minister himself. The only senior Civil Servant around the table was Eugene Skerritt who is his Permanent Secretary.

Our host David Brandt gave a short speech, and sweeping his arms around the small room at McChesney's where we had gathered, he announced *"These people here are the salt of the earth, the ones that are keeping Montserrat going"*.

Prince Andrew was at what Rose calls *"the people level"* and in a jovial mood. The conversation was chatty and the company convivial. Prince Andrew arrived dressed casually in fatigues and amid much laughter regaled us with several amusing anecdotes.

He told us of a recent Ministry of Defence briefing. The team had been discussing the possibility of Montserrat suffering a catastrophic or cataclysmic volcanic eruption. Prince Andrew had thought they were the same thing, and demanded a definition. He was informed that after a catastrophic eruption *"You wake up on the island, but it's in bits around you"* whereas after a cataclysmic eruption *"You wake up in bits on another island!"*

I was a little apprehensive that I would slurp my soup or splat ketchup into the Royal lap, but I need not have worried. The buffet was idiot proof and extremely simple, with neither soup nor ketchup. A large communal bowl of minced lamb tastefully garnished with a crown of bones, another of minced chicken, a plate of sliced tinned ham, a dish of diced tomatoes, a second of potato salad and a third of chopped lettuce.

Rubbing elbows we lined up to self-service scoop. Alan, a strict vegetarian, contented himself with a small roll and chopped lettuce. My husband found himself at the end of the line, by which time the minced lamb resembled an abandoned carcass savaged by starving vultures.

We were treated to one glass of wine each, but the Duke of York declined, preferring to drink a glass of bottled water, which he later followed with a lemon tea.

I was talking to Father Larry while we waited for the Duke of York to arrive. Unusually, Father Larry was in his 'uniform' and he looked very smart in black shirt, dog collar and light grey suit. He said he couldn't find his shirt at first and had panicked, thinking he had mislaid it.

He has been relocated so many times that all his things are in a great muddle. He still does his paperwork inside his van, filling in forms and such, but he has recently been given rooms in a house which used to be the home of the Anglican Minister.

"Very ecumenical!" said Father Larry cheerfully.

The Anglican Minister, Father Larry tells me, left in a hurry. He only lasted a month. Shortly after his arrival he woke to hear pumice falling on his roof, and he saw the trail of cars heading north and concluded we must be evacuating the island, and the poor man gathered up his belongings and fled. He left Montserrat and he hasn't returned. Father Larry feels a bit guilty, saying he really should have explained things a bit better and warned him what to expect.

Father Larry had spent the morning before our Royal lunch up on the roof of the villa they have taken over for the Catholic School, with a trowel and a bucket cleaning ash out of the gutters. He says he was so nervous he kept looking at his watch to make sure he wouldn't be late.

The last time he went on to the roof to clean it, the lad who was supposed to be holding the ladder wandered away and didn't return. Father Larry had to wait for almost an hour before a passer-by walking her dog came to his rescue. She thought it was very funny to see the priest stuck on his roof.

I did suggest that Father Larry might like to change his vocation and come and clean our gutters too. The gutters collect inches of weighty ash and have to be cleaned out regularly. It is a real problem for us all.

We employed Llewellyn to clean out our gutters last time. He arrived at 6.30 a.m. and clumped around on the roof for five hours with hose, broom, bucket and trowel. He had just finished when the skies opened and a torrential downpour flushed, gurgling and splashing, through the clean gutters.

During his brief visit to Montserrat, Prince Andrew flew over the volcano in the Temsco helicopter, landing briefly on the abandoned W.H. Bramble Airport runway at Trant's.

On his last visit, eight months ago, Prince Andrew had been able to drive into the evacuated capital of Plymouth, where he stood on the dock and talked to the stevedores before climbing down to look at Fort Ghaut. That whole area is now entombed under several feet of ash, and down at the waterfront only the top of the red phone box is visible. Prince Andrew must have noticed a dramatic and tragic difference.

Prince Andrew met Peter Edwards, who was evacuated two years ago and has lived in a shelter ever since. He was just moving into one of the new houses constructed at Davy Hill for evacuees when Prince Andrew arrived to look round.

There is only a mattress on the floor, but Peter is thrilled to be in his own home at last. Prince Andrew went from room to room checking everything. He even flushed the toilet *"And it works"* he reported triumphantly!

There are 742 people currently in shelters and 41% are single, non-elderly. On the 6th November, thirty-five 'special needs' people, mainly sick and elderly, left Montserrat accompanied by thirty-one relatives on a special flight to the UK. Some of the patients are confused and frail, and there are mixed feelings about their removal from Montserrat.

According to a social survey conducted by the Statistics Department of the Ministry of Finance and Economic

Development, there were some 3,609 Montserratian residents on island on 30th November (including those temporarily absent) in 1,599 households. Over a quarter of these have not had to relocate their homes. 64% of people currently in work do the same job as before relocation.

The House of Commons Select Committee Report was issued in November. In something of an understatement they confessed that there was a *"less than happy relationship"* between the UK Government and the Government of Montserrat.

They recommended a *"frank and impartial report"* be prepared by HMG into the whole affair. Clare Short has expressed particular regret concerning her off-the-cuff remark implying that *"They would be asking for golden elephants next"*.

However the Report did specify that £45.8 million has already been committed by DFID to Montserrat, making our island the second largest recipient of UK Aid after Bangladesh.

The Committee were *"Amazed"* that no comprehensive survey of the population has yet taken place and urged immediate action. They also recommended a single off-island evacuation plan providing for a coordinated regional response, and advised a *'simulated exercise'*.

The Report continues *"The north of Montserrat is not perfectly safe, merely significantly safer than elsewhere in the island. At present all planning and commitment of funds must take account of the possibility that the north itself might have to be evacuated."*

So here we are, now we being told that even our 'safe' north is no longer safe. If this is indeed an accurate assessment of the situation, why are we all still here?

28 - DECEMBER 1997

BOXING DAY LATERAL BLAST

December began innocently enough, with Christmas activities getting underway early. During the first week I helped the Governor's wife with a School Christmas party at Palmhurst.

It was a trial run for a much larger party organised for the 17th December, at which all the island's 169 primary school children (currently in the wooden buildings at Brades) were invited to attend.

We had 95 very excited children having a thoroughly good time. It was a thunderously noisy and fun party with Governor Abbott making a very amiable Father Christmas, a role normally fulfilled by Father Larry. This time Father Larry was allowed to enjoy the party as a spectator, watching the proceedings and eating ice cream with the teachers.

We played Musical Chairs and Pass the Parcel. Pass the Parcel proved very popular and great 'ripping' fun, with some of the youngsters completely disregarding the rules and shredding several layers at once.

The game Simon Says went on interminably because everyone was so good at it. But mostly the children seemed to just enjoy dancing to the music playing on the tapes.

During December HMS *Newcastle* arrived on a visit and the crew did their best to organize parties and fun for the island. A group of approximately two hundred adults were invited on board (no children and no-one over sixty) and we sailed completely round the island. A malicious rumour circulated that it was actually a trial evacuation exercise. I was so pleased to have been invited!

Fortunately the sea was unusually calm when the small ferry took us across to HMS *Newcastle*. We had to wait until both platform and ferry levelled in the swell, and on the command 'jump' we were launched from the rear and grabbed from the front by two lusty sailors who safely plucked and dumped each individual onto the small metal platform beside the gangplank.

On our 'cruise' it was interesting to see the vast new deltas of flat land caused by the pyroclastic deposits that had erupted from the mountain and which fanned out into the sea at Plymouth, O'Garros and Tar River.

As the ship passed offshore in front of Plymouth, we ran through a blanket of smelly sulphurous smog that sat heavily over the mountain and stretched out in a thick ribbon across the sea. We all complained of grit in our eyes.

While HMS *Newcastle* was visiting, their Lynx helo was used to send a team into the Exclusion Zone around Harris to search for a man reportedly tied to a tree. It seems that the man had been discovered looting a neighbour's property in Harris. The neighbour had arrived unexpectedly, caught him, and tied him to a tree, before returning to the safe zone and informing the police.

The helicopter had trouble locating the man. *"Which tree?"* they repeatedly asked, getting more exasperated as they flew backwards and forwards across the area. They finally found him, rescued him, and delivered him to hospital.

During the first few days of December, when the volcano appeared to be quiet, the MVO agreed to allow people into the Exclusion Zone on the condition they went under official escort. Within hours of the information being broadcast over one hundred applications for passes had been received.

Some individuals, keen to make the most of the window of opportunity, turned up at the police barrier with lorries and a crew of men, ready and willing to escort themselves into the Exclusion Zone. They were most indignant when they were prevented from passing through and told they could only proceed with an official escort.

People gave various reasons to the authorities for wanting to enter the danger zone. ZJB Radio Montserrat said they needed to go to their old studios in Plymouth to collect some Christmas tapes that had been left behind in the scramble to evacuate. Rams Emdee supermarket wished to bring out crates of beer and soft drinks that had been left in their Plymouth store. One individual went into Plymouth and returned with four lengths of pipe he said he needed urgently. Others wanted to bring out their fridges, ovens, and beds.

Shortly after the visits began a dome collapse over Galways *"with only seconds warning"* occurred. It did not deter the caravan of people wishing to go into the Exclusion Zone. But some of us, with the tragedy of 25th June still strong in our memories, have expressed grave misgivings about these forays into the danger zone.

When part of Gages Wall collapsed and a pyroclastic flow unexpectedly came over the top, the MVO maintained that it was *"too dangerous"* to go in and the escorted trips were immediately suspended.

The scientists were right to be cautious. During the week before Christmas the hybrid earthquakes recorded at the MVO increased in number and intensity. By midnight on Christmas Day the earthquakes had merged into a continuous signal, clipping the edges of the drum, and at 3.00 a.m. on Boxing Day there was a massive collapse of the dome.

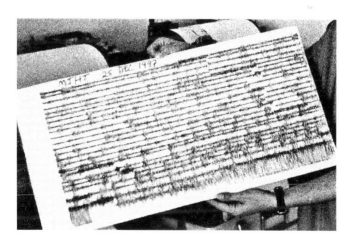

Print-out of Seismicity on 25th December 1997

The dome had been growing behind Chances Peak and was 400 ft. higher than the peak, a new record. Galways Wall, on the southwest side of the volcano, was unstable and collapsed. A large landslide had occurred at Galways Wall and simultaneously a vast pyroclastic flow with a destructive surge travelled down White River Valley. It was the first lateral blast to occur at the Soufrière Hills Volcano.

Part of Galways Wall and approximately 55 million cubic metres of dome material shot down the flanks of the volcano and into the sea. Travelling at 250-300 km per hour it took less than a minute to slice a 7 km wide arc of devastation across southern Montserrat.

A delta 2 km wide spilled into the sea causing a small tsunami to roll along the coast, smacking into the jetty at Old Road Bay and rising up across the golf course before receding back again.

The horizontal swathe of destruction stretched from Kinsale to O'Garros. In a matter of moments the two evacuated villages of St. Patrick's and Morris on the southwest side of Montserrat had vanished. They had, quite literally, been blasted out of the landscape.

It was at least five times larger than the previous largest eruption and was the most intense so far. Lightning, two explosions and a roaring sound were heard, with the ash cloud rising over 14 km into the air.

The vastness, and unexpected violence of this eruption with its destructive force, has frightened us all and reminds us how vulnerable life is in Montserrat. The scientists tell us that the eruption was bigger than that of Mt. Pelée in 1902, which took the lives of 29,000 people in Martinique.

At the moment the island feels rudderless. The House of Commons Select Committee Report has created an opportunity for a thorough pruning of the British Aid delivery system to Montserrat, but it has yet to be put in place. However, we hear via the grapevine that DFID is to leave the equation, and EMAD (the emergency wing) is also being wound-up. Instead a specially created 'Montserrat Unit' is to be set up in London to administer both policy and budget. It is hoped this new arrangement will speed up Aid and create an improved working relationship between the British and Montserrat Governments.

On the 9th December we learned that 2,305 Montserratians have now left the island on the special relocation scheme, while the total number who have registered on the scheme is now 4,396.

Stanley is one of those to recently register. He finally decided to accept the offer of a Caribbean 'compensation' package, and during December he left for Trinidad. Although he lived in Trinidad as a young boy, he has returned only once in over forty years. He has started drinking heavily again and I worry that his cash compensation package of EC$10,000 will make him a comparatively rich man in Trinidad, and an easy target for unscrupulous friends. I suspect the money will vanish quickly and Stanley will be back in Montserrat within a few weeks, destitute.

Some of those who have left Montserrat are doing very well for themselves in their new lives away from the volcano. One Montserratian we met in Antigua told us he was *'delighted'* with his Caribbean relocation package, and beamed with gratitude at the unexpected opportunity he had been given to better himself.

He had sent his two children to England to live with relatives, and had bought himself a new car with the money. He was now a taxi driver in Antigua and he told us it would not be long before he could buy himself some land and build a house. He added coyly that he was also still receiving food vouchers from 'the Government'.

Our old friend Alfred flew back to Montserrat for a two-week visit. He had been so nervous and apprehensive about leaving that it was good to see how well he had settled in England. He has been given a flat and is expecting to move into a house shortly. His boys are settled into school, and his wife is studying.

But Alfred himself can't get a job. He returned to see whether it would be possible to pick up some construction work in Montserrat, perhaps leaving his family in England. But in the end he has decided to return to his family, and he caught the flight back in time to spend Christmas with them in England.

We left the island for the UK and our own family Christmas during the last week of December. We spent two nights in Antigua before our London flight, hoping to relax a little in the Caribbean sunshine.

It was early evening and dusk was settling in as we gathered up our suitcases and took them along to the front desk reception, ready for the taxi to Antigua airport.

We returned to our hotel room to collect the 'carry-ons' and our coats, and I was sitting on the bed waiting for my husband to come out of the bathroom, when from the corner of my eye I thought I saw the hotel room door slowly opening.

Thinking it must have come unlatched, I stood up and reached for the handle and registered with surprise a black hand gripping the handle from the other side. My gaze travelled from the black hand up the arm, to a masked face, then swiftly to the other hand, which was holding a revolver levelled straight at me. Behind the first intruder stood a second, unarmed but also masked.

You never know until it happens how you will react to a situation like this. Strangely, my initial response was to laugh out loud. I thought it must be some sort of practical joke. A Christmas charade perhaps, performed on unsuspecting guests as they prepared to leave the hotel. But I quickly realised this was no joke.

My husband emerged from the bathroom as the gunman was pushing me backwards with the barrel of the revolver pressed firmly against my chest.

The intruders did not speak. I was propelled backwards towards the open bathroom door. I hesitated a moment and the gun was waved in my face. I was pushed roughly into the bathroom and thrust against the back wall, the gun jammed into my ribs, just above my heart.

The other masked intruder had grabbed my husband and was pushing him backwards into the bathroom with me.

The atmosphere felt charged, threatening and unpredictable, but I was surprised at how cool and rational my husband and I appeared to be, almost detached. My mind was sifting rapidly through various possibilities. I debated the advisability of tackling the gunman, a knee jerk in the groin perhaps, but thought better of it. I remembered once being advised that in such situations it is wisest to hand over your cash, or whatever they want, since resistance provokes attack.

I learned later that my husband was having exactly the same thoughts, but he was also fighting a strong masculine inclination to 'have a go'. His main concern was the fact that I had a gun pressed against my chest and any sudden move by him, several feet away, would most likely result in the gun being fired. A risk he was not prepared to take.

He was desperate to diffuse the situation. He began an amiable non-stop chatter in a casual, familiar, confident manner with the two masked men.

"Hey Man!" *"What's all this about, man?"* *"Beautiful island this!"* *"You don't want to spoil it man!"* *"You don't want to do anything stupid man!"* *"You want money, hey?"* *"We're tourists, just leaving!"* *"Spent all our money!"* *"No money left man!"* *"See, look, the taxi is waiting to take us to the airport!"*

He kept it flowing, but he was getting no response from the two men, and it was then I realised they were both high on drugs.

Another useful piece of advice flashed into my mind as the gunman frisked me for bracelet, necklace and watch, and that was *"try and remember a description"*.

I tried to concentrate. Both men were masked and both wore hats. One had a black peaked plastic cap and the other, rather incongruously I thought, wore a black straw hat. The gunman wore baggy knee-length canvas shorts. I remembered being told to look at shoes. A thief will change his clothes but rarely bothers to change his shoes. The gunman was wearing black and white plastic soled sneakers, beach shoes. Unusual, the sort to wear when wading out across stones to a boat.

I looked at the revolver. You don't forget a revolver when it is so close to your face. I noticed that part of the barrel was worn to shiny bare metal, presumably the result of years of handling.

The men were very jumpy but determined. My husband reached into his back pocket and drew out a folded wad of dollars.

"Here!" he offered the money to the second man. *"That's all we've got left."* *"It's our taxi money!"* *"Take it and go."* His tone suddenly changed, from amenable to authoritative.

"Go!" he ordered, then added *"Our taxi's waiting and they'll be coming for us any minute, go now while you can!"*

The accomplice seemed ready to obey and moved towards the door, but the gunman who had snatched the money from my husband's hand bent to count it. He spoke for the first time.

"Not enough!" he shouted angrily, and waved the gun wildly at us. I realised that the purpose of the robbery was to get cash to buy more drugs, and what we had given him was not enough.

We were pushed back into the bathroom once again and the gunman, still holding the revolver in his hand, grabbed my left hand and tried to pull off my wedding and engagement rings, struggling to get them off my finger. Both rings refused to come over my knuckle, but still the gunman struggled. I worried the gun might discharge accidentally. Meanwhile his accomplice was tugging at my husband's watch.

In a forlorn attempt to appeal to any sensitivity the gunman might possess I said pathetically

"You wouldn't take a woman's wedding ring, would you? What would your mother say?" and for added effect I lied *"this was my grandmother's engagement ring. It is the only thing I have to remember her by!"*

I am not sure whether this plea worked but the second man looked at me and spoke for the first time.

"Leave dem, leave dem" he ordered the gunman, and turned for the door.

But at that moment he noticed my handbag lying on the bed. He reached forward and tipped the contents roughly onto the floor. My purse tumbled out and he lunged for it. Inside he found a bundle of notes, which he grabbed. The gunman dropped my hand and backed away, he'd seen my husband's camera case on the bed. Inside were our airline tickets and credit cards. He flipped through the credit cards and seemed undecided what to do.

"No good to you man, no good at all!" said my husband, and as if in response the gunman tossed them onto the floor.

"Whah dis?" he demanded, holding up the battery for the video camera.

"Just a battery, no good to you man!" repeated my husband. The gunman was just about to throw it on the floor with the cards but suddenly changed his mind.

"Fingaprins!" he said triumphantly, waving the battery in our faces *"Fingaprins!"* he said again, and he put it in his pocket. My husband's change of tone to a more authoritative one seemed to be

having some effect. He ordered them to leave again, and almost without thinking they moved to obey.

"Go! Go! Go!" My husband repeated urgently *"I hear the taxi, quick"*. The accomplice opened the door and as he did so he took off his mask, ready to leave, then he turned to stare at us, seemingly unaware that we had now seen his face. But he didn't seem to realise what he had done. The gunman moved to the door, and almost as an afterthought he casually picked up my jacket from the bed before running out of the room.

The door had no sooner closed behind them, than my husband sprang towards it and wrenched it open, taking the steps down the stairs which led to the beach two at a time.

The men had stopped running, they were now sauntering towards the bright lights of the beach bar and restaurant a few yards away. They tried the door of another room, and my husband vaulted the low restaurant wall and shouted to the barman to call the police before giving chase as the men suddenly sprinted away into the darkness of the beach. It was useless, they quickly disappeared into the bushy undergrowth beside the sand and were lost in the darkness of the night.

Our taxi had arrived and was waiting to take us to the airport. We were already late for check-in for our London flight. The barman, who seemed more shaken than we were, gave us the money to pay for the fare.

By the time we reached the airport three of Antigua's CID were waiting to interview us. We discovered our overnight flight to London was delayed for two hours, and we spent the time sitting up in the bar with the CID, giving them our statements about the armed robbery.

Eventually the flight was called and eight hours later, in the early hours of the following morning, we arrived at Gatwick Airport. No coat, no money, no watch, tired and still a little shaken, but it was great to be back home in time for Christmas.

We consider ourselves very fortunate, it could have been a lot worse. We heard that the week following our robbery, a barman at the opposite end of the beach had been robbed, then beaten up by three armed men and was in a bad way in hospital.

29 - JANUARY 1998

NOWHERE TO GO

The British Airways flight from London to Antigua after our Christmas break was delayed for four hours on the runway at Gatwick Airport. We sat on board and waited. Something to do with a baggage door not closing properly they said.

Unfortunately, because of this delay, we had to overnight in Antigua before going on to Montserrat, something we would have preferred to avoid after our armed robbery experience last month.

We were pleased to board the morning Temsco helo for Montserrat. We put on the obligatory orange life jacket for the twenty-minute flight, and settled ourselves in beside fellow passengers Barry (who is currently our Commissioner of Police in Montserrat), a young lady burdened down with groceries and gifts, and a gentleman who told us he was a 'banana consultant'.

The final passenger was a large, overweight American who had to be levered in from behind because his legs *"couldn't climb"* and had collapsed under him.

Barry had his wrist in plaster and so I completed his Immigration forms for him. He had broken his wrist, he explained, as a result of a fall while he was on his way to the Aid Management Office Christmas party. *"Not"* he insisted *"as I was leaving the party"*. The pain had sent Barry to an orthopaedic specialist in Antigua, who looked at the X-rays and said it was very definitely broken and sealed his wrist into a fibre-glass cast that has not to be removed for six weeks.

The helicopter is often used for medivacs and we had two more during January. A heavy ashfall from the volcano shortly before the second medivac meant the Fire Brigade had to be called to quickly hose down a landing area for the helo.

A man had accidentally cut off his finger with a circular saw, and had eight hours to get it sewn back on. Although his hand was heavily bandaged the man did not seem in any pain, and he joyfully demonstrated the fact by lifting his arm up and down to prove it.

Unfortunately the private clinic in Antigua that was supposed to meet and treat him, refused to do so, saying they are owed money by the Government of Montserrat. So the patient was sent by taxi to the General Hospital where he was treated as an emergency admission.

The Boxing Day blast has made everyone nervous, and the volcano shows no signs of slowing down. It is still burping volumes of ash on a daily basis, much of which seems to be falling in the far north.

The 'hole' created by the Boxing Day eruption is rapidly filling as the volcano enters a new dome building phase, extruding now at a rate of 8 cu. metres per second.

On the 21st January the Governor's Office and the Government of Montserrat issued a joint statement to the public, although later the Chief Minister denied that it had received his approval. We read the notice with mounting incredulity and disbelief. It stated that all those residents in the buffer area of Zone 3 are being recommended to move out.

The release is quite specific in its advice.

Firstly *"No-one should live in the Salem area or any other part of the exclusion zone"*.

Secondly *"People are strongly recommended to leave the north Olveston/Woodlands area. Anyone deciding to remain should be fully aware that they are at greater risk from volcanic activity than those living north of Lawyers River."*

The release continues *"Those living in area 3 should relocate and fully understand the risks of not doing so."*

Zone 3 relocate? Where to? Surely there must be some mistake? Approximately 800 people live and work in this narrow zone, including ourselves and many of the Government offices. Are we being asked to leave the island?

The Exclusion Zone has been effectively re-drawn across Lawyer's Mountain, making two-thirds of Montserrat a no-go area. This leaves approximately ten square miles. Deduct the uninhabitable mountains of Silver Hills in the far north and Centre Hills and in effect we have approximately four square miles of residential space for 3,400 people.

My neighbours are close to despair and simply do not know what to do.

People do not remain in the 'buffer' Zone 3 from choice. There is, quite simply, nowhere else for us to go. The recommendation not only applies to us, it also applies to the Royal Bank of Canada, the Post Office, the Governor's Office, the Aid Management Office, the Chief Minister's Office and many others.

Our current home is 500 metres from the border drawn between areas 2 and 3. It is protected from behind by a hillside with no main road to the front or rear (which reduces the health risk from re-circulating ash), and has direct access to Woodlands beach (for a sea escape if necessary). It has well-fitting louver windows, an air-conditioned bedroom, and a steeply pitched roof (for shedding falling ash) but we are being advised to move.

The *"Advice to Residents of Montserrat"* seems to be forcing us into making the decision *"shall we remain here in this house, or return home to England?"* because unless the British Government is prepared to rent property in Antigua and fly their personnel over each working day, there appears to be no other alternative.

We took the personal decision to ignore the advice and remain where we were at Woodlands.

30 - FEBRUARY 1998

SAFE NORTH GETS HUGE ASHFALLS

On the morning of the 4th February I have written in my diary *"I am reminded of the thick yellow 'pea-souper' smogs of Victorian London 'Jack The Ripper' conditions!"*

But this Caribbean 'smog' is not the result of coal fires and industrial chimneys, it is caused by fine, volcanic ash, blown about by a fickle wind.

The MVO are quoted as saying that during the first week of February we suffered *"the most significant ash fall on the north of the island since the eruption began two and a half years ago"*.

An estimated 60,000 tonnes of powdered rock were deposited over the northern half of the island. The dust-trak measurements are reading *"high"* and *"alert"* in the Woodlands area and we are being urged to wear our masks *"at all times outside, and in ashy conditions"*.

Ash is getting into everything. The computers at the office just suddenly stopped functioning. The new Commissioner of Police says that his house is getting a lot of wind-blown ash inside. He has an open dining area, which he can't use, and he doesn't have an air-conditioner installed, which makes the bedroom very hot and stuffy when the windows are tightly closed against the ash.

Robin Cook, Secretary of State for Foreign and Commonwealth Affairs arrived on the 14th February for a fleeting five-hour visit.

Moments before his arrival the volcano belched a well-timed black cloud into the air and rolled a couple of white-hot pyroclastic flows down the south-eastern flanks. The fall-out drifted north and shrouded most of the Woodlands and Salem area and dusted St. John's in the north.

Up at Gerald's the waiting media were sand blasted by the fog of ash swirled up by the helicopter rotors as our VIP landed. The BBC, *'News of the World'*, and Nicholas from the Panama Office of the *'Financial Times'* were obliterated for several minutes to emerge coughing, white and wind-blown.

We were anticipating quite a heavy media coverage of the visit, but most of the anticipated press had raced off to Iraq to cover the 'surgical strikes' threatened by the US and UK, more politically newsworthy than our erupting volcano.

Robin Cook was wearing a dark business suit more suitable to Whitehall than the Caribbean. He appeared alien in our Montserrat landscape, which looks grey, empty and unloved. He had no sooner arrived than he climbed back on board the helicopter for a quick overflight of the island.

Eight of them squeezed in behind Don the pilot, including the Governor. As the helicopter clattered off in a cloud of dust Robin Cook had to be admired for his composure, sitting serenely beside the open helo door attempting to comb his hair. A helicopter overflight of the volcano with open doors is certainly not for the faint-hearted.

There was hardly anyone around for Robin Cook's visit. Many were indoors listening to the West Indies versus England cricket match live on the radio. To most Montserratians that is a far more interesting event than the visit of a British politician.

Even Chief Minister David Brandt carried a radio in his hand as he trailed behind the Secretary of State, only removing his headphones when asked a direct question.

It was a great result for the West Indies by the way, with England all out for a miserable 145.

After a working lunch there were visits to the Salem shelter, the hospital at St. John's School (where Robin Cook shrewdly observed the school books were still on the shelves in the wards), the Look Out housing site and the portakabins of the secondary school. A brief press conference to ten people completed the tour.

"I've seen how the people are suffering in the shelters, and I've seen the other end of the spectrum with the new housing" said the Foreign Secretary, but nothing else of significance for the listening audience.

The visitors departed as rapidly as they had arrived. As Robin Cook boarded the helicopter for his flight back to Antigua, the Fire Brigade (not wanting a repeat of the embarrassing sand storm arrival) were liberally hosing down the area, flooding the site into a thick, muddy quagmire.

But despite the Fire Brigade's best efforts, ash was once more whipped into a stinging cloud as the helo rose into the air, and the few spectators who had waited to watch the Foreign Secretary leave, limped home dispirited, caked in mud and ash.

A more welcome visitor arrived during the last week of February. Our son paid us a flying visit for a brief, four-day, photographic shoot. It was a spontaneous visit, which fortuitously coincided with the solar eclipse on 26th February.

Montserrat, together with Antigua and Guadeloupe, was considered one of the best places to view the eclipse. The last one visible from the island was on 3rd February 1916, and the next one will not be until the year 2212.

Many Montserratians expressed concern about the eclipse. There is a primal fear associated with it. So much so, that the nurses at St. John's hospital gathered together about thirty of the mentally disturbed Montserratians and treated them to lunch, as a means of keeping them contained and under supervision during the three hours of the passing of the moon across the sun's surface.

The volcano was huffing and puffing and churning out clouds of grey ashy steam and we wondered whether it would obscure the few precious moments of the total eclipse, but we were in luck. At around 2.30 p.m. we experienced a couple of minutes of twilight zone, a drop in temperature and an eerie brown darkening of the landscape. I could see a star or planet hanging just below the sun, which I was told was either Venus or Jupiter, but no-one seemed to know for sure.

The total eclipse lasted two minutes fifty-seven seconds in Plymouth, but we viewed it from an 'eclipse party' just outside the town. Our island photographer Kevin West decided to slip into the Exclusion Zone near W.H. Bramble Airport, so that he could capture the eclipse and the volcano in the same shot.

But our son decided to remain with the party, and as well as the eclipse, he took some candid shots of slack-jawed spectators gazing heavenwards, wearing the specially distributed cardboard and foil 'viewing' spectacles.

For part of his photo-shoot our son shadowed two of the scientists, going with them in the helicopter, suitably bagged head to heel in a red 'noddy' protection suit. He flew over the volcano and the devastated southern part of the island. He also visited the hospital at St. John's, and the ZJB Radio Montserrat studio where he met Soca King 'Arrow' doing a live interview. Later he toured the north of Montserrat taking photographs of all the British Aid projects.

Our son's most memorable excursion was a visit into Plymouth with Governor Tony Abbott and four of the HMS *Newcastle* crew.

The original plan had been to go in to retrieve records from the Court House safe, which had been left behind when Plymouth was evacuated. But unfortunately the tumbler fell off the combination lock and the only way to open the safe was with explosives, and none suitable could be found on either Antigua or Montserrat. So, instead of blasting the safe and rescuing the records, the convoy of three vehicles decided to continue through Plymouth and up to the abandoned and mothballed Government House.

Police checkpoint February 1998

They made their way beneath the volcano, across Plymouth along the west coast sea road, up to Fort Barrington and then doubled back to Government House.

It was like a nuclear moonscape. There were no landmarks. No roads were visible, and deep ravines dissected the ash, which lay between five and fifteen feet deep, with huge boulders strewn across the surface.

In some places the roofs of buried houses were level with the vehicles as they snaked carefully past. The navy men in the lead had to keep getting out to shovel a way through. My husband and son brought up the rear and had to stop frequently as the ash created by the two vehicles ahead caused complete 'white-out' conditions.

Governor Abbott had never been to the old Government House above Plymouth, and he was curious to see for himself the condition of the property after months of volcanic activity.

The familiar sentry box was still standing, and inside a dusty copy of 'Country Life' lay open. The team worked quickly to prise the nailed timbers off the front door, hurriedly hammered across for security when the building was vacated.

They pulled off the big old bell, and two plaques either side of the entrance.

With torches, they entered the dark and shuttered building and set to work to collect as much as possible.

Glasses, china, pictures, books, were hastily handed out, and piled high inside the three vehicles.

They were looking for a particular portrait of the Queen, but no-one could find it. However, a painting of Dover cliffs by James Savage was discovered tucked behind a sofa in one of the bedrooms, and grabbed. And another painting, a present to Governor Savage from his Personal Assistant, was also seen and seized and thrust onto the growing mountain of rescued items.

Down in the basement of the old Government House, huge toads had taken up residence, and blinked in the torchlight. While our son took hundreds of black and white images, my husband walked from room to room recording what he saw with a video camera.

Back at our villa in Woodlands I was listening to the short-wave radio, and I heard the scientists saying that the seismicity was increasing.

In Plymouth, at Government House, my husband was also monitoring the frequency, and I could hear him calling the MVO, seeking more details of the increasing activity, but he was getting no response. He could hear the MVO but they could not hear him, yet I could hear both of them.

I went outside and looked up towards the mountain and saw a black ash cloud roll down towards the sea over to the southwest in the general direction of Plymouth.

At Government House the convoy saw it too, and hastily crushed the last of the saved items into the vehicles in a race to get out of the Exclusion Zone as fast as they could. As the convoy began to crawl back towards the safe zone, they experienced a light ash-fall but fortunately nothing worse.

It took them over an hour to return to the Governor's new residence at 'Palmhurst' in the safe zone, where they unloaded the contents of the vehicles into the Governor's garage.

My husband and son were gone for a total of almost three hours, and when they finally returned home they were dusty, dirty, and 'emotionally drained', but yet exultant. They said there were no words to adequately describe the sensations they had experienced and the scenes they had witnessed during those three extraordinary hours.

Our son was concerned about his cameras, which after the excursion through Plymouth sounded 'gritty', but he maintained jovially that it was well worth the risk to his equipment in order to capture some fantastic and unique shots.

Among his images was one the Governor, Tony Abbott, ash mask on, arms akimbo, standing beside the official vehicle and watching the navy men digging the ash flat for the convoy to continue.

Another image captured for posterity the old red telephone box beside the post office in Plymouth, almost totally buried in the ash, with its roof just twelve inches above the surrounding granular grey surface of the ash deposit. His shots catch the tragic mood of disintegration surrounding Government House with rooms still curtained, carpeted and still containing some beautiful furniture.

Governor Abbott attempts to reach old Government House
Plymouth, February 1998

We have been told that the House of Commons have demanded, *"A frank and open report on the administration and handling of the crisis"* in Montserrat. Certainly the quality of life in Montserrat has deteriorated dramatically over the past twelve months and the authorities could, perhaps, have done more.

A fire at Monlec has meant that our electricity supply has been off more often than on this month and we are suffering unpredicted 'outages'. Supplies of LPG cooking gas, essential to us all, are irregular and limited, with cylinders being shipped to the neighbouring island of Nevis for filling.

A dozen eggs I bought yesterday contained two that were black when cracked open, the stench causing my stomach to churn.

As I look outside there is the now familiar thick mist of ash over the sea and a fine film of grey dust has settled on the outside tiles that I washed clean this morning.

My husband's present contract in Montserrat finishes in three months' time. I know he would stay here for another term if asked, since he feels he still has something to contribute. But personally I think three years on the island under such extreme and extraordinary conditions is long enough. It's time for us to go home.

31 - MARCH 1998

THE PINK MEALY BUG

It is as if the volcano is aware that many of us are reaching breaking point. During March it gave us a much needed respite. There have been no pyroclastic flows, nor any eruptive activity, for the entire month, and suddenly people are thinking the unthinkable, could the volcano be going back to sleep?

There is even talk of returning to Salem, and the Police barrier seems to be permanently open now with free movement backwards and forwards.

"It's either sleepy or preparing for the big one!" says the current MVO Chief Scientist cheerfully, neatly hedging his bets. But although there has been little obvious sign of activity to us, it appears that the 'line' between Harris and White's is shortening, and the instruments at the MVO show that the belly of the mountain has swelled three inches in seven weeks, and there is also a huge spine rising up out of the middle of the rubble.

Strong winds at the beginning of March blew the old ash off the streets in foggy, opaque whirls across the landscape. We closed up all the windows and shutters and for several days we lived in our bedroom, grateful for the air-conditioning.

The air-conditioner worked so hard I had to call Grenville in to give it a service. Grenville is a man of multiple talents being an electrician, a chicken farmer, and a mobile greengrocer. He arrived promptly, looking unusually smart and cheerful. He was extremely chatty and to my surprise he spent most of the hour while he checked my air conditioner singing the praises of the British Government.

Apparently five months ago Grenville's wife and two children (ages six and nine) reluctantly decided to leave Montserrat and they took advantage of the relocation offer to the UK.

It must have been quite a traumatic experience initially, when she first arrived in London, but according to Grenville she has settled in wonderfully and now has a supportive and caring group around her. She joined the local church, and discovered to her delight that the Pastor and over one hundred of the congregation were from Montserrat. She has a house in Tottenham, is studying, and the children are in school.

According to Grenville, the level of maths is apparently lower than in Montserrat, but the children's reading skills have improved greatly. He flew over to see them at Christmas and plans to go back again for Easter.

In Grenville's words he was *"offered an open door"* by the British, and he intends to make full use of it. Because all the electricians have left Montserrat his business is booming and he is now in great demand. His fresh vegetable business is also flourishing. He told me that all the Montserratians he knows in England are very pleased with their new life, the only complaint he has heard is about the weather.

Alfred says the same. Having returned to London and his family, he is now renting out his house in Montserrat to the Aid Management Office and at present the Senior Health Advisor (a consultant from DFID) is living there.

DFID are appointing several more Technical Co-operation Officers, expected to arrive on island very soon. Four of them are engineers in various disciplines.

The majority of the new recruits are here on short-term unaccompanied contracts. We have been told that they are expected to find accommodation in the 'safe' north, beyond Lawyers River, or they could find themselves penalised, but accommodation is very scarce and I know of nothing available at present. There is a suggestion that an apartment block might be built in the north to accommodate all TCO's, and the feasibility of renting in Antigua and commuting daily by ferry is also being investigated.

Tighter controls are currently being introduced regarding the distribution of British aid money in Montserrat. Auditors from London are presently trawling through the books, and discovering some interesting anomalies.

There is a rumour circulating that several months ago a cheque that should have been written out for US$387, had actually been signed and sent out in the sum of US$387,000. The error was only discovered on the death of the recipient, when his family returned the cheque, confident that it would have been quite impossible for the deceased to have legitimately earned such a large amount of money.

We did wonder if the shock of receiving the cheque had caused his demise!

A fire broke out at one of the new wooden shelters erected at Manjack this month. Thirty-two people who had just moved out of the inferior Brades shelter into the new wooden Manjack shelters have lost everything they owned and are now back at Brades.

It is thought that a child playing with matches in a bedroom started the fire, which was fanned by the strong wind and quickly spread to two adjacent shelters, subsequently destroying all three.

It was Sunday and fortunately most of the people living in the wooden shelters were across the road at the Church service, and no-one was injured. However the fire department has been criticised for not supplying extinguishers and for not responding adequately to the situation, but they maintain that several parked vehicles 'obstructed' their approach.

But there has been a magnificent response by everyone on island to the plea for help with money, clothing and goods for those who lost everything in the fire. David Brandt came on the radio immediately, pledging EC$1,000 cash to each person to enable them to go out and purchase essential items.

We had the annual St. Patrick's Day holiday on the 17th March, but it was a bittersweet occasion since the little village of St. Patrick's was blasted out of existence in the massive Boxing Day eruption.

There was a Group Therapy Session especially for the residents of St. Patrick's who are now in shelters or temporary accommodation.

The whole St. Patrick's Day celebration, normally such a festive occasion, was muted and reduced to a Domino Tournament, a Freedom Run and a video for the children to watch.

Beryl and Rob's Ruby Wedding party, two days earlier, had turned out to be a welcome diversion from the island's stresses for the huge number of invited guests. It was an evening of feasting and entertainment. The tables groaned with Beryl's culinary efforts and no matter how much we ate, more miraculously appeared from the depths of the kitchen.

Sometime earlier Beryl had stumbled across a photographer and journalist from the *'Discovery Channel'* and had invited them along to the party. They were visiting Montserrat for a month, having been advised by the scientists *"now is the time"* for something to happen.

Unfortunately for them, now is the time when nothing at all appears to be happening. They have wandered along behind the scientists, interviewed local people, looked for the national bird of Montserrat (the Montserrat Oriole), and are seriously beginning to run out of things to film. They drooled with jealousy when they heard about our son's photo-shoot in Plymouth, which was the last occasion there was a pyroclastic flow.

There is an unconfirmed story going around the island about a journalist claiming to be from the *'Discovery Channel'* who arrived in Montserrat recently with a rough terrain-tri wanting to *"drive up the volcano"*.

Permission was flatly refused, but the journalist quietly hired two Montserratians to guide him and was found filming the men cutting the chain on the road barrier as he entered the restricted zone. He was summarily arrested and immediately deported.

The police establishment in Montserrat should be ninety-five, but they are now down to seventy-two, of whom forty-seven are Constables. It makes policing the island very difficult, and in addition the Police Department is trying to assemble relevant paperwork and written evidence for the Inquest into the deaths of the victims of the 25th June eruption last year. Many of those who were involved in the tragedy have now left the island and once a date has been fixed for the Inquest they will need to return.

Now that the ash has been washed off the garden we can see that something is very wrong with all our plants, especially the hibiscus bushes. Everyone has the same problem. Leaves are curling into tight deformed balls and falling off. We thought it was the result of constant ashfalls but apparently not.

My neighbour Salo tells me that the hibiscus hedge which surrounds his property at Woodlands, and is much admired when all the blooms are out, is completely covered with something called the Pink Mealy Bug and it is this little pest which is doing all the damage.

Salo has been doing some research and has discovered that it came originally from South-East Asia and was apparently brought across to the Caribbean in 1994, seemingly imported into the island of Grenada with vegetables purchased from Asia. It spread rapidly and raced up the Caribbean chain.

Montserrat was free from infection until quite recently. The Pink Mealy Bug particularly likes hibiscus and can destroy a bush in a matter of days. Salo has tried the usual remedies. He cut his hedge right down to the ground in an attempt to halt the spread, but it hasn't worked. He tried spraying, but that didn't work either.

The Agricultural Department thought they had the pest under control, but obviously they have not. They are currently recommending a 'slash and burn' policy, but say that the only real solution is to import large numbers of a specific ladybird, which feeds on the Pink Mealy Bug. Pest control through natural means, but in the meantime all our vegetation is being destroyed.

Montserrat is a sorry sight, if the ash doesn't damage the vegetation then the Pink Mealy Bug does.

32 - APRIL 1998

TOUR OF EXCLUSION ZONE

For the first time in nine months I have visited the Exclusion Zone, still officially a no-go area.

The road barrier at Salem has been pushed to one side and the police on duty happily waved us through. As we passed Ram's supermarket, a few hundred yards beyond the barrier, I glanced inside and saw a queue of customers waiting with laden trolleys at the checkout.

A young mum and a schoolboy in white shirt and dark trousers, his haversack on his back, were strolling down the main street of Salem. Three men and a youth were working on a car, its bonnet up, by the side of the road, and waved cheerfully to us.

It looks like a thriving little community has quickly re-established itself in Salem, even though it is still officially designated as part the Exclusion Zone.

There is a more positive feeling on island. Some evacuees who took up the original UK package offer are now asking if it is safe to return to Montserrat. Apparently approximately three hundred families who are currently in the UK have asked if the British Government will pay their fares back to Montserrat.

As we drove on through Salem we passed the Roman Catholic Church, now boarded up. I remember when the Church was an evacuation shelter and school children sat beneath the tree for their lessons, ash masks to hand in case of emergency. There are still 51 people in emergency shelters but they are now in churches and schools in the safe north.

Beyond the empty Salem Police Station four old men and a woman were sitting on the veranda of a house, strings of washing straining in the sunny breeze. People wandered out in front us and waved cheerfully as we passed. Goats, cows and cattle meander freely or are tethered by the roadside.

Except for evidence of dusty ash lining the streets, Salem has all the appearance of a quiet and peaceful residential village on a sunny tropical island in the Caribbean. This was not my expectation of how it would be in the Exclusion Zone and I was very surprised.

I know there is a Rastafarian commune up in the hills near Molyneaux. They melt away into the bush when the police patrol arrives. The Rastas earn their living maintaining the gardens of the villas in the safe zone.

The leader is middle-aged, lean and wiry, with a serious weather-beaten face. He wears a torn purple vest and old jeans cut off at the knees, and his Rasta locks are held up and away from his face inside a big brown Hessian sack which hangs stiffly to his shoulders. His quiet young companion keeps his dreadlocks tucked up beneath a green beret.

The day we went into the Exclusion Zone the volcano was stunningly clear, a steaming mountain of pale grey rock rubble silhouetted against the brilliant blue of the sky. So often it has been veiled in cloud with ashy plumes obscuring the summit.

A sharp incisor of a spine is now protruding from the top of the dome. An inverted cone perched on the highest part of the heap and reaching 3,368 ft. into the sky. As we watched, steam and gulps of ash vented gently around the summit, but otherwise there was no obvious activity.

On the left flanks of the volcano, the slope across Farrell's is now a smooth slide of grey ash, many, many metres thick. This is the area where a few short months ago there had been green and fertile fields.

The MVO is saying that things are currently very quiet and the evening up-dates are beginning to sound like a cracked record. We are told that there are three possible reasons for this 'lull' in activity. It may be that the volcano is finally going to sleep, or it could be entering a period where the cycles of activity and inactivity are longer, or it could simply be a pause before more activity starts. As the scientists are fond of telling us, volcanology is an inexact science.

We finished our tour by visiting the deserted Vue Pointe Hotel and driving back through Old Towne to Lime Kiln, past our two previous homes, now firmly in the Exclusion Zone.

The Vue Pointe Hotel looked incredibly sad, abandoned to the volcano, grey and derelict. The big tapestry that hangs beside reception is still there, very dusty and dirty, but just recognisable. As we walked around the hotel, our feet leaving a trail of grey impressions in the dusty ash, we remembered Mike and Marife's wedding here, and Father Larry's Sunday services, and the rooms hastily converted into a supermarket at the beginning of the crisis, and Carol's shop where I bought my cards and gifts, and the dances, the laughter, the camaraderie of the place.

It is almost impossible to picture the hotel as it used to be, a buzzing place where there was always a friendly welcome, where there was always something exciting going on, and where the grilled Mountain Chicken was the best in Montserrat. Perhaps one day soon, when the volcano finally goes back to sleep, it will be restored and brought back to life again.

There are some small signs of renewal, a defiant Bougainvillea bush resolutely struggling for survival, and some tall grasses that have seeded themselves in the ash at the bottom of the empty pool.

Loose cattle have moved onto the land and were wandering around the garden, eating what little they can scavenge, and trampling on the rest.

Cattle are still managing to survive beyond the ashy slopes of the volcano to the southeast of the island. A helicopter reconnaissance of the Tar River/Long Ground area near the airport revealed that there are approximately 65 cattle roaming about out there. There are plans to try and drive them north, out of the danger area, using the police and the helo, down to the coast and along the beach at Trant's into the safety of Pelican Ghaut. As the ash is still very hot in the Trant's area they cannot go overland.

Seven months after the September 1997 pyroclastic flows the temperature of the ash two metres below the surface is registering between 257 to 283°C.

There was a massive exodus of expatriates over Easter, all wanting to escape from Montserrat for a stress-buster break.

A few of us remained, and found ourselves volunteering to help in the *Swimming 98 Clinic* organised jointly by the Community Department and Red Cross.

We had seventy-two children in total, age range eight to twelve, and we were attempting to teach them to swim during an eight-day intensive coaching session over Easter which included Good Friday and Easter Monday.

I managed to get permission to use the pool of the villa *'Sea Song'* and together with my two neighbours, Salo and Linda, I found myself supervising nine lively water babies who had never been in a swimming pool before.

It was very hard work but great fun being a 'Teacher' and the children were fantastic. By the eighth day every child in our little group could do at least three strokes before sinking, some considerably more. But the main triumph was that the children had fun, thoroughly enjoying the experience. Each one made huge strides in personal confidence.

When they were first introduced to the pool, the boys circled the edge hesitantly, peering into the water. But after an hour they were screaming with delight and confidence and just wanted to run, jump in, splash and play. We managed to encourage them into putting their heads underwater by throwing coins for them to retrieve. The girls took it all much more seriously, and responded well to the reward of Smarties.

On the first day Marlon arrived without a towel or trunks, but we managed to find something suitable. Later, we discovered it was his birthday and rustled up some biscuits and embarrassed him by loudly singing 'Happy Birthday'.

When he left we found he had forgotten his shoes. Unfortunately he did not return for another lesson, being barred by the organisers as too old for the group, and we had to parcel up his shoes to be dispatched to him at Brades.

The children used the bathroom of the empty villa as a changing room, and there was always something left behind, especially after the girls had been in. Delrose, with beautifully braided long hair, was always forgetting her hairpins, or watch, and Sharese once left her costume in a limp soggy bundle behind the door.

The girls really enjoyed using the bathroom, we could hear their giggles as we waited patiently for them to emerge. Eventually they came out, smelling deliciously of hand cream, which they had liberally applied to legs, arms and body.

Each morning the girls brought little presents for the 'Teachers'. A tamarind ball 'sweet' made of tamarind flesh mashed with sugar placed around a tamarind seed and wrapped like a toffee in cling film. Or a tamarind pod hidden within layer upon layer of cling film and foil, in the manner of the party game 'pass the parcel'.

I was watched with great amusement as I dutifully cracked the pod, sucked the seed clean, then with fat cheeks and big breath 'blew' it as far as I could.

The girls picked the hibiscus flowers that had escaped the attention of the mealy bug, and laughing infectiously they tucked them into our hair.

Sedrika, more thoughtful and reserved than the others, had the most determination to learn to swim. She is nine and has a little half-brother aged three. Until August last year Sedrika lived in the Pentecostal Church as an evacuee with her mother and brother. Before they were evacuated she used to go to school in Plymouth and she told me she was very sad when they had to leave the school, adding in a quiet, sad little voice, that her art and science books had been inside her desk when the school burned down after one of the volcanic eruptions. She said many of the teachers had sobbed when they heard their school in Plymouth had been destroyed by fire.

Ellyson was the most mischievous of the boys. He thoroughly enjoyed teasing the girls, spraying them with water from the hosepipe beside the pool, and hiding their clothes. One morning he came tottering out of the villa giggling loudly, having put on Sharese's black patent shoes.

Young Diren was the complete opposite to Ellyson. Initially quiet and cautious, when he had overcome his fear of the water he surprised us all by doing handstands on the bottom of the pool, which quickly became his 'speciality'.

After the course we were all invited to the *'Sea Pointe'* villa in Palm Loop, and each participant was presented with prizes and certificates, regardless of level of achievement. Every child brought a towel and swimming costume and in front of proud parents and friends (all shouting encouragement) each child demonstrated his or her ability in the pool.

Diron did his width underwater (he still hasn't quite mastered the technique of swimming on the surface) then finished with a handstand on the bottom to loud applause. And Annesta and Sharese both managed to do an amazing full length of the swimming pool in breaststroke, quite an accomplishment for two girls who had been complete non-swimmers before the 'clinic'.

Linda, who came to help with the swimming lessons, is my nearest neighbour. She and her Montserratian husband Harry (who left Montserrat for England when he was just thirteen) returned to the island in November 1996 to retire here, and they are busy trying to complete the house they began to build a year ago on the hillside behind me.

I phoned Linda early on the morning of the 22nd April with the news that I had just seen a whale spouting far out to sea, the first of the season. Harry answered my call, and told me that Linda was in hospital at St. John's, having been rushed there as an emergency patient the previous evening.

Linda had been visiting me, and it seems that after leaving me she had decided to take her two dogs for a short walk along the rough track between our two houses.

Suddenly a small calf had emerged from the scrubby bush beside the road and bounded up to the two dogs, obviously full of curiosity. Unknown to Linda, the mother cow was behind her and must have seen the two dogs as a threat to her baby calf. In her haste to reach and protect the calf, the cow knocked Linda to the ground and trampled across her.

When Linda tried to get up, lifting her face from the mud, she thought the cow must have urinated over her, but quickly realised with horror that it was her own blood gushing from a wound in her head. She told me later that she wondered how it was that I did not hear her screams. Fortunately for her, Harry did, and he very quickly rushed her up to the hospital, where she stayed for two nights.

I went up to see Linda at the temporary hospital at St. John's. She was in one of the metal 'shelters' that has been pressed into service as the Women's Ward while refurbishment work is being carried out on St. John's School, the intended new hospital.

I had to negotiate the building site of the new works to get to the ward. Inside the building eight beds lined the walls, and a small cot with a young baby in it was tucked just inside the door.

Three elderly, frail, but fully dressed ladies lay quietly on three of the beds. At the end of the ward was the toilet and shower, separated by a door, which Linda told me was locked at night. She knew because she had been bursting to use the toilet all through the first night and was unable to unlock the door.

The first night Linda had her blood pressure and temperature taken several times, but the second night no-one came near her. She could hear snoring coming from the next bed, which had screens round it, but in the morning when the screens were removed the bed was empty, leading us to speculate that either a patient had died in her sleep and been whisked away while Linda showered herself, or the night nurse on duty was taking a little nap!

Linda appeared to be asleep when I arrived, clutching my grapes, bananas and a copy of the *'Guardian Weekly'* for her to read. The window was open and a pleasant breeze cooled the room, but it also allowed the flies in and they were dancing around Linda's face. Her head had been shaved and bandaged, seven stitches having been inserted by Dr. Anand. Her hand was strapped in a bloodstained bandage and she thinks she may have broken her little finger, but she won't know until a radiologist visits Montserrat to take an X-ray. In the meantime it will be put in a splint.

When Linda returned home two days later she received a visit from the Rasta who owned the cow that trampled over her. He was almost in tears and said that he had been *"Tol' dat a white lady bin attack frum mi cow"*. Linda says she felt so sorry for him, and told him she doesn't intend to prosecute. All she asks is that he keeps his cow well-tethered in future, and away from the track.

On the 23rd April David Brandt presented the annual Budget to LegCo. It is the largest budget amount ever in the history of Montserrat, with 70% of the sum being provided by Her Majesty's Government courtesy of the British Taxpayer.

On the 28th April, I listened to the Budget debate, which was being broadcast live from McChesney's. Most LegCo members seemed to be using the opportunity as a platform to score points against each other. It was an acrimonious moaning session with each member taking an hour or more on average to have their say.

Reuben Meade, who had refused the British Government offer of 1,000 houses in the north in 1995 during the early days of the eruption, had to be called to order by the Speaker when he said, *"If nineteen people hadn't died last June then we'd still be waiting for the British to supply houses!"*

But Reuben did have a point when he complained about the supply of LPG cooking gas. Many people, including Linda, have been reduced to cooking outside on open charcoal fires because they cannot get their LPG cylinders filled.

We are supposed to take our empty tanks to the depot (in the back seat of the car) and they are sent over to St. Kitts for filling, and then returned to the island. A number system has been introduced to try and cope with the demand but it does not seem to be working very effectively.

Rob was issued with number 251 seven weeks ago, and he has to listen to the daily broadcast to hear whether his number is ready for collection. Since they have only just reached number 125 it may be that Rob will have to wait many more weeks before he is called to collect his cylinder.

Another contentious issue raised during the Budget debate was the new police launch. Recently arrived and named *'Shamrock II'* in a champagne splashing ceremony it replaces the larger police vessel *'MV Shamrock'*.

'Shamrock II' has had a humiliating start, having been unflatteringly referred to as the *"Police Fishing Boat"* and *"a dinghy with an outboard motor"*. It is an open boat only 26 ft. long, which requires a three-man crew but has the capacity to hold ten to twelve people.

Concern has been expressed that this new police launch will be unable to tow an island fishing boat out of trouble, especially in a heavy sea. Certainly it could not tow the ferryboat. But it was apparently purchased with the assurance that it can tow something up to 50 ft. long. The main advantage being claimed for the boat is that it is unsinkable, but someone was quick to respond with the question *"Does that mean it will float upside-down if capsized?"*

The old, larger, *'MV Shamrock'* kept breaking down and needed a complete refurbishment that would have cost up to EC$400,000, so the decision was made to sell it on, and commission this new boat from St. Maarten. The islanders had expected something on a grander scale, bigger and better than the *'MV Shamrock'* and were naturally disappointed when *'Shamrock II'* arrived and they discovered what they had got. Reuben was the main spokesman again, expressing concern that there are no facilities on board for responding to the calls of nature. He presumed those on board would have to do whatever was necessary *"over the side"*.

To my mind Bertrand Osborne raised the most sensible question during the Budget debate. He commented that if the ferry and helicopter are costing the British Government US$5 million per year, wouldn't it be cheaper to build a small airstrip suitable for Twin Otters?

He is right of course. Since Montserrat's existing airport lies in the Exclusion Zone and in the path of potential pyroclastic flows down the eastern side of the volcano, it is most unlikely it will ever be re-opened.

How long can Montserrat rely on the ferry and a helicopter for access to the island? Wouldn't it be better to think long-term and begin the process of providing for a new airstrip? Perhaps similar to the one that existed at Salem many years ago before W.H. Bramble Airport was built.

33 - MAY 1998

THE GREAT BARCLAYS BANK ROBBERY

The island is buzzing with gossip about a burglary at the abandoned Barclays Bank in Plymouth.

It seems to me very strange to rob a bank that has been closed for several months. But apparently EC$1,000,000 of lovely new money belonging to the Eastern Caribbean Central Bank was being stored in the vault of the abandoned bank, and this proved too much of a temptation for someone.

There are various versions of the 'Barclays Bank Robbery' story in circulation, but basically it is alleged that sometime between the end of February and mid-May (when the theft was discovered) a senior employee of said bank supplied person or persons unknown with the key to enter the building. A big round hole was then 'blown' in the vault by *"several other persons"*.

As a result of investigations six men were arrested on 28th May in connection with the burglary, and many more were interviewed, including several senior figures in the Montserrat community who were allegedly involved in the 'laundering' of the stolen money. Also, two senior police officials have been suspended pending investigation. So many suspects have been arrested that one of the Defence Force wooden buildings at Gerald's has been taken over in order to accommodate them.

Apparently, before the investigation, it is alleged that the police had found a paper bag containing over EC$9,000 with a passport resting on top, beside the road at St. Peters. The police had thoughtfully returned both bag and contents to the owner of the passport.

One version of the story going around Montserrat maintains it was a suitcase not a paper bag, but all versions agree on the name of the owner of the passport, and the contents.

It seems the stolen money from the vault has already been distributed all around the Caribbean. Since the notes were new, and not issued as legal tender, they are still the property of the ECCB, which means that anyone innocently holding these five, ten, twenty, fifty and one hundred dollar notes has been instructed to take them to the nearest police station.

Once the offending numbers had been publicised we all checked our wallets, and many of us discovered to our surprise and dismay that we were in possession of some of the *'funny money'*.

I have one EC$50 note which was given to me in change at the Big Banana Restaurant at Antigua Airport, but I am not returning it to the police, I shall keep it as a souvenir.

Some people have found themselves very badly out of pocket. I feel particularly sorry for Rose who has been saving carefully over the past few weeks for a trip to Gibraltar, a radio conference she wants to attend. When she took her money into to the Royal Bank of Canada to pay for her currency, she was told that EC$2,000 of it was part of the stolen money. Another friend tells me that the Royal Bank of Canada had unwittingly issued him with EC$500 of *'funny money'* before the theft was discovered, and now he wants to know who is going to compensate him for his loss.

The *'funny money'* has the suffix 'M' and we hear that many businesses and taxi drivers in Antigua are refusing to handle any money with the suffix M because trying to memorise the naughty numbers that follow is far too difficult, it is much easier to refuse any M's.

Charlie, paying his bill at the Big Banana Restaurant in Antigua, checked his change and discovered one of the notes was from the burglary. Being a policeman he promptly handed it back, and then watched in astonishment as the waiter casually replaced it in the till.

According to David Brandt, one family were paying for groceries in Antigua when their notes were inspected at the checkout and discovered to be part of the stolen money. Through no fault of their own they suffered the humiliation of having it confiscated, and were then subjected to the indignity of having to replace the contents of their trolley back onto the shelves.

In addition to the notes a substantial number of EC$1 coins have also been stolen, all with the minted date of 1997. Since no EC$1 coins have ever been issued with that date, it is easy to notice them and it was no surprise to discover I had one in my purse.

We spent the early part of May back in England, having decided on impulse to return to celebrate our son's 21st birthday with him. It was as we passed through Antigua airport on the way to London that I was given the EC$50 *'funny money'*.

Both our outgoing and incoming BWIA flights were delayed. After a delay of an hour in boarding at Antigua, the plane (packed to capacity) was kept on the runway while engineers tried to release a 'stuck' air intake valve on engine two.

In all seriousness they informed the restless passengers that they *"didn't have a tall enough ladder"* to reach into the engine. Eventually, in desperation, the pilot whimsically suggested starting engine three in the hope that the required rush of air might release the stuck valve. It worked, and we finally left Antigua running three hours late.

The return flight was also fully laden, and included sixty footballers in the rear of the plane intent on partying and having a good time. They insisted on strolling down the aisles and forming chatty, boozy, groups. In a vain attempt to make them go back to their seats the pilot kept putting on the seatbelt sign.

We came into Antigua two hours late, and having missed our connecting helicopter flight to Montserrat we were obliged to overnight, courtesy of BWIA in the Rex Halcyon Hotel.

Montserrat is very hot and humid at the moment, with temperatures up in the nineties. It has brought bouts of heavy rain with accompanying thunder and lightning. The rain has created mudflows down the flanks of the volcano, but apart from these everything is quiet. We have been told the dome stopped growing in March, and the authorities are now very 'optimistic' that the volcano has actually gone back to sleep. There is talk of cleaning-up the Salem, Old Towne and Frith's areas for an early return.

But the scientists remain cautious and are waiting until their July brainstorming session. In the meantime the Governor is planning a meeting with the Public Works Department and Fire Brigade to discuss the matter of cleaning the buildings and streets in parts of the current Exclusion Zone.

The Salem barrier is now pushed aside in the ditch and there is a free flow of cars and pedestrians into Zone 3, although 'officially' anyone entering this area still does so at their own risk.

There is even a rumour that W.H. Bramble Airport could be re-opened if a new terminal building was built higher up the hillside, and 'walls' of some sort were constructed to direct any mudflows away from the runway. It sounds rather risky to me, since pyroclastic flows are no respecter of walls, but the fact that it is being suggested is an indication of the optimism in the air.

During May a new *'Residents Guide to Evacuation of the Central Zone'* was issued. This brief booklet is specifically aimed at those of us living in the narrow strip of Olveston and Woodlands, between Nantes River and Lawyers River to the north of the Exclusion Zone that starts at Salem, and it seems to blatantly contradict the positive view that the volcano has finally gone back to sleep.

The first paragraph begins *"In the event of an increase in volcanic activity directly affecting the Belham Valley area or if environmental conditions cause serious health hazards in the Central Zone of the Risk Map of Montserrat, an Evacuation Order may be issued for those areas."*

The leaflet then continues with details on 'Alert and Warning', 'What to Do if the Evacuation is called', and how to conduct oneself when arriving at the Brades shelter, and finishes with several short paragraphs on what to take, including clothing, toiletries, medical supplies, food, water and papers.

The final check list before leaving home in the event of instructions to evacuate advises *"Turn off gas at your tank"*, *"Turn off electricity at the main switch"*, *"Turn off water at main stop valve"*, *"Check your emergency bag is packed and ready to go"*, *"Lock doors and windows"* and finally, *"Release all pets"*.

Peter (Dr. Doom) Baxter reflects the caution expressed in the new leaflet. He came out to present his February findings into asthma in the island's children. The results seem to show that one

251

in ten children are suffering from asthma, a statistic similar to that of Barbados.

Children less than twelve are more likely to have had wheeze and asthmatic symptoms if they have been exposed to ash within the last twelve months, and those living in Salem and Woodlands were the ones who tended to show a decline in lung function after exercise.

It has been suggested that concrete or tarmac aprons are laid around schools so that they can be easily hosed down to keep the ash to a minimum.

Although current ash levels in the air are low, a 'clean-up' of Salem will not necessarily mean that those areas will then be safe for children with asthmatic tendencies. The cristobalite content of the ash varies between 5% and 20%, with pyroclastic flows producing a higher proportion of cristobalite than explosive eruptions.

When tested with cell cultures the ash produced a toxic response. It was also discovered that the toxicity was not reduced by washing in water. By implication this suggests that the ash in Montserrat will remain toxic for a long time.

The optimistic belief that all could soon be back to 'almost normal' has created something of a scramble in the property market, with keen purchasers making offers on empty villas that have been up for sale in Old Towne and Woodlands for many months. For instance Montserrat's Soca King 'Arrow' has bought our old villa in Lime Kiln, although it is still officially in the Exclusion Zone.

Before the volcano erupted in 1995, the villa next to us in Woodlands was bought, unseen, for US$300,000 by purchasers in the US. The owners visited three times before trying to sell it, and it has been on the market for some considerable time at US$250,000. Now, at long last, it has been sold. Lennie has been working on the villa, painting the outside in readiness for the new owners.

Lennie who is from Ghana, recently received his Montserratian work permit and residency status after years of trying. He is thrilled and has become much more confident, gaining himself a reputation as a reliable handyman, and he is doing very well for himself. He told me he has now applied for a Montserratian passport.

Like Grenville, Lennie is one of those who seem to have benefited from the volcano, one of the winners.

Villa owners letting property to Government officials are also among the winners. Rents are still very high in the safe north, and property is a secure source of income.

Villas in Woodlands and Palm Loop that rented out to the American University of the Caribbean students at US$600 per month in July 1995, are now renting at an astounding US$2,000 per month. Some villa owners are even managing to persuade the tenants to pay for building improvement work.

The Aid Management Office has just relocated to a warren of a house at Manjack in the north. The house was formerly a Doctor's, then Tina's Pizzeria and shelter accommodation. DFID have just spent over EC$200,000 renovating the property, and in addition are paying a high monthly rent to the owner.

The new houses being built at Look Out in the north have now been allocated. Mostly to civil servants and others, but sadly not to those evacuees still living in shelters.

Over two hundred people applied for a Look Out house but as they are renting out at EC$500 per month, few can afford the price. Shirley told me that some nurses she knew had gone along to the interview, but simply could not afford that sort of rent.

The Davy Hill houses, built quickly as emergency 'immediate' housing specifically for those in shelters, and viewed by HRH Prince Andrew during his visit, are of a much cheaper construction to the Look Out properties, and are renting out at EC$150 per month, or less, or even free if the 'incumbent' cannot pay.

Well, the time has come for us to make the decision whether to ask for an extension to my husband's contract here in Montserrat. After much heart-searching, and wrestling with guilty feelings of defection, we have reluctantly decided that we should leave.

I have been asked repeatedly why we have stayed so long, and I answer that while we still feel we have something to contribute to the island and her people we have remained. But three years of living under the shadow of the volcano has used us up, both emotionally and physically.

It is time to go home, rest and recover, and move on to pastures new.

We are currently living out of two suitcases, having packed everything that needs to be returned to the UK into crates for shipment. Devoid of all our personal bits and pieces, our villa feels naked and bleak. But it does mean that if the volcano starts up again and we have to evacuate in a hurry, we have just two cases to carry.

Harris Police Station after 25th June 1997

34 - JUNE/JULY 1998

A SENSE OF OPTIMISM RETURNS

The 25th June was designated a Day of Remembrance for those who died in the eruption last year. The little hexagonal Brades Pentecostal Church was packed with people and the congregation spilled outside, crowding the entrance and pressing forward to listen to the service through the open windows.

Twenty-one names were listed on the service sheet, including my friend Beryl from Harris. Two persons were un-named, giving an apparent total of twenty-three deaths for that fateful day. But this is not accurate. I noticed that at least two of the names on the list refer to one individual, and the exact number of fatalities will not be known until the formal Inquest is held later this year.

The service was very moving, with hymns, scripture readings, a musical tribute and the laying of wreaths. It was completely inter-denominational with Rev. Morgan, Rev. Banks, Pastor Meade, Rev. Riley, and Father Larry, all taking part in the proceedings.

Most of those who perished were farmers working the ground on the slopes of the volcano at Farrell's, but baby Allister Joseph was just three months old, and his young mother Alicia, in whose arms he died at Farms, was barely twenty-three.

Many Montserratians whose loved ones perished in the tragic eruption of 25th June 1997 are still very badly traumatised, and life is extremely hard for them.

Life is also difficult for those remaining in shelters, but every Montserratian is struggling in various different ways. The island is without cooking gas, and many people are still making their meals on pot-stoves in the yard. When I went to see Linda to look at the artwork for a charity Christmas card she has designed, her husband Harry was carefully fanning a small pot-stove into life before setting the crock on top to cook their dinner. They have been out of LPG for several weeks.

Harry had heard on the morning radio bulletin that LPG supplies had at last arrived on island, and holding his numbered ticket he drove off as quickly as possible to claim his cylinder. It seems, however, that everyone had the same idea and converged on the distribution centre at Carr's Bay where there was pandemonium.

Allegations were flying round that some people, arriving late and without tickets, had been given several tanks, while others, who had queued patiently for four hours in the sun and held allocated tickets, were turned away.

One old gentleman had arrived at 8.00 a.m. and was eighth in the queue. He stood patiently waiting in line in the hot sun, then at mid-day he was told the supplies had run out and he was sent away empty-handed.

Harry, whose number was in the low 200's, saw the confusion and gave up in frustration. He didn't bother to wait and returned home. He'll go back and try again with the next radio announcement, probably in a couple of weeks' time.

Linda is a very talented artist and the Christmas card she has designed is exquisite. It depicts Father Christmas and reindeer flying across a night sky while below a volcano steams beside a church (which closely resembles Cavalla Hill Church where the old folk are sheltering) all surrounded with bright exotic flowers and foliage. Beryl has volunteered to arrange for the card to be printed in England, and it will be sold to raise money for island charities.

Linda and Harry had been invited to attend the annual Queen's Birthday Reception, held by the Governor at 'Palmhurst' on 13th June, but they decided to decline the invitation.

Normally the pomp and ceremony of the Morning Parade, with the uniformed march past and the Governor's salute, attracts an interested crowd. But this year not many people bothered to go to Gerald's to watch.

However the evening 'bun bash' was very well attended, with over 580 guests turning up. Initially there was an element of chaos as the poor constable on gate duty at Palmhurst attempted to turn away those guests not able to produce their embossed invitation.

I had left our invitation skewered to the fridge beneath one of Beryl's volcanic ash magnets, but just as we were turning the car around to return home to collect it, Sammy, the Governor's driver, saw us and motioned us through the gates and down the 'Palmhurst' drive.

Normally 'smart casual' or 'jacket and tie' would have been printed opposite the RSVP on the invitation, but this year there was no indication as to dress code and as a result the complete clothing spectrum was represented, from T-shirt and shorts to dinner jacket and bow tie.

David, who had attended last year's function wearing a T-shirt, was resplendent in full DJ and sporting such a stunningly colourful waistcoat that my special chemically-sensitive tinted glasses began to darken while we spoke.

It was not the usual sedate gathering, where the guests sip cocktails and murmur politely to each other. The appearance of fresh strawberries flown in from Antigua on the helicopter almost caused a stampede, and as the evening wore on and the guests visibly mellowed, it turned into a lively affair complete with dancing and singing, enthusiastically led by Governor Abbott and his energetic wife.

A selection of our son's photographs, taken during his brief visit to Montserrat in February, were displayed along one wall of the reception room and created a great deal of interest. People who had not been allowed into the Exclusion Zone or seen the devastation caused in Plymouth by the eruptions, were particularly fascinated.

As confidence grows that the volcano may now have finished activity, curiosity is encouraging sightseers into the Exclusion Zone. One of the scientists told me that on the 12th June he had counted eleven cars driving through the road barrier into what is still officially the Exclusion Zone and heading for Plymouth, each vehicle full of passengers with cameras primed ready to take pictures of the destruction in town. The scientists urge caution, but no-one seems to want to listen.

Ahead of us lies the annual hurricane season. In anticipation Dr. William Gray at the Colorado State University has just released the alphabetical list of this season's proposed hurricane names, which include Alex, Bonnie, Danielle, Earl, Frances, and Georges.

He predicts ten named storms with six of these becoming hurricanes and two developing into major hurricanes. The hurricane season peaks on the 10th September, and apparently there have been over fifty hurricanes on that particular date during the past 100 years of monitoring.

June is generally quiet with any storms that arise coming out of the Caribbean and the Gulf of Mexico rather than off the African coast.

Although we may not have had a hurricane, June has brought us several sudden heavy squalls, with one leaving behind six inches of rain. This briefly disturbed the quiescence of the volcano and sparked off a series of mudflows down the flanks.

Belham Valley came off worst with rock and pumice debris littering the road and mud covering the bridge.

The MVO describe the mudflows as *"hyper-concentrated stream flows"* which have scoured new watercourses through Plymouth. Five new river tracts have formed in the town, with several areas where trapped water is forming lakes, and new springs have appeared in the Farms and Trant's areas to the east of the volcano.

A river now flows straight down the old George Street, and another actually passes through the empty Plymouth Secondary School, while a third flows through the derelict Police Station.

The landscape of Montserrat is changing radically with each passing month. The island bears no relationship to the views I knew when I first arrived in Montserrat in July 1995.

Although the dome of the volcano is no longer growing, for some reason the sulphur dioxide emissions remain high, and all month a blue haze has hung over the Soufrière Hills.

The dust-trak measurements were also high at the end of June, but the scientists said this was due to 'Sahara dust' passing over Montserrat and was not caused by ash from our volcano.

Mr. Best the butcher came with his pick-up on the 30th June to collect the last of our belongings for shipment back to the UK. He told me he has been 'moonlighting' as a delivery truck for the shipping agents. In the morning he had meat carcasses in the back, and in the afternoon our boxes. But he assured me that he had thoroughly hosed the back of the truck between his two commitments.

Many people sincerely believe that the volcanic activity is now over. They say my husband and I are leaving at a positive time in the island's history.

But before our departure the volcano decided to have the last word. At 3.00 a.m. on the 3rd July there was an unexpected and enormous eruption with almost 20% of the old dome being removed. A large spine in the centre had collapsed, causing a pyroclastic flow down to the sea at Tar River.

Ash and mud rained down on the island for the first time in months. Then at 10.00 a.m. the following morning an explosive eruption sent an ash cloud 40,000 ft. into the air. The inky filth swept across the landscape for the first time in many weeks, plunging us into the old familiar darkness and leaving behind a heavy grey, brown blanket of sodden ash.

The eruption left us feeling profoundly dejected. It looked as if perhaps all the recent optimism had been misplaced. My husband and I found we were completely 'burnt-out' as Frankie puts it. Unable and unwilling to make the effort, we decided to leave the ashy mess for someone else to clear up.

On the morning of the 5th July we picked up our two suitcases, took one final look around the villa and locked the door for the last time. We climbed into the car and headed, through the swirling ashy fog created by the other road users, for the heliport at Gerald's and our last flight from Montserrat.

The 'tropical igloo' being used as the island's Immigration and Customs Terminal was empty. Parts of the torn plastic flapped and rippled noisily with the downdraught of the small blue helicopter as it landed to collect us for our flight to Antigua.

The helo was newly emblazoned with the words *'Montserrat Air Support Unit',* and the pilot was unknown to us, an Englishman standing smartly to attention in his white shirt, epaulettes and dark trousers. 'Kamikaze Jim' with his tousled head of hair, blue shirt and shorts, has gone. Probably now chasing polar bears in the Arctic, or ferrying oil workers to the rigs off the Gulf of Mexico.

We boarded the waiting helo with a strange assortment of feelings. Huge regret at leaving Montserrat and our friends after three long years, but yet an immense sense of relief that we were going to be free at last from the stressful pressure of living in the shadow of this unpredictable volcano.

As we said an emotional goodbye, the words of the Montserratian politician, spoken in July 1997, came to my mind. *"We are a worn out people"* he had said, and the overwhelming sensation as we left Montserrat for the final time was one of profound fatigue.

My husband sat in the co-pilot's seat and I sat behind him. As we lifted gently up and away, swinging round to head for Antigua, I gazed out to my right, towards the Soufrière Hills and the volcano that had ruled every moment of our lives for three long years.

With the thump of the helicopter blades resonating in my ears, I studied the volcano in solemn silence, believing this to be the last time I would ever see it. I did not know I would be returning to Montserrat in 2007.

Grey and smouldering, the peak shrouded by ashy emissions, the volcano was a menacing presence, dominating the southern landscape. I knew then, with a chilling and absolute certainty, that the volcano had far from finished with Montserrat.

Volcano from MVO 2007

35 - INTERVENING YEARS

1998 TO 2015

A few short weeks after our departure from Montserrat the authorities began to believe the Soufrière Hills Volcano had finally stopped growing and was going back to sleep.

1ˢᵗ October 1998 saw the reoccupation of Salem, Old Towne and Frith's begin and many Montserratians who had evacuated overseas decided to return home.

11ᵗʰ January 1999 and the Inquest into the deaths of those Montserratians who were caught in the massive eruption on 25ᵗʰ June 1997 commenced. Nineteen persons were named. The verdict finally delivered criticised both the British and Montserrat Governments. The Coroner taking the most unusual step of adding his own comments on the situation.

12ᵗʰ March 1999 and the scientists stated the risk to populated areas of Montserrat had fallen to levels of other Caribbean islands with dormant volcanoes.

1ˢᵗ May 1999 an assisted passage scheme was introduced for Montserratians wishing to return to the island. Plans were also underway to re-open W.H. Bramble Airport at Trant's.

27ᵗʰ November 1999 a new lava dome was observed to be growing at the Soufrière Hills Volcano, confirming the disquieting fact that activity had recommenced. The optimism generated during the previous twelve months evaporated overnight. The plans to re-open W.H. Bramble Airport were immediately abandoned. A new airport was proposed, to be sited at Gerald's in the north, with construction expected to commence by spring/summer 2003.

20ᵗʰ March 2000 a year after the scientists had declared the volcano dormant, there was a massive collapse of the dome with all the new growth going down Tar River. Heavy rainfall was blamed.

29ᵗʰ July 2001 another massive collapse, described as *"a significant eruption"* occurred. A huge amount of the dome, 45 million cu. metres, went down Tar River to the east. The airports of St. Maarten, Puerto Rico and Antigua were temporarily closed and the whole of Montserrat was covered with heavy ash.

A Maritime Exclusion Zone was imposed around the southern part of Montserrat that extended two miles beyond the coastline. Access to Plymouth and the old W.H. Bramble Airport was prohibited.

The 2001 hurricane season continued to de-stabilise the dome and brought mudflows into the valleys.

August 2002 and the Soufrière Hills Volcano was described as *"a persistently active volcano"* that could continue *"for 10, 20, 30 years even"*. Two months later the Belham and Old Towne areas were evacuated because of concerns about potential volcanic activity.

22ⁿᵈ October 2002 intense rainfall produced mudflows down Belham Valley. The entire width of the valley floor at Belham Bridge was flooded with standing waves up to 2.5 metres travelling down the valley. By early that afternoon pyroclastic flows from the northern flanks of the dome had travelled into Tuitt's Ghaut then crossed into White's Bottom Ghaut. Tar River valley on the east also had pyroclastic flows. After this event the two-mile Exclusion Zone was brought right around the island as far as Lime Kiln Bay on the west coast.

These lahars down Belham Valley after heavy rain became commonplace and by 2005 the Belham Valley had been infilled by approximately 15 metres of sediment. The Belham Bridge (which we used to decorate with crimson flamboyant flowers to celebrate

Emancipation Day) was buried 4 metres below the new ground level. The jetty at Old Road Bay was also buried with the new Old Road Bay coastline 500 metres further seawards.

8ᵗʰ December 2002 and another dome collapse with *"energetic pyroclastic flows down White's Ghaut to the sea at Spanish Pointe."*

3ʳᵈ January 2003 a purpose-built Observatory with a helicopter landing pad was opened at Flemming's. High on the southern slopes of the Centre Hills it had perfect views of the Soufrière Hills Volcano, less than three miles away.

12ᵗʰ July 2003, starting at around 8.00 p.m., the worst eruption to date took place and continued without pause until approximately 4.00 a.m. on the following morning. Over 100 metres (in height) of mountain disappeared overnight. Heavy rainfall all day was blamed for de-stabilising the dome. Explosive activity at the volcano produced very heavy ashfall which was particularly bad to the northwest of the island. Approximately 210 million cu. metres of dome material was estimated to be in the collapse.

The massive, island-wide, clear-up operation required the importation of special equipment and took weeks to complete. It was the largest historical dome collapse since the volcanic activity began in July 1995.

July 2003 to August 2005 there was relative quiet at the volcano, but after two years the dome began building again.

20ᵗʰ May 2006 another major dome collapse occurred (the second largest to date) with an estimated 115 million cu. metres of material ejected over a three-hour period. The accompanying ash cloud rose 55,000 ft. into the air, the highest so far recorded. Mudflows down the flanks were extensive and tsunamis were reported in the neighbouring islands of Guadeloupe and Antigua.

According to the MVO *"a large part of the dome remnant above Gages Valley disintegrated"* during this eruption.

September 2006 and the dome was building again very quickly at an extrusion rate of 8 cu. metres per second.

December 2006 a vent opened at Gages.

8ᵗʰ January 2007 and an explosive event took place during the early hours. Although it was only a partial collapse and small by previous eruptions, pyroclastic flows came down Gages Valley and Tyres Ghaut reaching as far as Cork Hill.

Very little material was removed from the growing dome during this collapse, but the scientists became increasingly concerned that further activity would bring larger pyroclastic flows down Tyres Ghaut endangering the people living in Lower Belham Valley and Isles Bay and an evacuation of 50 homes, including the Vue Pointe Hotel, was ordered.

7ᵗʰ February 2007 another additional 40 homes in Old Towne were evacuated as a precautionary measure.

A public service reggae song was released, very catchy and tuneful, which offered advice on being 'volcano aware'. The lyrics included the phrase *"we don't know when the dome might go, better safe than sorry, when the siren blow get ready to go."*

Eight large sirens were strategically placed around the island. At mid-day Monday to Friday the hills resonated with the melodic sound of the Westminster Chimes. In an emergency no-one could possibly miss the alarm signal from these sirens, they are equipped with a digital voice urgently repeating the instruction *'Evacuate! Evacuate! Evacuate!'*

11ᵗʰ February 2010 another partial dome collapse of approximately 50 million cubic metres, the largest on the northern flank since the eruption began in 1995. Pyroclastic flows reached 400 metres out to sea. W.H. Bramble airport was buried. Extensive ashfall in Guadeloupe closed the airport and schools.

From 2010 to early 2015 the volcano remained relatively quiet with no significant activity.

It is very closely monitored by a resident team of volcanologists, each with specialist duties. A weekly report on the status of the volcano is produced by the MVO. This keeps Montserratians fully aware of activity at the Soufrière Hills Volcano, their troublesome and unpredictable neighbour.

In addition six very experienced volcanologists (known as the Scientific Advisory Committee) meet annually on Montserrat to assess the state of the volcano. The Committee keeps a watching brief over the volcano and advises both the MVO and the Government.

The current Chairman (2015) of the Scientific Advisory Committee is Professor Jurgen Neuberg from the University of Leeds. A previous Chairman was Professor Geoff Wadge who co-wrote the original *'Wadge and Isaacs Report'* that warned of the possibility of an eruption at the Soufrière Hills before anyone on island saw activity. He is very well respected in Montserrat by everyone.

Another valuable member of the Scientific Advisory Committee is Professor Willy Aspinall (currently Cabot Professor of Risk at Bristol University) who has been associated with the Soufrière Hills Volcano since 1970 when he first went to Montserrat to service the primitive photographic seismograph.

Slowly a sense of optimism has returned to Montserrat. Living with an active volcano is now part of normal life for the 5,000 residents. Indeed, it has brought some unusual benefits and opportunities they are enthusiastically embracing.

The north of Montserrat, so long neglected in the years before the volcano erupted, has sprung into life. The whole Little Bay area is being developed. It will become the new capital for the island with bars, restaurants, hotel, waterfront and marina planned.

Work on the Little Bay area has uncovered the remains of an old Manor House and village and this will now be treated as an historic site and of special archaeological interest. A team of visiting archaeologists from the US spent a few weeks during March 2007 investigating the site.

It seems that Sir William Carr, an Irishman from St. Kitt's, arrived at Carr's Bay and Little Bay in the seventeenth century. He started a plantation and began by experimenting with growing indigo, then cotton and finally sugar. It is his Manor House the team believe they have uncovered. There is evidence the Manor House had been burned down and rebuilt several times. They have found a number of pieces of pottery of African/Caribbean plain 'red ware' primarily used as cooking pots, and also some European ceramics.

There also seems to have been a densely populated labourers' settlement at Little Bay, and unfortunately the new Little Bay road will go through this settlement. Before they left Montserrat the archaeologists mapped the area using GPS.

The island now has a new airport at Gerald's in the north. What had been a cricket pitch converted to provide a helicopter pad in 1998 now boasts an impressive runway with smart terminal buildings.

The ferry services from Little Bay have been greatly improved and provide a fast and efficient inter-island sea link.

A thriving complex of Government Offices (including a sparkling green and white Governor's Office), business premises, shops and banks line the roads in the north.

New houses climb the hillside at Lookout and a new Primary School is being built.

Geothermal energy is being actively developed with the drilling of a third well anticipated soon.

Sand is again being exported from Plymouth Jetty.

Tourism is being actively encouraged, with excursions to the MVO to view the volcano, and it is anticipated land tours into the old capital of Plymouth will be offered from February 2015.

Sir George Martin (Record producer and arranger, owner of Air Studios in Montserrat) has built an impressive Cultural Centre at Little Bay. It is a very imposing building and equipped with some of the best sound systems available. There is no doubt it is a tremendous asset to the island.

And there is talk of renovating Sir George's original Air Studios as a tourist attraction. This ultimate paradise Recording Studio was built in 1977 and produced some of the biggest selling hits of the 1980's. Legendary superstars who recorded here include The Beatles, The Rolling Stones, Sting, Phil Collins, Elton John, Eric

Clapton, Stevie Wonder, The Police, Duran Duran. All were here in Montserrat recording with Sir George at Air Studios until Hurricane Hugo swept through in 1989 destroying the island.

The volcano has inspired some really good music in Montserrat. So many of the soca, reggae and calypso lyrics sing of the love of Montserrat *'Montserrat Still Nice, Always Paradise' 'Montserrat nice, nice, nice'.*

Arrow, the undisputed 'King of Soca', Montserrat's famous son who died on 15th September 2010, produced some great music based on the volcano. A highlight of his career was when he was invited to perform at the opening ceremony in Jamaica for the World Cricket Cup on 11th March 2007.

This beautiful Caribbean island is now infused with a feeling of vibrancy and hope. The birth of this new mountain has been a traumatic experience for the island of Montserrat, but Montserratians are very special people, endowed with an extraordinary resilience and an optimistic determination to succeed. They will never give up or give in. Together they will restore Montserrat to create a lively and exciting community on an island grown even more beautiful than it was before.

Life is good again and the future is looking very positive. With a broad smile every Montserratian will proudly tell you,
   "Montserrat still home, still nice, still paradise"

COMMENTS:

"As time moves on and memories fade, this unique, compelling book will serve as an important and accurate first-hand record of traumatic events, faithfully and sensitively recounted by Lally Brown".
Professor Willy Aspinall, Cabot Professor of Risk, University of Bristol.

"Whatever you do don't miss this book. A moving and detailed story of a courageous people with insights only an eyewitness can give."
Terry Waite, CBE

"Your summary of the disaster of June 1997 is brilliant and says in a few carefully chosen words what others have failed to say in thick volumes."
R. N. Thompson, Durham University.

"A very rich, warm and marvellous read. Elegantly phrased by someone with a flair for writing!"
Professor R.E. Nelson, Colby College, Maine, USA.

"You have captured the heart of the island."
"Excellent, edge of the seat stuff ... and true!"
"Had us laughing and in tears at the turn of a page."
"I could not put this book down!"
"An excellent read, highly recommended."
"A must-read for sure."
"Absolutely brilliant!"

ABOUT THE AUTHOR

Born and bred in Yorkshire, England, **Lally Brown** embraced the Swinging Sixties with naïve enthusiasm. As a teenager in search of adventure she trekked overland to war-torn Israel, working on a small kibbutz driving a tractor and picking oranges to earn her keep. She managed to hitch-hike around the country staying in Haifa, Jerusalem and Acre. This amazing, and occasionally dangerous experience, was the spark that ignited her lifelong love of adventure and travel.

Lally has lost count of the number of homes she has had over the years, but says her most memorable are those on remote St. Helena Island (where Napoleon was imprisoned), Montserrat in the Caribbean, Turks and Caicos Islands and the British Virgin Islands.

Now, in her twilight years, Lally is writing about her adventurous life using the journals she kept at the time.. Her books prove that truth can indeed be far stranger than fiction, with erupting volcanoes, hurricanes, earthquakes, evacuations, abduction, drug smugglers, people smugglers, armed robbery, hangings, stowaways, bribery, corruption, political intrigues, riots, and much, much, more.

ALSO BY LALLY BROWN

'THE COUNTESS, NAPOLEON AND ST HELENA'

A fascinating true story about Countess Françoise Elisabeth 'Fanny' Bertrand who, with her husband and children, accompanied ex-Emperor Napoleon into exile to the remote island of St Helena.

Researched from primary source documents.

'I congratulate you on your research efforts and dedicated work'
Ben Weider, founder of The Napoleonic Society.

'HIGH AND DRY IN THE BVI'

Lighthearted memoir of life in the British Virgin Islands in the early Seventies. A banana boat to Trinidad and Tobago then island-hopping to Tortola. Experience life in the BVI before cruise ships and tourists. Meet the colourful characters and celebrities who called Tortola home.

Printed in Great Britain
by Amazon